THE NEW ZEALAND CPI AT 100

HISTORY AND INTERPRETATION

THE NEW ZEALAND CPI AT 100

HISTORY AND INTERPRETATION

Edited by
Sharleen Forbes and Antong Victorio

VICTORIA UNIVERSITY PRESS

TE WHARE WĀNANGA O TE ŪPOKO O TE IKA A MĀUI

VICTORIA

UNIVERSITY OF WELLINGTON

VICTORIA UNIVERSITY PRESS
Victoria University of Wellington
PO Box 600 Wellington
vup.victoria.ac.nz

National Library of New Zealand Cataloguing-in-Publication Data

The New Zealand CPI at 100 : history and interpretation / edited by
Sharleen Forbes and Antong Victorio.
ISBN 978-0-86473-966-7
1. Consumer price indexes—New Zealand—History. 2. Prices—New
Zealand—History. I. Forbes, Sharleen, 1948- 2. Victorio, Andres
G. III. Title
338.5280993—dc 23

Printed by PrintStop, Wellington

Contents

Preface

Introduction to the Consumers Price Index (CPI)

The Consumers Price Index (CPI) is a single index number used as a general measure of the overall rate of price change over the range of outlets and locations where goods and services are purchased. It is designed to measure the combined price movements of the huge number of retail transactions undertaken by people throughout New Zealand in a specified period. Any such statistical indicator is bound to have limitations for particular users and uses.

The CPI provides a broad measure of changes in prices as they affect New Zealand consumers in general. It includes an extensive list of goods and services, and each household purchases some combination of these, but rarely all. The CPI, therefore, does not reflect the price changes experienced by any one particular individual or household. Rather, it represents the spending habits of all New Zealand consumers as a whole.

The CPI covers goods and services purchased for the purpose of consumption (i.e. use) by private New Zealand households, using information on household expenditure obtained from Statistics New Zealand's Household Economic Survey (HES). The HES also provides information on the proportion of total consumers' expenditure on specific items. This proportion (relative importance) is called the 'weight' of that commodity in the CPI.

Expenditure that is not for consumption is excluded from the CPI. For example, expenditure on investments, such as superannuation, shares and collectors' items, is excluded, as well as expenditure on residential sections (because the land on which a house stands is not 'used up' and is therefore a type of investment). Charitable donations, income tax and court fines are also excluded, because they are not payments for a specific good or service which can be consumed. Until recently, interest charges were excluded too, as these typically bore no direct relationship to actual quantities of specific goods and services acquired. And some goods and services (such as paintings, antiques, pets and gambling) are excluded simply because prices for them cannot be adequately measured.

To ensure that the changes in prices are not due to changes in the quantity or quality of the goods and services purchased, whenever possible, prices are collected for exactly the same items in each time period. A selection of goods and services is surveyed. This selection, a CPI 'basket' of goods and services, represents the price movements of the much wider range of items that households purchase. The basket and the expenditure weights of items in it are reviewed and recalculated approximately every three years. The last five major revisions of the CPI included a full review of the field outlets considered; these were done in 1999, 2002, 2006, 2008 and 2011. To be considered for inclusion in the CPI, the selected goods and services must:

- be a representative sample of goods and services purchased by consumers.
- have price movements which will accurately reflect those of a broad grouping of similar products.
- have a high probability of being available in the future, in order to reduce the difficulties of pricing items that have been replaced.

The current CPI includes an extensive range of goods and services, ranging from apples through to dental fees, postal charges and new cars. In all, over 700 different goods and services have their prices surveyed and are categorised into nine groups, 21 subgroups and 73 sections, in such a way that similar goods and services are grouped together.

The nine groups currently in the New Zealand CPI are:

- Food
- Housing
- Household Operation
- Apparel
- Tobacco and Alcohol
- Transportation
- Personal and Health Care
- Recreation and Education
- Credit Services

A separate group, Interest Charges, is also calculated. Until 1999, interest charges were not separated from the 'all groups' CPI. Their separate calculation allowed users the flexibility of excluding interest when measuring inflation.

Prices for the 'basket of goods and services' are taken from selected outlets (supermarkets, department stores, specialty stores, liquor outlets, dairies, travel agents, dentists, mail-order outlets and service stations), across 15 main urban areas (Whangarei, Auckland, Hamilton, Tauranga, Rotorua, Napier/Hastings, New Plymouth, Whanganui, Palmerston North, Wellington/Hutt Valley, Nelson, Christchurch, Timaru, Dunedin and Invercargill). They are collected by Statistics New Zealand interviewers, postal survey, the Internet, telephone or e-mail. Some items, such as telephone call charges, are monitored on a quarterly basis. Others, such as fresh fruit and vegetables, are collected weekly, whereas items such as other food and non-food groceries, electricity, gas, petrol, alternative motor fuels, tobacco, alcoholic drinks, newspapers and domestic and international airfares are surveyed monthly. To ensure that price movements truly reflect the buying experiences of consumers, a range of regularly purchased brands and varieties is surveyed. The price recorded is the price consumers pay for the specified quantity and quality of the good or service. 'Specials' and 'sale' prices are accepted but the prices of 'obsolete' stock are not.

When all the prices have been checked for accuracy and validity, an average price is calculated for each item in each urban area. Movements in these averages are then weighted again, this time according to the population of each urban area. This ensures that the price movements in bigger urban areas like Auckland have a greater effect on the CPI than those of smaller areas like Timaru. The CPI is calculated from thousands of prices. It involves calculating the total expenditure required in the current period to purchase the same selection of goods and services that was surveyed in a previous base period. The ratio of this expenditure to that in the base quarter is then multiplied by 1,000 to give the current index number.

About this book

The overall theme of this book is that the New Zealand CPI is not just an index of prices. It can also be seen as a history of conflicting interests and machinations, as a beacon for social norms, as a representation of endurance and obsolescence, as a leading progenitor of economic policy, and even potentially as a measure of consumer satisfaction, regional integration and social progress.

The CPI is described by Brian Easton as exceedingly contentious – to unions and employers haggling over what constitutes a decent wage, to public officials wanting to portray stable prices, and to lobby groups fearing benefit cuts if their wishes are excluded. Conflicts are also presented by Sharleen Forbes, Corin Higgs, James Keating and Evan Roberts. These arise from prescriptive views concerning what items were to be included in the CPI, and from urgent demands that domestic wages conform to international reforms and the pursuit of world peace. Roberts describes the history of housing surveys as also having been coloured by such concerns. From these conflicts, there eventually emerges an enlightened consensus that is positivist: the CPI should reflect what households themselves choose to buy, even if controversial items are included.

This view is shared by Gary Hawke and Antong Victorio in their description of historical conceptualisations. A chronology of pivotal developments that may have expressed these interests is provided by Chris Pike for the years after 1949. Were it not for the pragmatic decisions that resulted from this contentiousness, the modern CPI may not have emerged as an index with such considerable public trust.

What households buy is described by Forbes as a changing mix. Some items have been in the CPI for a hundred years, for example, milk, cheese and flour. Some have been there for less than a hundred years, but enduringly from the time of inclusion. A few, like telegrams, have disappeared. The chief culprits of such change are thought to be technological change, the commercialisation of house work, the increasing importance of leisure goods, changes in government policy and, naturally, the unpredictable dictates of fashion. It is clear that consumer preferences are not immutable.

Alan Bentley suggests how a positivist approach can be improved by disaggregating households into specific groups with specific needs, such as with the elderly. Ekaterina Sadetskaya and Les Oxley conduct an equally useful geographical disaggregation, according to how New Zealand provinces were previously defined. This disaggregation shows a convergence of agricultural prices, possibly because of technology, transportation and regional integration in ways that may have been unique to New Zealand.

Michael Reddell traces how the CPI evolved, from being a reference for a wage, to being an indicator of monetary policy and of Reserve Bank independence and effectiveness. In the interim, there was a period during which the CPI was seen merely as an appendage to the vagaries of international economic shocks, and to the constraints of fixed exchange rates. It appears that policies are influenced by the intellectual reasoning of their time, and that the ones that emerge are presumably the ones that survive the most criticism.

While Reddell discusses the CPI's weakness in measuring true inflation, John Gibson and Grant Scobie query whether the New Zealand CPI overstates inflation by around 1.4 percentage points a year. They reason that the New Zealand CPI has not been adequately adjusted for the declining importance that households place upon food expenditures. If this is true, many Western democracies may be targeting inflation at a more aggressive rate than necessary to maintain the real value of their welfare provisions.

Victorio describes how an overstatement of the costs of maintaining a given standard of living might arise as a consequence of many other inadequacies in the CPI. His starting point is bolder: that of maintaining a given level of *satisfaction* that underlies a given cost of living, based upon a reasonable model of consumer preferences. From this starting point, he shows how an overstatement of satisfaction can occur if consumer substitution is not fully considered, such as for commodities that are cheaper, newer, or of better quality. Frances Krsinich follows through by describing how such overstatements might be empirically identified, such as with modern methods that quantify desirable characteristics and which include spending on new items without delay.

Towards the end, Hawke and Victorio conclude that the many perspectives offered by the CPI arise from differing conceptualisations. These conceptualisations suggest that the CPI must be regarded innovatively: not so much as an index "whose purity must be preserved", but perhaps instead as a genuine barometer of social and economic progress.

Prescriptivism to Positivism? The development of the CPI in New Zealand

Sharleen Forbes, Corin Higgs, James Keating
& Evan Roberts

Abstract

Retail price collection in New Zealand has a long history. Early indices were prescriptive, with price changes measured in items prescribed as staples. The development of a price index to meet the conflicting demands of government, domestic labour, and international organisations was an imperfect process and these conflicts gradually changed its nature and purpose. This chapter documents the history of retail prices in New Zealand, from the compilation of basic commodity prices in the 1840s through to the beginnings of the Consumers Price Index as we now know it, an objective, positivist index based on actual household consumption (expenditure) patterns.

Introduction

Prices are intrinsic to the study of economics. Price data support micro-economic analysis of market structures, and macro-economic analysis of overall price levels and changes. Long-term price series provide substantial insights into changing economic structure and performance. They are vital for converting nominal entities into real entities, and historians use them to assess economic activity in the absence of adequate production measures.

There is a long history of the collection and analysis of price data in New Zealand by professional and amateur economists, and statisticians. Over time, the methodology of price collection has changed considerably. In order for price changes to be used to assess real changes in economic outcomes, it is important that price series are consistent, and the changes in them well understood, lest artefacts of data collection be mistaken for real change.[1] To this end, this chapter provides an overview of the development of the measurement of price changes in New Zealand, leading eventually to the Consumers Price Index (CPI).

The collection of retail price data in New Zealand began with the compilation of basic commodity prices soon after the establishment of a Crown Colony in

1840. Colonial administrators sent early price data to the Colonial Office in London as part of the required collection of statistics across the British Empire. By the late nineteenth century, colonial politicians, administrators and labour leaders were searching for 'objective' measures to end industrial unrest. The establishment of a Court of Arbitration in 1894 provided a forum for the determination of basic wages, initially derived from the wages paid by 'reputable employers' but by the early twentieth century derived from an estimation of the basic living requirements of a working-class family (Holt, 1986, pp.66–70). This was reflected in the composition of early price surveys, which charted price changes in 'staple' goods, such as food, rent, fuel, and light. As a founding member, New Zealand shared the 1919 League of Nations' conviction that a basic living wage was fundamental to the construction of an equitable society. Nevertheless, the primary purpose of price indices was domestic, for example, providing the government with accurate price information to maintain price and wage restrictions during the Second World War (Baker, 1965, pp.280–291, 309–312).

The development of indices to meet the often conflicting demands of government, domestic labour, and international organisations was necessarily an imperfect process, and throughout the early twentieth century, New Zealand's price indices existed in a state of flux as government statisticians responded to a complex mix of political and economic demands, not to mention the difficulties of collecting appropriate data. The conflicts between workers' desire for fair wages, the government's inflationary controls, and international demands for consistency and comparability gradually changed the nature and purpose of New Zealand's price indices. Early indices were prescriptive, with the Department of Labour (and later the Census and Statistics Office) measuring price changes in items prescribed as staples. The consumer boom that followed World War II prompted the government to reassess this prescriptive approach and expand the basket of goods beyond necessary items of expenditure to make it more reflective of what New Zealanders were actually buying, with the advent of regular household surveying providing the government with accurate estimates of the relative expenditure on individual items.

Price levels and price changes have been an important part of economic policy in New Zealand since the 1890s, when the Industrial Conciliation and Arbitration Act 1894 ensured a role for government in labour negotiations. The contemporary importance of the CPI in New Zealand's political economy has been enshrined in the Reserve Bank's Policy Targets Agreements (PTAs) since 1990. Under the Reserve Bank of New Zealand Act 1989, the Governor of the Reserve Bank negotiates an agreement with the government to try and maintain inflation (as measured by a proxy, currently the CPI) within a specified range, currently between 1 and 3 per cent over the medium term. The use of the CPI in successive Policy Targets Agreements ensured that there is now regular public and media attention to the way in which in the CPI is collected, and to changes in the index. This history lists important changes in definitions and methodology from the advent of the measurement of prices in New Zealand through to the establishment of the modern CPI as we know it.

The early history of price collection in New Zealand

The collection of retail price data began with the compilation of basic commodity prices after the establishment of a Crown Colony in 1840. During the Crown Colony period (and beyond, 1840–1858), Colonial Blue Books recording retail prices were sent to London (Wood, 1976, pp.1–4). After the New Zealand Constitution Act 1852, national prices began to be collected, recorded and published. Beginning in 1858, the New Zealand Statistical Report annuals were published, containing price data for the previous four years. Alone, these provide incomplete records of consumer prices and expenditure patterns in the late nineteenth century. During the 1880s, colonial politicians, administrators, and labour leaders sought 'objective' measures to end the industrial unrest that wracked the country. The landmark Industrial Conciliation and Arbitration (IC&A) Act 1894 established a Court of Arbitration to provide a forum for the determination of basic wages. Initially wage rulings were derived from the wages paid by 'reputable employers' (Woods, 1963, pp.96–97). By the early twentieth century there was a growing realisation, based in part on union demands, that workers' wages should match the basic living requirements of a working class family. This was reflected in the composition of early price indices, which charted price changes in 'staple' goods – food, rent, fuel, and light. Price levels and changes became an important input to wage setting under the IC&A Act, and continued to be so for a century.

While there was no formal agreement between New Zealand statistical agencies and the Court of Arbitration, the workings of the Court relied heavily on government price indices. An amendment to the IC&A Act in 1918 formalised what had been common practice by giving the Court the power to increase (but not decrease) nominal wages to maintain real wages. The cost-of-living and price statistics were thus an explicit part of the legislation for wage setting in New Zealand. Even before the Act prescribed adjustments for the cost of living, it was a common union basis for claims for wage increases. Following one of the Court's early cases, the Westport Coal Company dispute, the *Otago Daily Times* noted approvingly that "For the first time . . . in the world . . . a competent court has adjudicated . . . in an industrial dispute, taken evidence on all sorts of details, such as the *cost of living*, . . . and has been able . . . to arrive at a decision which must be regarded as a fair one".[2] Conversely, employers wanted to deny or limit any agreement that the cost of living had increased.[3] Disputes over the cost of living went beyond merely national estimates of consumer prices. While the Court had the power to make awards in industrial districts (corresponding to the old provincial boundaries), many awards spanned districts, raising the question of whether prices and costs were the same across the country. Union and employer claims that wages should be different in different places then rested on evidence that the cost of living did, in fact, differ in different places.[4]

Thus, impartial evidence on changes in the cost of living was crucial to the workings of the Court of Arbitration. Although at that time people were not always aware of long-term trends in prices, the first 30 years of the Court of Arbitration were contemporaneous with the transition in the 1890s from a long decline in prices to steadily rising prices until World War I, followed by very high inflation in the early 1920s. In late 1920 the Court of Arbitration was "prepared to grant . . . a bonus of 9s[hillings] per week in order that wages should keep pace with the increased cost of living, as revealed by the Government Statistician."[5] With prices rising very rapidly, the exact way in which the cost-of-living figures were calculated came under serious question from the media. The dispute turned largely on which months' prices were included in the index used to justify the bonus, and the method of annualising the monthly figures for food prices.[6] Although there was significant discord over the increase in wages paid in 1921, and whether nominal wages should fall when prices began falling in 1922, there was universal agreement that the Court was well-served by the Government Statistician collecting accurate price indices.[7] The 1921–22 dispute over how price indices were computed was an exception to the normal pattern of disputes before the Court. For the most part, parties before the Court accepted the accuracy of national and regional figures on prices. What they disputed was the relevance of the basket of goods in the price indices to the current case before the Court. With only infrequent surveys of what consumers were purchasing, it could be an effective rhetorical strategy to argue to the Court that workers in the current case spent their money on different items than 'working men' surveyed in 1893 or 1912.

New Zealand authorities had particular difficulty in collecting accurate statistics on consumer expenditures. Rare instances of records on consumer budgets, such as the 1875–1876 Karamea government store ledger book, fill important gaps in New Zealand's economic history by showing detailed expenditures over a year for an admittedly remote and atypical group of households.[8] An 1893 survey of 146 working-class family budgets was the first, and arguably most successful, such survey conducted by any government department until the Household Economic Survey began in the 1970s.[9] The small and irregular collections of household expenditure data meant that the composition of New Zealand price indices changed infrequently. Simply put, the

New Zealand authorities did not know with much confidence what proportion of consumer expenditure was going towards broad commodity categories such as food or clothing. They knew even less about how households substituted between goods in response to price changes. In comparison to countries such as the United States or Britain, we lack information on consumer spending behaviour in New Zealand for substantial periods of our history (Burnett, 1969; Stapleford, 2009, pp.22–58).

Price index figures were first officially collected and published in New Zealand in 1908, when Dr John Findlay, Minister for the Registrar General's Department, discussed price and wage increases at public meetings in Wanganui and Wellington ('Dr. Findlay's Address', 1908, p.4; 'Wages and the Cost of Living', 1908, p.8).[10] In 1911, James McIlraith's seminal doctoral thesis expressing wholesale (as opposed to retail) price changes between 1861 and 1910 was published as *The Course of Prices in New Zealand* (McIlraith, 1911). By expressing price fluctuations through index numbers and examining their causes, McIlraith hoped to provide information on purchasing power in New Zealand that "had been available for some time to statesmen and economic investigators generally in England and America" (Hight, 1911, p.3). In the same year, the Department of Labour conducted a budget study of 2,000 'bona fide workers' and their families. Modelled on a similar survey of 1,500 households in Australia, the *Inquiry into the Cost of Living in New Zealand* hoped to produce reliable data on the cost of living. Yet, as the report admitted, the survey was a failure. Of the 1,800 household account-books distributed in the four main centres (a larger study encompassing the entire Dominion was planned, but scrapped for financial reasons), just 69 were "of any practical use" (Collins, 1912, pp.7–9). Nevertheless, the Department of Labour persevered with the publication of its tentative findings, "in the absence of any prior statistics on the matter" (Lomas, 1912, p.3).

1912 Royal Commission on the Cost of Living

The 1912 Royal Commission on the Cost of Living was appointed to investigate increases in the cost of living and suggest anti-inflationary measures. The Commission enquired broadly into changes in the cost of living between 1894 and 1911, with emphasis on price changes over the previous decade. Commissioners placed particular emphasis on the inflationary impact of price monopolies and cartels, tariffs, land prices, labour legislation, the advent of refrigeration and the increased demand for exports, and the rural–urban population drift. Foreshadowing a trend that would characterise the development of New Zealand's price indices throughout the twentieth century, the report had an international focus, comparing domestic price movements with patterns in

"English Speaking Countries" (the United Kingdom, United States, Canada, South Africa, New South Wales) and large European economies (France, Italy, Germany). The Commission did not collect new price information, but relied on data collected during the Department of Labour 1910–1911 budget study, James McIlraith's doctoral thesis, and the examination of 270 witnesses from trade unions, small businesses, and merchants.[11]

Adjusted for changes in the quality of consumer goods, the Commission found that the cost of living increased "by at least 16 per cent" between 1894 and 1911.[12] The figure was low by international standards – the report noted that New Zealand prices generally lagged behind "any other country of which we had reliable records".[13] Among the factors considered to have stimulated inflation, the report emphasised the impact of higher wages and the increased supply of money, the increased international demand for agricultural exports, anti-competitive practices and price collusion between retailers and importers, increases in customs duties and taxation, and the wastefulness of contemporary society.[14] Its proposals to reduce inflation included tariff reductions, municipalisation of bread and milk supplies, breaking retail and transportation cartels, and the addition of economics education to the national primary school curriculum.[15]

In addition to providing technical suggestions for the collection and analysis of price information, and suggesting anti-inflationary measures, the Commissioners envisaged a stronger role for the Government Statistician (a position created in 1910). Their proposals for ameliorating the impact of rising prices hinged upon the establishment of an independent statistics advisory board under the direction of the Government Statistician. The Commissioners feared that the lack of a permanent bureaucracy dedicated to statistical analysis reduced the quality and reliability of the country's official statistics. Essentially, they wanted price indices and the bodies that created them to have a greater influence in the determination of national economic policy.[16] Despite the wide-ranging recommendations, the report was largely ignored by the conservative Massey Government.

By 1912, the Court of Arbitration was using retail price data to form basic indices to assist judgement in employment cases. The Court formed the cornerstone of the Liberals' ambition to "end . . . the evils of industrial war".[17] The intent of the IC&A legislation was to settle industrial disputes in a "civilised" manner, but it quickly became an important "state mechanism for fixing fair wages for breadwinners" (Martin, 2010, p.170). Initially the Court adopted a "fair wage policy" – deriving basic pay rates from the wages paid by "reputable employers", rather than any assessment of the living requirements of an unskilled worker (Woods, 1963, pp.96–97). However, in the first decade of the twentieth century, the broad consensus on "fair wages" that had characterised the Court of Arbitration's first round of awards had evaporated (Holt, 2001, pp.152–53). In order to secure wage increases, trade unions argued their necessity based on the increased cost of living. Worried that the increased cost of living undermined the IC&A Act's intent, the Court, in conjunction with the Department of Labour, pioneered early cost of living surveys to provide a statistical basis for assessing workers' demands (Martin, 2010, pp.172–73). As the price indices rose, the Court increased the minimum wage for unskilled labour correspondingly, so that workers could retain a constant purchasing power. Between 1908 and 1916, the 'reasonable' living wage rose from £2 to £2.12s. per week (Woods, 1963, pp.96–97).

1915: First official index of retail prices

Surging wartime inflation prompted the compilation of the earliest official index of New Zealand retail price figures – the *Report on the Cost of Living in New Zealand, 1891–1914*, published in 1915 (Fraser, 1915). A precursor to the creation of the Retail Price Index (RPI) in 1921, the purpose of the exercise was two-fold: to compile historical price data, and to establish a continuing system of data collection and index compilation (*Consumers Price Index Revision Report 1993*, 1995, p.13). Government Statistician Malcolm Fraser sought data reaching back to 1891 with the intention of creating a series of base prices, explaining that "since the nineties . . . New Zealand Labour and Social Legislation has developed".[18] The early index monitored price data on food, rent, fuel and light collected in the four main centres of Auckland, Wellington, Christchurch and Dunedin. Between 1891 and 1907, the index only contained information on the 60 items categorised as food and rent (although Christchurch food prices were not included until 1899). In 1907, upon the addition of a 'fuel and light' category, the basket expanded to 67 items. For the years prior to 1914, Fraser inexplicably failed to include the annual return of retail prices in the publication *Statistics of New Zealand*, questioning the reliability of his early findings. From 1914, prices were collected by surveying retailers in 25 towns, but the index base remained linked to prices in the main centres (Arnold, 1982). Beginning in 1912, a series of household surveys collected information on consumer expenditure and retail prices, published in the *Monthly Abstract of Statistics*. The period these figures covered dated back to 1907 (though food and rent data obtained from the 1915 report stretched back to 1899: *Consumers' Price Index 1955 Revision*, 1956, p.5).

The range of price information collected by the Census and Statistics Office (later the Department of Statistics) dramatically increased in December 1918, when Parliament passed the War Legislation and Statute Law Amendment Act. The amended legislation required the Office to collect price data on: clothing and drapery, footwear, household furnishings, household ironmongery, crockery, train and tram fares, and newspapers and periodicals. Wartime economic pressures prompted the expansion of the early basket of goods, and the revised index was reserved for exclusive use by the Court of Arbitration to determine wage rates (*Consumers' Price Index 1955 Revision*, 1956, p.12).

Following World War I, as a founding member of the League of Nations in 1919, New Zealand shared the organisation's conviction that world peace would be achieved through social and political reform. Fundamental to the idea of the "makeable society" – the notion that the state was central to the construction of an equitable society – was universal access to a "basic living wage" (Van Daele, 2005, p.435). Established alongside the League of Nations at the Versailles Conference, the International Labour Organization (ILO) operated under the assumption that "universal and lasting peace can be established only if it is based upon social justice" (International Labour Organization, 1919). Central to this goal was the standardisation of social and economic statistics for comparison between nations in support of the ILO's labour activism. While the New Zealand government eagerly participated in these international endeavours, price indices continued to serve a primarily domestic purpose.

1921: Retail Price Index

In 1921, a new Retail Price Index (RPI) was created. The construction of the RPI expanded on the work undertaken by Malcolm Fraser in 1914, when he compiled the *Report on the Cost of Living in New Zealand 1891–1914*. Correspondence regarding the creation of the RPI reveals that its primary purpose was to determine basic wages and their relationship to the prices of staples. In order to determine a 'truly representative' average working wage, wages in different industries were weighted by the numbers of workers enrolled in various trade unions (with precautions taken to avoid duplicate memberships).[19] Price information for the new index was collected in a Household Budget survey. Participants charted their household expenditure over a period of six months in an account book with sections for a list of prescribed products (thus the survey only addressed spending on certain predetermined goods, rather than on total household expenditure). The existing categories of food, rent, fuel, and lighting collected in 1914 were augmented by the addition of clothing, drapery, footwear, and miscellaneous items.[20] As in 1911, the survey was a failure. Only 318 out of 20,000 household account books were completed correctly and returned, thus the revised index was based on earlier data (Wood, 1976, p.76). Though it was compiled in 1921, the new index was not published until 1924. In the intervening three years the Court of Arbitration used the index as a confidential wage-setting tool (Wood, 1976, pp.87–88).

The Census and Statistics Act 1926 provided for the prosecution of businesses that persistently failed to comply with the Government Statistician's requests for price information. The provision of punitive powers to the Census and Statistics Office was an attempt to ensure compliance with a government organisation that had no permanent field organisation, and no branch offices outside Wellington.[21]

1930: Family budget inquiry

Under advice from the ILO, the Census and Statistics Office undertook another family budget inquiry in 1930. The aim was a revision of the RPI "to ensure more ready and exact [international] comparability".[22] One of the main uses of the information collected in the RPI was the collation of global prices by both national and international organisations. The figures were used in conjunction with international data to trace relative worldwide price movements.[23] The household budget survey would be the last conducted by the Census and Statistics Office until 1973. In a break from previous surveys, the inquiry was not limited to 'working class families', yet the index weightings were still based on a 'working class' living standard (Wood, 1976, pp.76, 91). The collection of household budget data was undertaken by selected families in 25 towns, with cash prizes (of up to £100) advertised in metropolitan and regional newspapers as incentives to complete the survey. Households were instructed to complete the 'Householder's Diary Account Book' which detailed individual household income and expenditure (Wood, 1976, pp.75–76). As with previous revisions to price indices, the standard minimum pay rate for unskilled workers was calculated against the revised RPI by the Court of Arbitration so that real wages would retain their purchasing power.

1932: Farmers' Price Index (FPI)

During the early 1930s, there was also pressure to compile an index that measured movements in farming costs as well as movement in the prices of farm produce. Farmers displayed little interest in the arbitration system and price collection, but grew increasingly agitated with decisions that concerned agricultural labourers in the mid-1920s (Holt, 1986, pp.165–89). Amid growing rural unrest with the arbitration system, P. A. de la Perrelle, the Minister of Internal Affairs, suggested that a new index be created as New Zealand was "a farmers country" and that in other countries similar figures were collected.[24] The proposed index would cover produce prices, farm expenses (machinery, seeds, fertilisers, wages, buildings) and domestic purchases (boots, drapery, groceries, etc). In order to construct the new index, which was applied retrospectively with 1914 as the base year, around 2,000 farmers ('representative of all classes') were selected as respondents for a survey of agricultural prices over the previous 12 months.[25]

Table 1. Excerpt from the Farmers' Price Index

Year	Farm Expenditure	Export Prices (Pastoral and dairy produce)	Percentages of Export Prices to Farm Expenditure index number	Relative Value of 20 Shillings to a Farmer
1914	1000	1000	100	20
1915	1096	1142	104.2	20/10
1916	1195	1350	116.3	23/3
1917	1284	1519	118.3	23/8
1918	1452	1544	106.3	21/3
1919	1511	1632	108	21/7
1920	1661	1666	100.3	20/1
1921	1606	1575	98.1	19/11
1922	1543	1235	80	16
1923	1593	1479	92.8	18/7
1924	1586	1649	104	20/10
1925	1582	1748	110.5	22/1
1926	1555	1407	90.5	18/1
1927	1574	1396	88.7	17/9
1928	1642	1553	94.6	18/11
1929	1636	1492	91.2	18/3
1930	1628	1168	71.8	14/4
1931	1490	881	59.1	11/10
1932	1250	795	63.6	12/9
1933	1150	792	xxx	xxx
1934	1150	995	xxx	xxx

1942: Wartime Prices Index (WPI)

On 31 December 1942 the War Cabinet indefinitely suspended publication of the RPI and replaced it with the Wartime Price Index.[26] The design and collection of data for a new price index was central to the Government's wartime plan for economic stabilisation. The Parliamentary paper addressing the WPI noted that "the decision that wages and other forms of remuneration should be linked to the prices of essential commodities and services (including rents) entering into the cost of living of the average New Zealand family" was fundamental to the stabilisation of the domestic economy.[27] Price information on a new schedule of commodities and services was recorded at the discretion of the Minister of Industries and Commerce. As with previous indices, the WPI provided a reference point from which wages could be adjusted to match changes in the retail prices of 'essential' goods and services. The weighting of the new index was slightly revised from the RPI – in addition to the 1930 family budget inquiry, the Department of Scientific and Industrial Research 1938–1939 budget inquiry and "emergency adjustments" influenced the final weighting of the index (*Consumers' Price Index 1955 Revision*, 1956, p.13).

The objective of the economic stabilisation scheme was to keep inflation, as measured by the WPI, below the 2.5 per cent threshold that would trigger increases in wages and farm payouts (Baker, 1965, pp.288–297). In aid of this goal, the Fraser Government implemented a series of price controls and inveighed against cost increases. Where cost increases were unavoidable, extensive government subsidies were applied to a range of commodities (including wheat, coal, gas, meat and railway fares) to prevent price rises from influencing the WPI (Hawke, 1985, p.171). During the Second World War, the government needed accurate price information to maintain price and wage restrictions, and to limit inflation. Rigorous data collection was required to accurately determine the relationship between basic wages and the price of staples, a task complicated by wartime economic pressures and the emergence of a burgeoning consumer economy. At this time also there was a test case of the prosecution powers provided in the Census and Statistics Act 1926. A 1948 charge against Thomas McFarlane, a butcher, who only listed price maximums on his price forms, was dismissed by the Whangarei Court.[28] Clearly, the provision of accurate information would rely more on persuasion than enforcement.

1949: Consumers' Price Index (CPI)

As a post-war economy emerged after 1945, tensions manifested between visions of the WPI as a tool to limit wage movements, a measure that would allow wages to match the cost of living, and a means of 'insulating' New Zealand exporters from price shocks (Hawke, 1985, pp.163–173). Trade unions, in particular, urged the government to construct a revised post-war price index, as they recognised that the WPI tended to understate price movements – thus Arbitration Court estimates for wage increases made from the index were typically conservative.[29] Political interference, in the form of subsidies, and the failure to record the prices of substitute products prompted suspicions that the WPI was "loaded against the worker" (Woods, 1963, p.161). With these concerns in mind, in 1948 the Fraser Government established a committee "to investigate the need and method of establishing a revised cost-of-living index" (Woods, 1963, p.161). Cabinet adopted the committee's report, and the Government Statistician was instructed to begin compiling the new index. Work began in November 1948, and in 1949, the Census and Statistics Office introduced a new price measure, the Consumers' Price Index. The new index was first published in the June–July 1949 issue of the *Monthly Abstract of Statistics* (*Retail Prices in New Zealand with Special Reference to the Consumers' Price Index*, 1949).

The 'Index Committee' noted that the group of commodities and services selected to represent 'reasonable wartime standards of consumption' could not be regarded as a suitable gauge of post-war prices. Some of the major changes noted since the 1930 family budget inquiry were the greater use of electricity and household electrical appliances, and increased relative consumption of fruits and vegetables, breakfast cereals, milk, and ice cream. While past indices had been governed by the primary criterion of 'essentiality', the new index was intended to incorporate normal living expenses in the average home – including expenditure regarded as "non-essential or socially undesirable".[30] This remit was not entirely fulfilled. Part of the Committee's mandate was to consider whether "the index should cover only *necessary* items of expenditure or *all* items of expenditure?" The report on the construction of the CPI noted that "it was felt that some line must be drawn to exclude what might be regarded as luxury spending". Luxuries were not defined specifically, but alcoholic liquors, private motoring, holiday travel, hotel accommodation, sports expenses, domestic services and telephone rentals were all excluded on these grounds (*Retail Prices in New Zealand with Special Reference to the Consumers' Price Index*, 1949, p.4).

Thus, although the Committee boasted that the new regimen encompassed "the whole range of commodities and services used in the average household – with representation as far as possible, of the amenities of modern living", it represented an ongoing compromise between competing conceptions of the CPI.[31] Ultimately the Census and Statistics Office continued to record 'respectable' rather than actual consumer expenditure.[32] The main groups of commodities and services covered by the new index were food, housing, fuel and lighting, clothing and footwear, and a broad range of miscellaneous items (including household goods, medicines, education, and services). Within these groups a selection of 300 'key items' (308 items were eventually represented) was to be made, for which prices would be collected and weighted to represent all other similar items. The Committee noted that an index representing 300 priced items would make the New Zealand CPI the most comprehensive in the world.[33]

No survey was undertaken to establish new weightings, but the Committee provided a proposed weighting system based on recent production, trade, and manufacturing data, and compared it to the weightings given for the WPI.[34] Furthermore, the construction of the new index followed the recommendations and statistical standards of the 1947 ILO Statisticians Conference "as closely as possible".[35]

Table 2. Revised CPI weights in 1949

Group	Weighting (%)		
	Proposed CPI	WPI	Government Statistician's Series (1926–1930) Index
Food	35.50	43.00	38
Housing	16.75	23.00	21
Fuel and Lighting	3.75	6.50	7
Clothing and Footwear	19.25	13.50	18
Miscellaneous	24.75	14.00	16
	100.00	100.00	100

The Census and Statistics Office took over price collection from the Department of Labour. Recognising that the efficacy of the CPI as a measure of price changes depended more on accurate data than on the technical basis of the index, the office appointed a team of field researchers at considerable expense. Prices were collected in 21 towns across New Zealand with the aim of accurately representing all urban localities.[36] For the collection of food prices, the country was divided into four sectors, each visited by a 'price collector' in March 1949. March was chosen as figures collected could be compared with January and February numbers, giving the Statistics Office the opportunity to verify an entire quarter.[37]

1955: Expansion of the basket of goods

In 1955, the basket of goods was expanded significantly (from 308 items to 375) as the CPI underwent its first revision. Items previously considered to be 'luxuries' (alcohol, private motoring, private telephones, recreational goods, insurance) were now included in the index. The 1955 CPI covered around 85 per cent of personal expenditure, compared with 65 per cent in the 1949 index. One explanation for the dramatic expansion of the 1949 basket of goods was that "conditions were more favourable for this revision than in the immediate post-war period" (*Consumers' Price Index 1955 Revision*, 1956, p.15). Rationing ended in 1950, the post-war supply problems and currency fluctuations that rendered consumer goods scarce began easing in 1952, and economic conditions stabilised following the transition to peace.[38]

The 1955 revision was aided by the availability of a range of new research and information. Since 1946 the Census and Statistics Office industrial production statistics had been 'recast' to provide a more detailed analysis of individual commodities. In 1949, Customs introduced new statistical classifications providing specific data on individual imports that had previously been grouped together under general headings. Additionally, the first 'Census of Distribution' was undertaken during the year ending March 1953. The census supplied previously unavailable information on wholesale and retail sales by commodity groups. Also in 1953, the Public Service Association (PSA) released its (1952–1953) household budget survey, and the Department of Statistics conducted a national census. Between 1950 and 1956, Canada, the UK, Australia and the US all revised their retail price index numbers – experiences that the 1955 revision drew upon and incorporated (*Consumers' Price Index 1955 Revision*, 1956, pp.6–8).

Within the Department of Statistics (renamed in 1955), the expansion of the basket was believed to represent a tendency towards "more liberal thinking on the part of index number statisticians" (*Consumers' Price Index 1955 Revision*, 1956, p.5). Two important additions to the index were areas of expenditure previously considered 'borderline': private motoring and alcoholic liquor. The former was included because post-war New Zealand was considered among the most highly motorised countries in the world, and because motoring price data was now included in the Canadian, American and British indices. Again, the inclusion of alcohol was noted as following the accepted practice of most other comparable countries (excluding Australia and South Africa), and it aligned with the Department's policy of making the CPI more representative of actual household consumption habits (*Consumers' Price Index 1955 Revision*, 1956, p.22).

1965: Stability and expansion

The 1965 revision of the CPI followed the same procedures as the 1955 revision, and incorporated only minor changes to the index. Notably, the revision continued to trend towards a more inclusive and representative index, accounting for approximately 90 per cent of consumer expenditure. In accordance with the Department of Statistics' desire to include 'luxury' items, 136 new commodities were added to the basket of goods, including household electronics, professionals' fees, beer and long-distance public transport costs. As with previous post-war indices, the 1965 index was based on the expenditure patterns of households in large urban areas and small towns. Though the number of municipalities covered by the Department of Statistics' price surveys expanded from 21 to 25, the publication of individual urban indices was reduced to the largest 14 towns, with the remaining 11 aggregated into groupings of smaller centres for the North and South Islands (*Consumers' Price Index Revision Report 1993*, 1995, p.15).

1972: CPI advisory committees

In May 1972, the Department of Statistics established a committee to examine the Consumers' Price Index, which had remained unchanged for seven years. The 1965 revision reflected household consumption patterns from 1963, and was thus felt to inadequately represent contemporary expenditure patterns. The 1972 committee was composed of representatives from national federations of employers, farmers, retailers and labour; the State Services Organisation; the Consumer Council; and the National Council of Women; as well as academic and technical experts (*Report on Consumers' Price Index Revision*, 1976).

The committee delivered a range of broad recommendations on the CPI, including the suggested revision of the index to reflect actual private household expenditure; expanding the geographical coverage of the index to include all "larger centres" and a "selected range of smaller centres"; and scheduling regular revisions to the index every five years to weight the relative importance of goods in the basket according to the current consumption patterns of the average New Zealander (*Household Sample Survey: Handbook for Field Interviewers*, 1974, p.1).[39] The change in the conceptual base of the CPI from an index charting notional consumption to an index that measured actual household expenditure was fundamental. The new index allowed a broader understanding of consumer spending, as commodities in the basket of goods would be weighted in proportion to household expenditure, as measured by the Department of Statistics (*Consumers' Price Index Revision Report 1993*, 1995).

Reflecting this transition to an objective, positivist index, the report of the 1972 Review Committee described the Department of Statistics' task as "essentially the ascertaining of a set of facts about the real world of contemporary existence" (*Report on Consumers' Price Index Revision*, 1976, p.9). To obtain the data required to implement the new weighting system, the Department introduced the first comprehensive Household Economic Survey since the family budget inquiry in 1930. In the intervening 43 years, revisions to price indices were based on estimates of average consumption derived from production, retail trade and external trade statistics, as well as "limited special sample surveys" of merchants and retailers. By the early 1970s, statisticians were increasingly aware that such estimates provided unsatisfactory data on actual household consumption patterns (*Household Sample Survey: Handbook for Field Interviewers*, 1974, p.1).

1973: Household Economic Survey

The 'Household Expenditure and Income Survey' had three major aims: to collect household expenditure data for use in the revision and weighting of the CPI; to prepare the proposed New Zealand system of National Accounts; and to provide household socio-economic statistics. Beginning in 1973, the survey sampled 4,600 households in the North and South Islands (Stewart Island and dependencies were dismissed as too expensive to survey) over a period of two weeks. Those interviewed were given a personal expenditure diary and asked to record their daily expenditure, and return the diary to their field interviewer. For larger items of spending (automobiles, major appliances, houses) participants were asked to recall their spending over the previous 12 months.

The expenditure categories covered by the survey were: Food; Housing; Household Operation (fuel, furnishings, utilities); Apparel; Transport; Alcohol and Tobacco (which necessitated the use of retail figures to allow for under-reporting); and Other Supplies (medicines, toiletries, stationery and books, jewellery, recreational goods); Other Services (medical services, entertainment, insurance, education, holidays). As well as a fortnightly Household Expenditure Diary, the Household Economic Survey included an 'Expenditure Schedule' (housing, utility, rent costs) and 'Income Schedule'.[40]

The current CPI

The current CPI can be defined as a measure of the average rate of change over time in the prices paid by consumers for a set basket of goods and services. While the CPI's role in determining wages has waned, the trend towards broader uses of the CPI continues; in 1990 the index became an integral component of New Zealand's monetary policy when the Reserve Bank of New Zealand Act 1989 came into effect. The Act placed the implementation of monetary policy under the control of the Reserve Bank Governor, with the objective of "achieving and maintaining [price] stability" (Reserve Bank of New Zealand Act 1989, s.8). Previously, the Minister of Finance both devised New Zealand's monetary policy targets and determined the means by which these goals were to be achieved. In the interests of reducing economic uncertainty, and liberating monetary policy from daily political pressures, the innovative new system offered greater autonomy to the Reserve Bank.

Under the new framework, the Reserve Bank endeavours to meet transparent inflation targets (called Policy Targets Agreements) set in conjunction with the Treasurer and currently measured by the 'all groups' CPI (Reserve Bank of New Zealand, 2008). The Reserve Bank Act does not specify a particular measure by which 'price stability' is tracked, but since 1990, modified versions of the

CPI have been used as monetary policy targets. While the CPI is a reasonable proxy to the aims outlined in the Reserve Bank Act, other measures such as the GDP implicit price deflator or the Producers Price Index (PPI) could also be used to measure inflation. Perhaps the best explanation for the CPI's continued recognition in PTAs is that its long history has made it the most publicly accepted and understood measure of inflation (Reddell, 1999, pp.68–69). Under the terms of the initial agreement, the target for annual underlying inflation was set at 0–2 per cent. Policy Targets Agreements are periodically redrawn to reflect 'price shocks', international pressures, and changes in rates of indirect taxation. Although changes to state industrial relations mechanisms, notably the Employment Contracts Act 1991, minimised the function of the CPI in settling wage disputes, the index remains an important input in wage negotiations. It is also used to adjust commercial contracts, excise duties, and "New Zealand Superannuation and unemployment benefit payments once a year, to help ensure that these payments maintain their purchasing power" (Statistics New Zealand, 2011).

Discussion: Significant changes in the CPI

As the foregoing review makes clear, there have been significant changes in the construction of consumer price indices in New Zealand since official price statistics were first collected in the 1840s. Conceptually these may be divided into changes in the universe of consumers for whom the index is constructed, and changes in the prices included in the index.

The universe of consumers for price indices has changed significantly, with a movement from prescriptively defined nuclear families to a representative average of all households. Until the first survey of household budgets in 1893, price statistics in New Zealand were not collected to construct an aggregate index. Indices were computed separately for each type of good, or the raw nominal prices were published. From 1893 to 1949 the universe of consumers for price indices was families headed by a wage-earning man in largely urban industries (both secondary and tertiary). The men in these surveys represented a range of occupations, from unskilled labourers to skilled tradesmen, along with some salespeople and clerical workers. Managers and professionals were likely to have been under-represented in these surveys. Men and women living on their own, without children, or as boarders or lodgers, are also likely to have been under-represented in – if not excluded from – these surveys. However, this was also the universe for expenditure surveys in the US, the UK and Australia (International Labour Organization, 1926; Stapleford, 2009). Family budgets collected from samples of working men provided the expenditure shares for price indices until 1949.

From 1949 until 1973 the weights of items in the CPI were constructed from aggregate expenditure shares, and without reference to a survey of household expenditures. The universe of consumers implied by this method of construction is somewhat unclear. However, if the aggregate expenditure shares accurately distinguished household, government, and firm expenditure, then the household shares will implicitly include all households. The final expenditure shares will then be a weighted average of expenditure shares among different types of households.

Since the introduction of a household expenditure survey in 1973 – carried out by sampling households from Statistics New Zealand's master sampling frame – items in the CPI are weighted by expenditure shares from a representative household survey. The expenditure shares derived from the survey are then a weighted average of the expenditure shares by different forms of households in New Zealand. Some populations may feel that their expenditure patterns are sufficiently different from the average that the CPI is not an accurate representation of changes in their cost of living. For both political and demographic reasons, a CPI weighted to the expenditure shares of superannuitants was first published in 1995 as a research index. The index has not been adopted as an official price index by Statistics New Zealand. However, the 2004 CPI Revision Advisory Committee recommended that the CPI "take account of changes in the cost of living for different population subgroups such as superannuitants, wage and salary earners, low-income households, and recipients of government transfer payments" (Statistics New Zealand, 2004). The price indices that would allow interested groups to publish a re-weighted CPI are available on Statistics New Zealand's Infoshare service, but detailed information on expenditure shares by different household types are not widely available. Thus, the century-long historical pattern of some groups being under-represented in the CPI is likely to continue.

As well as expanding to cover all households in New Zealand, the CPI has also expanded its coverage of the goods and services purchased by consumers. As shown in Table 3, early price indices missed some significant items of consumer expenditure. Most importantly, until 1955 the CPI excluded items regarded as 'luxuries', even when a substantial proportion of the population consumed those items. Alcohol, tobacco, and motor vehicle acquisition and running costs were the most significant exclusions that were brought into the index in 1955.

Housing – a necessity consistently included in the index – has been subject to multiple changes. Housing has made up between 13 and 25 per cent of household expenditure for the past hundred years (Collins, 1912; Statistics New Zealand, 2010). Reflecting the prevalence of renting in household expenditure surveys, in the early twentieth century the CPI measured housing by including a measure of rental prices for private households. Surveys of rental contracts, and information on rental prices from the quinquennial census were used to update the index.[41]

Table 3. Changes in major categories of expenditure in the CPI, 1914–2006.

Food	Food was included from 1914 (when the series started). Confined to staples until 1949, when restaurant meals, confectionery, and soft drinks were added. Seasonal fruit and vegetables were also included from 1949. The value of home-produced fruit and vegetables was included from 1949. The value of home-produced fruit and vegetables was excluded from 1974.
Alcoholic beverages and tobacco	Tobacco was included from 1914. Beer for consumption on licensed premises was included from 1955. Beer for consumption off licensed premises was included from 1965. Wine and spirits were included from 1974.
Clothing and footwear	Clothing and footwear were included from 1924 and the series was recalculated back to 1914.
Housing and household utilities	Electricity, gas, and solid fuels were included from 1914. Housing rentals were included from 1914. From 1949, a 'use' conceptual framework was used, with a weighting pattern based on actual or notional consumption. Home ownership was added in 1949. A 'user-cost' approach was adopted, incorporating depreciation, return on capital, repairs and maintenance, local authority rates, and dwelling insurance. Fees associated with the purchase and sale of dwellings (such as real estate agent and conveyancing fees) were included from 1965. From 1974, an 'expenditure' approach was adopted. In practice, this combined elements of the 'acquisition' and 'payment' conceptual frameworks. The new approach to measuring home ownership included the purchase of new and previously occupied dwellings, the purchase of residential sections, expenditure on alterations and additions to existing dwellings, land, interest payments on new mortgages, repairs and maintenance, local authority rates, and dwelling insurance. From 1980, there was fuller netting of house purchases/sales (which led to a lower weight), but the weight on mortgage interest was increased to cover all mortgages existing in the weight reference period. From 1974 until 1993, prices of both previously occupied and new dwellings were tracked. From 1993, prices of only new dwellings were tracked (this aligned more closely with the weight allocated to home ownership, which represented the value of the net increase in the stock of owner-occupied housing during the weight reference period). From 1999, an 'acquisition' conceptual framework was formally adopted. Mortgage interest payments and the purchase of residential sections (land) were removed from the scope of the index. An analytical 'all groups plus interest' series remains available. From 2006, a new method was adopted for estimating the weight for home ownership (which led to a lower weight). This method better reflected the falling rate of home ownership.

Household contents and services	Household utensils, crockery, and furnishings were included from 1924 and the series was recalculated back to 1914. Furniture was included from 1942. Household appliances were included from 1949 (refrigerators from 1955).
Health	Health services and supplies were included from 1949.
Transport	Train and tram fares were included from 1924 and the series was recalculated back to 1914. Bus fares, taxi fares, and cycle parts were included from 1949. Cars, vehicle servicing, petrol, and cycles were included from 1955. Domestic airfares were included from 1974. International airfares (prepaid in New Zealand) were included from 1980. Overseas package holidays (prepaid in New Zealand) were included from 2006 (previously they had been represented by international airfares).
Communication	Postage and telegrams were included from 1930. Telephone services were included from 1955. Internet services and mobile phone services were included from 1999.
Recreation and culture	Recreational and cultural services were included from 1949. Sports and recreation goods were included from 1955. Television sets were included from 1965. Holiday accommodation costs were included from 1974. Subscriber television services were included from 1993.
Education	Education services were included from 1974.
Miscellaneous goods and services	Cosmetics were included from 1949. All types of insurance were grouped together from 2006 (rather than with the goods being insured) and a change was made from weighting based on gross insurance premiums to weighting based on insurance service charges (premiums less claims). All types of credit services were grouped together from 1993. Interest payments were removed from the scope of the index from 1999. An analytical 'all groups plus interest' series remains available.

The 1949 revision to the CPI added a measure of the cost of owner-occupied housing to the index. Housing is a large component of household expenditure, and owner-occupied housing bundles several conceptually distinct items into one purchase. Like rental housing, owner-occupied housing provides shelter. The price of shelter can be approximated by rentals for private housing. However, the price of private housing also embodies, in part, an investment component. The investment component of housing can, in theory, be separated into land and dwelling values, which may move separately. Households typically support the purchase of dwellings with loans requiring repayment of the dwelling price, plus interest. Household expenditures on owner-occupied housing thus bundle shelter services, investment and interest payments. For both analytical and monetary policy purposes it is desirable to be able to separate these different aspects of housing expenditures. Reflecting the current primacy of monetary policy makers as consumers of the CPI, since 1999 mortgage interest payments and 'section' (land) prices have been removed from the published CPI (Statistics New Zealand, 2008; Smith, 2007). Thus, users of the CPI should be aware that the treatment of housing in the CPI has varied considerably despite the consistent inclusion of this broad category in the CPI since the nineteenth century.

Conclusions

State administrators have collected price information in New Zealand for over 150 years. Initially, these efforts were rudimentary, providing the Colonial Office with trade figures from a distant outpost of the British Empire. Yet population growth, industrial pressures, and the volatile impact of a global economic downturn in the late nineteenth century all prompted a growing realisation that state intervention in the domestic economy was both necessary and desirable. Reformist politicians and bureaucrats, influenced by the liberal tradition of state social engineering, sought to both understand and mould New Zealand's social and economic growth. Alongside these domestic concerns, the desire for international comparison drove the implementation of systematic price collection at the turn of the century. For much of the twentieth century these concerns operated in tandem, pushing the development of increasingly extensive and sophisticated indices, both to protect a 'reasonable' standard of living for New Zealand families, and to meet the country's growing international obligations.

The pre-war price indices that served to regulate workers' wages became useful inflationary measures during wartime, and their international significance heightened as New Zealand enthusiastically joined post-war institutions that promoted peace through the application of the living wage. Gradually responding to the development of a post-war consumer economy, the CPI became a positive index of New Zealand household consumer spending, a departure from its origin as a prescriptive list of state-sanctioned 'staples'. As the basket of goods grew to reflect consumer expenditure, and the collection and compilation of price indices became increasingly sophisticated, they evolved from strictly prescribed data sets constructed to meet the direct needs of government and the Court of Arbitration to far more 'open' sets of data with widespread implications for social, economic, and monetary policy. That is, the CPI has evolved from a haphazard survey of prices in the major centres, to a comprehensive index reflecting national household spending. The measurement of prices is nearly coincident with the entire history of New Zealand as a British colony and independent country. Inevitably it is a history of important changes in definitions and methodology, of which economists must be aware.

References

Arnold, M. N. (1982). *Consumer prices, 1870 to 1919 (Victoria University economics discussion paper no. 12).* Wellington: Victoria University Department of Economics.

Baker, J. V. T. (1965). *The New Zealand people at war: War economy.* Wellington: Historical Publications Branch, Department of Internal Affairs.

Burnett, John. (1969). *A history of the cost of living.* London: Penguin.

Collins, J. W. (1912). *Inquiry into the cost of living in New Zealand, 1910–1911.* Wellington: Government Printer.

Consumers Price Index 1955 revision (1956). Wellington: Government Printer.

Consumers Price Index revision report 1993 (1995). Wellington: Statistics New Zealand.

Dr. Findlay's address (1908). *Wanganui Herald,* 23 May 1908, p.4.

Explaining New Zealand's Monetary Policy (2007). Wellington: Reserve Bank of New Zealand.

Fraser, M (1915). *Report on the cost of living in New Zealand 1891–1914: Being an inquiry into the course of retail prices during the period 1891–1914; with monthly tables showing increases during war period – July, 1914 to August, 1915.* Wellington: Government Printer.

Hawke, G. R. (1985). *The Making of New Zealand: An Economic History.* Cambridge: Cambridge University Press.

Hight, J. (1911). Introduction. In J. W. McIlraith, *The course of prices in New Zealand: An inquiry into the nature and causes of the variations in the standard of value in New Zealand.* Wellington: Government Printing Office, pp.3–4.

Holt, J. (1986). *Compulsory arbitration in New Zealand: The first forty years.* Auckland: Auckland University Press.

Holt, J. (2001). Compulsory arbitration in New Zealand, 1894–1901: The evolution of an industrial relations system. In J. Binney (ed.) *The shaping of history: Essays from the New Zealand Journal of History.* Wellington: Bridget Williams Books.

Household sample survey: Handbook for field interviewers (1974). Wellington: Department of Statistics.

International Labour Organization (1919). *Constitution of the International Labour Organization.* Retrieved 10 March, 2011, from http://www.unchr.org/refworld/docid3bbd5391a.htm.

International Labour Organization (1926) *Methods of Conducting Family Budget Enquiries.* Geneva: ILO Studies and Reports, Series N, No. 9.

Lomas, J. (1912). Preface. In J. W. Collins, *Inquiry into the cost of living in New Zealand, 1910–1911.* Wellington: Government Printer, pp.1–3.

Martin, J. E. (2010). *Honouring the Contract.* Wellington: Victoria University Press.

McIlraith, J. W. (1911). *The course of prices in New Zealand: An inquiry into the nature and causes of the variations in the standard of value in New Zealand.* Wellington: Government Printing Office.

Neale, E. P. (1955). *Guide to New Zealand official statistics.* Third edition. Auckland: Whitcombe and Tombs Limited.

Reddell, Michael (1999). Origins and early development of the inflation target. *Reserve Bank of New Zealand Bulletin, 62*, 63–71.

Report on Consumers Price Index revision (1976). Wellington: Department of Statistics.

Reserve Bank of New Zealand (2008). *Policy targets agreement*. Retrieved 15 July, 2011, from http://www.rbnz.govt.nz/monpol/pta/3517828.html.

Retail prices in New Zealand with special reference to the Consumers' Price Index (1949). Wellington: Government Printer.

Smith, Mark (2007). Microeconomic analysis of household expenditures and their relationship with house prices. *Reserve Bank of New Zealand Bulletin, 70*, 39–45.

Stapleford, Thomas (2009). *The cost of living in America: A political history of economic statistics, 1880–2000*. New York: Cambridge University Press.

Statistics New Zealand (2004). *Report of the Consumers Price Index Revision Advisory Committee*. Wellington: Statistics New Zealand.

Statistics New Zealand (2008). Home ownership in the Consumers Price Index. *Price Index News*. January 2008. Wellington: Statistics New Zealand.

Statistics New Zealand (2010). Household Economic Survey: Year ended June 2010, *Hot Off the Press*, 25 November 2010. Wellington: Statistics New Zealand.

Statistics New Zealand (2011). *Our surveys*. Retrieved 10 March, 2011, from http://www.stats.govt.nz/survey_and_methods/our-surveys/cpi-resource.aspx.

Van Daele, J. (2005). Engineering social peace: Networks, ideas, and the founding of the International Labour Organization. *International Review of Social History, 50*, 435–466.

Wages and the cost of living (1908). *Evening Post*, 19 June 1908, p.8.

Wood, G. (1976). *Progress in official statistics 1840–1957: A personal history*. Wellington: Department of Statistics.

Woods, N. S. (1963). *Industrial conciliation and arbitration in New Zealand*. Wellington: Government Publisher.

Notes

1   E. P. Neale provides a detailed series of such 'cautionary remarks' related to technical and methodological issues with historical price indices. E. P. Neale (1955). *Guide to New Zealand official statistics*. Auckland: Whitcombe and Tombs Limited, pp.94–108.

2   *Otago Daily Times*, 5 October 1896, p.2.

3   e.g. 'Sitting at Orepuki', *Otago Witness*, Issue 2690, 4 October 1905, p.32.

4   'The Cost of Living: Conditions in Wellington and Christchurch', *Evening Post* (Wellington), 14 August 1901, p.6.

5   'The Bonus: Employers' Appeal to Court', *Evening Post* (Wellington), 29 November 1920, p.7.

6   'Real Wages and Unreal Prices', *Evening Post* (Wellington), 14 December 1920, p.6.; 'Index Numbers', *Evening Post* (Wellington), 3 June 1921, p.7.

7   'The Bonus Decision', *Grey River Argus*, 16 December 1920, p.2.; 'The New

Bonus', *Hawera and Normanby Star,* 14 December 1920, p.5; 'Real Wages and Unreal Prices', *Evening Post* (Wellington), 14 December 1920, p.6.

8   Karamea Store Book, 1875–1876, NP Series 23, Box 5, item 6, Archives New Zealand (ANZ).

9   The Department of Labour sent out surveys to 800 'workingmen' deemed likely to respond by factory inspectors, labour bureau agents, and union secretaries, and received 146 completed surveys. The survey measured 30 different commodities (including beer) and the Department divided respondents into two categories and hoped to add a third. Households earning less than £100 per annum were deemed 'working-class', while households earning more than £100 per annum were deemed to be part of the 'mercantile class'. Future surveys including the 'wealthier classes' (households earning more than £200 per annum) were mooted that year, but not carried out. 'Returns of Expenditure by Workingmen', Annual Report of the Department of Labour, *Appendices to the Journal of the House of Representatives (AJHR),* H-10, 1893, pp.40–51.

10 'Estimated Rise in Wages and Prices of Necessary Foods', *New Zealand Official Year Book,* 1908, pp.539–540.

11 'Cost of Living in New Zealand (Report and Evidence of the Royal Commission On)', *AJHR,* 1912 Session II, H-18, pp. ix, xi–xii.

12 ibid., p. xcix.

13 ibid., p.c.

14 ibid., p.cvi.

15 ibid., pp.cvii–cviii.

16 ibid., pp. lxxxvii–lxxxviii.

17 *New Zealand Parliamentary Debates (NZPD),* 1892, Vol. 78, p.181.

18 M. Fraser (Government Statistician), to G. H. Knibbs (Commonwealth Statistician), 13 March 1914, in STATS Series 1, Box 26, Record 22/1/7, ANZ.

19 M. Fraser, to The Secretary, NZ Seamen's Union, 20 October 1921, STATS Series 1, Box 29, Record 22/6/15, ANZ.

20 M. Fraser, to R. S. Parrington, 24 May 1918, in STATS Series 1, Box 26, Record 22/1/22, ANZ.

21 Cost of Living, Prices, Wages, Rent, Unemployment – Prosecution of firms for failure to furnish price returns, STATS Series 1, Box 30, Record 22/30/21, ANZ.

22 M. Fraser to Newspaper Editors, 10 February 1930, in STATS Series 1, Box 22, Record 22/1/82, ANZ.

23 J. W. Butcher (Government Statistician), to the Minister in charge of Census and Statistics, 24 February 1943, in STATS Series 1, Box 27, Record 22/1/71, ANZ.

24 P. A. de la Perrelle (Minister of Internal Affairs) to M. Fraser, 11 November 1929, in STATS Series 1, Box 34, Record 34, 60/1/6, ANZ .

25 P. A. de la Perrelle to A. Hamilton MP, 25 November 1929, in STATS Series 1, Box 34, Record 34, 60/1/6, ANZ.

26 The RPI continued to be collected, however, "to preserve the continuity of the series". The decision was contested, as trade unions had used the RPI, with its wider range of goods, to calculate wages and as a base measure in industrial

disputes; Memorandum, Director of Stabilization, to Minister in charge of Stabilization, 4 June 1943, in STATS Series 1, Box 27, Record 22/1/71, ANZ.

27 'The New Zealand Wartime Prices Index', *AJHR*, H-43, 1944, p.1.

28 There appears to have been trouble with butchers complying with price information surveys because their prices frequently exceeded government-established price ceilings and they feared prosecution if their deception were uncovered. Other retailers had previously been 'duped' by competitors posing as price collectors in order to ascertain more complete information about their rivals' businesses.

29 'Notes on Wages Fixation' in STATS Series 1, Box 29, Record 22/6/71, ANZ.

30 *AJHR*, H-48, 1948, p.5. Report of Index Committee, *AJHR*, H-48, 1948, pp.4–5.

31 ibid., p.48.

32 When informed that the Committee intended to include beer in the regimen, Peter Fraser reacted swiftly to ensure its exclusion, horrified at the possibility that wages would rise in sympathy with the price of alcohol. Wood, 1976, pp.95–96.

33 Australia had 160, the UK 230, Canada 152, the USA 160, and South Africa 208. ibid., p.22.

34 ibid., p.13.

35 G. E. Wood (Government Statistician) to R. B. Ainsworth (Director of Statistics, UK Ministry of Labour and National Service), 1 February 1949, in STATS Series 1, Box 27, Record 22/1/78, ANZ.

36 For a town to be included in the collection process it required a population greater than 4,696. G. H. Hawthorne, Acting Secretary, The Associated Chambers of Commerce of New Zealand, to M. Fraser (Government Statistician), 10 July 1951, in STATS Series 1, Box 27, Record 22/1/78, ANZ.

37 'Consumers' Price Index – Collection of Food Prices', in STATS Series 1, Box 28, Record 22/1/86, ANZ.

38 Presumably the Department also had more resources to devote to the project. Budgetary considerations have always limited the extent of price collection in the CPI. When new items are added to the basket of goods, collection costs are one of the factors considered by the revision committee. In the 1988 revision of the index, price surveys in Ashburton, Gore, Hawera, Taupo and Whakatane were discontinued 'as a cost saving measure'. *Consumers' Price Index Revision Report 1993*, p.17.

39 Since 1974, the CPI has been reviewed nine times, an average of once every 3.8 years. *Report on Consumers' Price Index Revision*, pp.6, 16–17.

40 Household Sample Expenditure Survey, 1975, in Department of Internal Affairs Series 6015, Box 226, Record 103/492/8/1C, ANZ.

41 'Rent Statistics', *Evening Post* (Wellington), 12 January 1924, p.1.

Acknowledgement

This chapter was first published in *New Zealand Economic Papers*, 46:1, 57–77, DOI: 10.1080/00779954.2011.645222 and is reprinted here with their permission.

CPI Frameworks, 1949–2014

Chris Pike

Abstract

The construction of the CPI requires the use of a framework for choosing what is contained in the market basket of goods and services, and how these are to be weighted. Different frameworks are explained and historical changes to the ones applied in New Zealand are described for the 65-year period from 1949 to 2014.

Introduction

The two main uses of the New Zealand Consumers Price Index (CPI) are as an inflation indicator – for the purposes of monitoring, or maintaining general price stability – and as a compensation index for adjusting a range of public and private payments and receipts.

Over recent history, there has been a desire to use the official CPI as the yardstick for measuring inflation, primarily for monetary policy purposes. This trend has also been evident in other developed economies, following the widespread adoption of formal inflation targeting. This, in turn, has affected the suitability of the CPI as an index for compensating changes in the cost of living. Most notably, the treatment of owner-occupied housing and interest payments are the areas where the requirements of an inflation index and a compensation index differ most.

1 What should the Consumers Price Index measure?

At the broadest level, two central uses are made of the CPI (Statistics NZ, 2004a):[1]

- As an inflation index – either for the household sector, or the wider economy. The CPI is widely used to assist central banks in maintaining general price stability.
- As a compensation index – to allow the adjustment of government transfer payments to households or income tax thresholds to compensate for increases

---

1   These relate to the public uses of the CPI. The CPI is also used extensively by statistical agencies as a deflator of household consumption expenditures in the National Accounts.

in the cost of living; or as information used by employees, employers, or goods or service retailers to seek adjustments in prices, wages, or profits to maintain income levels in the face of rising costs.

The use of the CPI as an inflation index for monetary policy purposes is largely pragmatic. In New Zealand, other official price indices, such as the gross domestic product implicit price deflator, producers price index, or other derived measures, are seen to have deficiencies, or are not sufficiently well understood to meet the perceived need for general public acceptance in the monetary policy regime.

The CPI is regarded as an appropriate barometer of inflation in the wider economy, although this is not reflected in its design. In many countries, the stabilisation of CPI inflation has successfully resulted in the stabilisation of economy-wide inflation expectations.

The use of the CPI as a compensation index also partly reflects its high profile and wide acceptance. These characteristics may be seen to outweigh any conceptual or technical deficiencies in the index itself.

2 Background

Since 1974, the New Zealand CPI has been designed to provide a measure of price change for New Zealand resident private households, based on the goods and services they actually purchase. This is a sufficiently general statement to embrace the two central uses of the CPI. In the 1970s, the emphasis was on using the CPI to determine wages. During this period and into the 1980s, wage bargaining took place at a national level and in a high-inflation environment, and the CPI was seen as a key indicator of the level of wage adjustment required to maintain the purchasing power of incomes.

After the Reserve Bank Act 1989 and Employment Contracts Act 1991 were passed, the use of the CPI as an inflation indicator became more important. This trend has also been evident worldwide in other developed economies, following the widespread adoption of inflation targeting by central banks.

During the early phase of formal inflation targeting, the Reserve Bank focused primarily on a variant of the CPI. The official 'all groups' index was recognised as treating certain items, such as housing, in a way that was not optimal for monetary policy considerations. The 1997 Policy Targets Agreement (PTA), between the Governor of the Reserve Bank and the Minister of Finance, formalised the policy target in terms of the analytical series, CPIX. This series was the 'all groups CPI excluding credit services,' which left out interest rates included in the 'headline' measure.

The desire to align the official CPI more closely to an inflation index suitable for monetary policy resulted in both interest rates and residential section prices[2] being excluded from the 'all groups' CPI at the June 1999 quarter review. Since that time, the monetary policy target has been defined in terms of the 'all groups' CPI in successive PTAs.

The 1997 CPI Advisory Committee recognised the importance of having a credible measure of the CPI that was suitable for monetary policy purposes (Statistics NZ, 1997). However, there were significant differences in committee members' views about the necessity of making changes to the CPI, given its history as a compensation index. In the end, the 1997 committee agreed that the official 'all groups' CPI would incorporate some conceptual characteristics that made it more suitable for measuring inflation. A so-called 'acquisition' framework was formally affirmed and refined. The CPI was to measure price change based on goods and services actually acquired by households, and would exclude interest payments (and residential section prices). However, the committee recommended that the official CPI be supported by two additional price indices that, in concept, would better suit compensation purposes.

There was to be an index based on all household payments for goods and services. This index would adopt the so-called 'payment' framework and include interest payments, allowing continuity with the CPI prior to the changes.

The other index was to be based on a 'use' framework and more closely approximate the concept of a cost-of-living index. The key difference was that it would use a 'rental equivalence' approach for owner-occupied housing costs, rather than the expenditure-based approaches of the other indices. Rental equivalence uses the rent paid for an equivalent house in the private sector as a proxy for the costs faced by an owner occupier. In other words, this answers the question, "How much would I have to pay in rent to live in a home like mine?" for an owner occupier.

The committee's recommendation for three price indices was not implemented, principally because Statistics New Zealand is not funded to produce multiple CPIs. Proposals to obtain the necessary funding to produce these additional indices were assessed by Statistics New Zealand, by Treasury, and by Statistics New Zealand's external Advisory Committee on Economics Statistics, as having lower priority than other investments to improve macro-economic statistics.

As a consequence, the 'all groups' CPI, incorporating conceptual features appropriate to its use as an inflation index suitable for monetary policy considerations, has remained the sole household consumption price index in New Zealand,[3] although an implicit price index can be derived from the current

---

2   The exclusion of section prices was on the grounds that expenditure on sections was predominantly an investment expense, which had no place in an index measuring prices of consumption goods and services.

3   Since the 1999 review, Statistics New Zealand has published an analytical series, 'CPI plus interest'.

and constant price estimates of household consumption expenditures in the National Accounts.

The 'all groups' CPI does, however, include non-market transactions – for example, government charges such as local authority rates and those for health and education. It can be argued that these inclusions make the CPI less suitable for monetary purposes, because price changes for services that are partly or fully provided by government do not reflect 'inflation' in the economy and are not amenable to monetary policy interventions. Excluding non-market transactions from the CPI would, however, make the basket less representative of household purchases, which might compromise the credibility of, and trust and confidence in, the CPI.

3 Guidelines for constructing CPIs

The characteristics of a good CPI are its credibility and timeliness, supported by good methodological practices.

The International Labour Organization (ILO) *Resolution Concerning Consumer Price Indices* (ILO, 2003) describes three frameworks that are used to underpin CPI design:

- acquisition
- payment
- use.

Under the **acquisition** framework, the CPI weights are derived from expenditure on the goods and services *purchased* by households during the 'weight reference' period (which is usually a year), irrespective of whether they were wholly paid for or consumed during that period. Prices enter the CPI in the period when consumers purchase the good or service, and at the full, agreed value, irrespective of what is paid.

Under the **payment** framework, the weights are derived from the total *payments* made for goods and services during the weight reference period, regardless of when the goods or services were acquired or consumed. Prices enter the CPI in the period that payment is made, which may or may not coincide with the period of acquisition or use.

Both of these frameworks are based on monetary expenditures. Most goods and services are fully paid for when acquired, but a different treatment is given to items purchased on credit. Under the acquisition concept, the full value of goods and services purchased during the weight reference period is used to determine their expenditure weights, regardless of whether those items were fully paid for when acquired.

Under the **payment** framework, only the actual payments made during the weight reference period are used. However, these payments may represent partial payment for items purchased during the weight reference period, plus any payments made for goods that had been previously purchased on credit. This framework also allows for the inclusion of interest payments.

Payments for previously purchased goods have no place in an index measuring prices for weight-reference-period acquisitions, and are therefore out of scope under the **acquisition** framework. Interest payments are also excluded in this framework, as the amount of interest paid bears a weak relationship to the actual quantities of goods and services purchased in the weight reference period. Bank account fees that are explicitly charged for are included in this framework and are included in CPIs compiled by many national statistics offices. The financial intermediation service that banks implicitly charge for when lending money out at higher interest rates than they pay to depositors falls within the conceptual scope of the acquisition framework, but is excluded from the CPIs compiled by almost all national statistics offices.

Under the acquisition approach, the insurance industry is viewed as providing an intermediation service in which the contributions made by policy holders are pooled and managed. The part of premiums that does not pay for the intermediation service goes into pools. The pools are managed by the insurance companies, invested to best advantage, and provide a source of funds for policy holders to use when they need to repair or replace insured property, pay for medical services, or obtain income.

Under this 'net' approach, the weight given to insurance relates to the administrative costs of providing the service (i.e. collecting premiums and paying claims), and the profits of insurance companies. In simple terms, this is equivalent to premiums plus investment income on premiums and reserves, less claims and changes in reserves. Under the net approach for insurance services, the weights of goods and services covered by insurance represent total expenditure on goods and services, whether funded by insurance or other means.

For practical reasons, most national statistics offices measure price change for insurance services by tracking change in gross premiums.

Under the **use** framework, the expenditure weight is based on the value of the goods and services *used* or *consumed* during the weight reference period. The emphasis is on the value of the commodity consumed, rather than what was paid for it. The value and cost of a commodity for 'use' will be the same for many items. The most significant difference under the use framework is the treatment of capital (or durable) goods.

Consumers are seen to benefit from the flow of services derived from durable goods rather than the purchase of these goods. The most important of these items in the CPI is owner-occupied dwellings.

Under the acquisition framework, the weight of owner-occupied housing in the CPI is the net acquisition of owner-occupied housing – that is, the value of the net increase in the stock of owner-occupied housing in the weight reference period.

Under the payment framework, the weight of owner-occupied housing is determined by the amounts actually paid out for housing – including mortgage interest payments for previously acquired dwellings. Deposits and principal payments paid by owner occupiers are not included, as they are viewed as not affecting household balance sheets.

Under the use framework, it is the value of the shelter services being consumed that is used to derive its expenditure weight. The value of shelter services can be derived by estimating either the equivalent rental value of the stock of owner-occupied housing or the estimated economic cost of use. The economic cost of use is estimated using interest rates, house price inflation, and depreciation rates.

The use approach is consistent with the System of National Accounts, which is a standard system that is adhered to internationally. In contrast, the three frameworks that are used to underpin CPI design are all endorsed in the ILO resolution on CPIs. While the use framework is universally adopted for household consumption expenditures in the National Accounts, all three approaches are common for CPIs, as there is a diverse range of primary uses of CPIs in different countries.

There has been a preference in some countries to include in CPIs only prices that can be actually observed and to exclude prices that are proxies or notional in nature. For example, rental equivalence uses the rent paid for an equivalent house in the private sector as a proxy for the costs faced by an owner occupier. Many countries have been reluctant to adopt rental equivalence in their CPIs and there has been widespread criticism in some countries that have, at times when private-sector housing rentals have changed in ways that have been perceived to be unrepresentative of changes in owner-occupied housing costs.

The design of the New Zealand CPI has been explicitly based on the acquisition framework since 1999. It is a price index for goods and services actually purchased by consumers. The ILO considers this framework the most appropriate for an inflation indicator, as it reflects the actual prices of goods and services transacted. The payment and use frameworks are conceptually more appropriate for compensation purposes. A decision to adopt a payment rather than use approach can reflect concerns over the possible lack of credibility of an index that incorporates a notional price component. Some have also made the distinction of adopting a payment framework where the aim is to maintain purchasing power, and a use framework where the aim is to preserve living standards.[4]

4   The **use** framework is also conceptually more suitable for the deflation of household consumption expenditures in the National Accounts.

While these frameworks help give shape to the CPI design, they do not provide all the answers. To determine the full scope of the expenditures and prices to be covered in the CPI, statistical agencies need to appeal to the purposes the index is to serve. An inflation index would differ from a compensation index in several areas. These differences need to be considered, irrespective of whether an acquisition, payment, or use framework has been chosen.

4 CPI advisory committees

The use of CPI advisory committees is recommended by the ILO. The ILO's *Resolution Concerning Consumer Price Indices* states:

> The ... agency ... should consult representatives of users ... particularly during preparations for any changes to the methodology used in compiling the CPI. One way ... is through the establishment of advisory committees.

Advisory committees undertake independent reviews of the practices and methods used to compile the CPI and make recommendations for change or to confirm current practice. The first 'modern' CPI advisory committee was appointed in 1948, and committees have also been convened in 1971, 1978, 1985, 1991, 1997, 2004, and 2013. The 1991 and 1997 committees had 16 and 14 members, respectively, and were chaired by the Government Statistician. The 2004 committee, which had seven members, was chaired by John McDermott (then Chief Economist of the National Bank). The 2013 committee, which had nine members, was chaired by Diana Crossan (former Retirement Commissioner).

5 CPI reviews

Reviews of the composition and relative importance of the CPI basket of representative goods and services (and, for some reviews, the conceptual framework or methods used to compile the CPI) have been undertaken in the years shown in Table 1.

Table 1. Changes to concepts, scope, and coverage of the CPI, 1949–2014

Year	Significant changes
1949	Replaced the Retail Prices Index. No longer limited to essential commodities. Home ownership added. A user-cost approach was adopted, incorporating depreciation, return on capital, repairs and maintenance, rates, and insurance. A 'use' conceptual framework was used, with a weighting pattern based on actual or notional consumption (e.g. the value of home-produced fruit and vegetables was included) . Prices collected in 21 centres. Monthly for food and fuel components..

1955	Private motoring, beer, refrigerators, household insurance, telephone rental, and sports and recreation goods were included for the first time. Monthly for food component.
1965	Prices collected in 25 centres.
1974	An 'expenditure' approach was adopted. In practice, this combined elements of the 'acquisition' and 'payment' conceptual frameworks. New approach to measuring home ownership, including interest payments on new mortgages. Weighting pattern based on the first Household Expenditure and Income Survey (HEIS), held in 1973/74. Basket expanded to include domestic airfares, holiday expenditure, and local package holidays.
1977	Minor review of expenditure weighting pattern.
1980	Fuller netting of house purchases/sales (which led to a lower weight), but the weight on mortgage interest was increased to cover all mortgages existing in the weight reference period.
1983	Minor review of basket and expenditure weighting pattern.
1988	Review originally scheduled for 1986; delayed until a HEIS free of the pre-GST spending boom was available. Price collection reduced to 20 centres. New or expanded price surveys were introduced, following deregulation of the economy.
1993	Advisory committee recommendations were to review the index five-yearly, to add term life insurance, and not to develop alternative CPIs but to consider a wider range of sub-indices such as for subpopulations (but only on a user-funded basis). Superannuitants Price Index subsequently produced from 1995 to 1999. All charges relating to credit were grouped together. Price collection reduced to 15 centres.
1999	Implementation delayed a year. Advisory committee recommendation that the CPI should be an acquisition measure that does not include interest (implemented), and that there should be two additional indices compiled on a payment basis and a use basis (not implemented). Other advisory committee recommendations included reviewing the basket and weighting pattern three-yearly (implemented) and calculating a retrospective 'superlative' index to indicate the effect of commodity substitution on the fixed-weight CPI (not implemented at the time). Interest payments and residential sections were removed from the basket.
2002	Minor review of basket and expenditure weighting pattern.
2006	Review delayed a year due to a decision (subsequently reversed) to delay the Household Expenditure Survey (HES) for a year (Statistics NZ, 2006). New expenditure classification, based on an international standard but modified for New Zealand use, adopted for the CPI and the 2006/07 HES. Geometric elementary aggregate formula adopted for goods and services that are subject to outlet substitution Retrospective superlative index calculated between 2002 and 2006, using both sets of weights, to indicate the effect of commodity substitution on the fixed-weight CPI Comprehensive review of field outlet samples and a reallocation of the sample more towards the larger centres.

2006 (cont.)	Extensive use of retail transaction (i.e. scanner) data for determining the expenditure weights, selecting representative products to track, and ensuring that the mix of sampled brands reflects market shares. The advisory committee recommended that the CPI remain an acquisition-based index. The committee also recommended another, annual. index or indices more suited conceptually to measuring changes in the cost of living for population subgroups, and a regional spatial index to measure differences in the cost of living in different regions (not implemented).
2008	Review of basket and expenditure weighting pattern (Statistics NZ, 2008). Retrospective superlative index time series extended from 2002 to 2008. High level of interest in basket changes (including *Campbell Live* item on food basket changes with Richard Till, a 15-minute slot on National Radio's *This Way Up*, and radio reports of runs on condensed milk and saveloys (which were removed from the basket) in Hawera.
2011	Review of basket and expenditure weighting pattern (Statistics NZ, 2011). Retrospective superlative index time series extended from 2002 to 2011, and to the tradables and non-tradables components of the CPI. A rolling review of field outlet samples and product specifications was implemented after the review.
2014	Review of basket and expenditure weighting pattern due to be implemented in October 2014. Retrospective superlative index time series will be extended to 2014. Retail transaction data for ten consumer electronic goods will be used to measure price change in the CPI, from the September 2014 quarter. Advisory committee recommendations included reducing the number of regional pricing centres from 15 to between 10 and 12, in order to fund other CPI-related initiatives, such as providing indices that measure price change for particular groups of households, and providing an analytical seasonally adjusting CPI time series. The committee also recommended that the CPI be provided monthly, with additional costs met by new funding.

Source: Statistics New Zealand

6 *Treatment of owner-occupied housing*

There has been a lack of agreement internationally on the appropriate treatment of owner-occupied housing in CPIs. The treatment adopted by a country depends on the main use of the CPI, the conceptual framework under which the CPI is compiled, and on the circumstances of the country's housing market.

As the treatment of owner-occupied housing differs across countries, international comparisons are often made after excluding housing and credit services (another area where there are measurement differences from country to country).

An example of the challenges involved in achieving consensus on the treatment of owner-occupied housing is the suite of harmonised indices of consumer prices (HICPs) compiled by European Union countries. From their inception in the 1990s, the HICPs have excluded owner-occupied housing costs (except for dwelling repairs and maintenance) – primarily due to a lack of agreement on how these costs should be treated, exacerbated by differences in national housing markets.

There has been longstanding work towards developing experimental owner-occupied housing series, based on the net acquisitions approach, to sit alongside the HICPs. During the past year, a regulation has been approved that will require member states to produce a stand-alone owner-occupied housing price index, using the net acquisitions approach – with the potential for full inclusion in the HICP at some point in the future. The regulation will come into force in late 2014. A decision on the inclusion of owner-occupied housing in the HICP is due to be made by September 2017.

The United Kingdom HICP is known as the consumer prices index (CPI). Due to strong user demand, the development of measures of owner-occupied housing has progressed more quickly than for the European Union as a whole. With guidance from the UK Consumer Prices Advisory Committee, the UK Office for National Statistics developed two approaches to measuring owner-occupied housing – the rental equivalence approach and the net acquisitions approach.

In September 2012, the Board of the UK Statistics Authority accepted the UK National Statistician's recommendation to use the rental equivalence approach to measure owner-occupied housing, following a report from the Consumer Prices Advisory Committee, a public consultation, and a review carried out by the National Statistician (Office for National Statistics, 2013). The UK series including the rental equivalence owner-occupied housing component is known as CPIH.

Housing rentals have been tracked in New Zealand since the CPI time series commenced in 1914. From 1949, a 'use' conceptual framework was used for the CPI, with a weighting pattern based on actual or notional consumption. Home ownership was added to the CPI in 1949. A 'user cost' (or economic cost-of-use) approach was adopted, incorporating depreciation, return on capital, repairs and maintenance, local authority rates, and dwelling insurance. Fees associated with the purchase and sale of dwellings (such as real estate agent and conveyancing fees) were included from 1965.

From 1974, an 'expenditure' approach was adopted. In practice, this combined elements of the 'acquisition' and 'payment' conceptual frameworks. The new approach to measuring home ownership included the purchase of new and previously occupied dwellings, the purchase of residential sections, expenditure on alterations and additions to existing dwellings, land, interest payments on new mortgages, repairs and maintenance, local authority rates, and dwelling insurance. From 1980, there was fuller netting of house purchases/sales (which led to a lower weight), but the weight on mortgage interest was increased to cover all mortgages existing in the weight reference period. From

1974 until 1993, prices of both previously occupied and new dwellings were tracked. Since 1993, only prices of new dwellings have been tracked. This aligned more closely with the weight allocated to home ownership, which represented the value of the net increase in the stock of owner-occupied housing during the weight reference period.

From 1999, an 'acquisition' conceptual framework was formally adopted for the CPI. Mortgage interest payments and the purchase of residential sections (land) were removed from the scope of the index. An analytical 'all groups plus interest' series remains available. From 2006, a new method was adopted for estimating the weight for home ownership (which led to a lower weight). The method better reflected the falling rate of home ownership. The CPI home ownership component is known as the 'purchase of housing index'. It measures the change in price of a newly built house, excluding the land the house is built on. The price of a newly constructed dwelling is surveyed from builders that build standard-plan houses.

In the CPI, the price of existing (second-hand) houses is not tracked. This is because the CPI uses the acquisition framework. Under the acquisition framework, only spending on newly built owner-occupied houses, and on alterations and additions to existing owner-occupied houses, are included. Sales within the household sector of existing owner-occupied houses are excluded because they do not add to the stock of owner-occupied houses.

7 Current uses of the CPI

7.1 Monetary policy setting

The 1997 CPI advisory committee accepted that the established role of the CPI in New Zealand's monetary policy regime meant that the index should retain an inflation focus rather than a compensation focus.

The Policy Targets Agreement between the Governor of the Reserve Bank and the Minister of Finance requires the Governor to keep annual CPI movements in the range of 1 to 3 per cent on average over the medium term (Reserve Bank of New Zealand, 2012). In doing this, the Governor increases or decreases the official cash rate, and changes in this rate have an impact on the mortgage interest rates that households pay on about $185 billion of housing debt.

7.2 Adjusting government benefit payments and excise duty

Another important use of the CPI is by government to adjust New Zealand superannuation rates, welfare benefit rates, and other payments each year (to help ensure that these payments maintain their purchasing power) and to adjust excise duty payments on tobacco and alcohol (Treasury, 2013). Excise adjustments are made using the 'all groups less credit services' index. The 'all groups less cigarettes and tobacco' index is being used to adjust benefit rates during the period in which there are supplementary excise duty increases for tobacco of 10 per cent per annum, which commenced in 2011.

7.3 Adjusting contract payments and price regulation

The CPI is used to adjust commercial and residential rental payments and a range of contracted payments for services, and to regulate certain industries; for instance, the CPI-X is used to regulate electricity line company charges, and increases in telephone residential line rentals are capped by the CPI).

7.4 Wage negotiations

Another common use of the CPI is by employers and employees in wage negotiations. In Statistics NZ's Labour Cost Survey, the main reason cited by employers for increasing pay rates is still to reflect changes in the cost of living.

7.5 Deflation

The CPI is used extensively as a deflator of the household consumption expenditure components of the National Accounts, to remove the effect of price change and produce gross domestic product volume series. The CPI is also used as a basis for deflating retail sales, to produce sales at constant prices.

8 Re-weighting frequency

The ILO recommends that CPIs are re-weighted at least once every five years. The 1948 New Zealand CPI advisory committee recommended consideration of five-yearly reviews, even though the ILO recommendation at the time was for ten-yearly reviews. In practice, reviews were undertaken infrequently until 1974, then three-yearly until 1983, then five-yearly until 1999, then three-yearly since.

Current practice compares with six-yearly reviews in Australia. This issue was considered in 2010 by the Australian CPI Advisory Group, which recommended a move to four-yearly re-weights, although the Australian Bureau of Statistics has not yet obtained additional funding to make this change (Australian Bureau of Statistics, 2010).

9 Frequency of compilation

The food group of the CPI is published monthly as the food price index. The CPI is produced quarterly. Australia and New Zealand are the only two countries in the OECD that do not produce monthly CPIs. This issue was considered in 2010 by the Australian CPI Advisory Group. The advisory group supported a move to a monthly CPI, although, again, the Australian Bureau of Statistics has not yet obtained additional funding to make the change (Australian Bureau of Statistics, 2010). More recently, the 2013 New Zealand CPI Advisory Committee recommended that the CPI should be provided on a monthly basis (Statistics NZ, 2013). The committee recommended that the extra resources required to produce the CPI on a monthly basis should be paid for by new funding rather than by reprioritisation across the suite of official statistics.

At the time of writing, Statistics New Zealand was consulting CPI customers and stakeholders, to help prioritise the committee's recommendations.

Table 2. Current scope and coverage of the CPI

Coverage Dimension	Inclusions	Exclusions
Reference population	New Zealand-resident private households living in permanent dwellings.	New Zealand-resident private households not living in permanent dwellings. Institutional dwellings (such as retirement homes and prisons) Other non-private dwellings (such as boarding houses).
Goods and services	Goods and services transacted at market prices. Government charges (such as local authority rates, vehicle and driver licences). Services partly or fully subsidised by government (such as health and education) and transacted at non-market prices.	Interest Residential sections Assets Financial investment
Place of acquisition	In New Zealand, by the reference population.*	In New Zealand, by other than the reference population (such as by non-private households, foreign visitors, non-profit institutions serving households, and general government). Abroad, by the reference population.

* Purchases via mail order or the Internet where the supplier is located abroad are included in the expenditure weights, and, in some cases, are price surveyed.

References

Australian Bureau of Statistics (2010). *Outcome of the 16th Series Australian Consumer Price Index Review*. Available from www.abs.gov.au

International Labour Organization (2003). *Resolution Concerning Consumer Price Indices*. Adopted by the Seventeenth International Conference of Labour Statisticians. Available from www.ilo.org

Office for National Statistics (2013). *Introducing the New CPIH Measure of Consumer Price Inflation*. Available from www.ons.gov.uk

Reserve Bank of New Zealand (2012). *Policy Targets Agreement*. Available from www.rbnz.govt.nz

Statistics New Zealand (1995). *Consumers Price Index Revision Report 1993*. Wellington: Author.

Statistics New Zealand (1997). *Report of the Consumers Price Index Revision Advisory Committee 1997*. Wellington: Author.

Statistics New Zealand (2004a). *What Should the Consumers Price Index Measure?* Paper prepared for the 2004 Consumers Price Index Revision Advisory Committee. Available from www.stats.govt.nz

Statistics New Zealand (2004b). *Report of the Consumers Price Index Revision Advisory Committee 2004*. Available from www.stats.govt.nz

Statistics New Zealand (2006). *Consumers Price Index Review*. Available from www.stats.govt.nz

Statistics New Zealand (2008). *Consumers Price Index, 2008 Review*. Available from www.stats.govt.nz

Statistics New Zealand (2011). *Consumers Price Index Review: 2011*. Available from www.stats.govt.nz

Statistics New Zealand (2013). *Report of the Consumers Price Index Advisory Committee 2013*. Available from www.stats.govt.nz

The Treasury (2013). *Financial Statements of the Government of New Zealand for the year ended 30 June 2013*. Available from www.treasury.govt.nz

The Changing Basket of Goods

Sharleen Forbes

Abstract

The basket of commodities priced in surveys on which price indices are based has changed over the last hundred years. Some changes were the result of conceptual changes to the price index, which has been based on household expenditure patterns since 1974. The commodities, and their relative importance in the basket, give a historical perspective of social and political changes. Selected commodities are examined from two perspectives: longevity in the basket, and type of change.

1 Introduction

The opening chapter of this volume, by Forbes and colleagues, states that early price indices did not have good expenditure and price measures. As the quality of these measures has changed, so has the scope of the basket of goods and services on which the index is based. The very earliest price indices (1891–1907) were only calculated on a limited range of food and rent 'staples'. Table 1 gives the groups used in pricing surveys a century ago (in 1914) and the weights associated with each group (which reflect their relative importance in the final index). The first price index to be called a Consumers Price Index (CPI) was introduced in 1949, with a basket of goods and services primarily, but not exclusively, focused on items deemed to be necessary for a working-class family. Items deemed to be luxuries (alcohol, private motoring, private telephones, recreational goods, insurance) were first introduced in 1955. Since 1974, the basket has been based on the actual average expenditure pattern of New Zealand households, as determined by Statistics New Zealand's Household Economic Survey (initially called the New Zealand Household Survey). Changes in the spending patterns of New Zealand households increasingly reflect wider societal changes and the national impact of globalisation. The first section of this chapter examines the longevity of different types of items in the basket. A different perspective is taken in the second section, which analyses the types of social and political changes reflected in the basket of goods surveyed in CPI pricing surveys.

40

Table 1. 1914 pricing groups and associated weights

Group or subgroup		Weight as % of total
1. Groceries		16.67
2. Dairy Produce		9.05
3. Meat		13.28
4. Housing		23.21
5. Fuel and Light		5.97
6. Clothing		15.87
(a) Men's & Boys' overwear	2.51	
(b) Men's & Boys' underwear & hose	2.51	
(c) Women's & Girls' overwear	2.51	
(d) Women's & Girls' underwear	2.51	
(e) Household Drapery	2.51	
(f) Men's shoes	1.10	
(g) Women's shoes	1.10	
(h) Children's shoes	1.10	
7. Miscellaneous		15.94
(a) Household furnishings	3.43	
(b) Household ironmongery, brushware	2.29	
(c) Crockery	2.29	
(d) Train & Tram fares	4.00	
(e) Newspapers & Periodicals	2.86	
(f) Personal expenditure	1.09	
TOTAL		100%

Source: Statistics New Zealand

The change in focus from the basics, to the necessary, then to actual expenditure is reflected in the growing proportion of actual household expenditure that is included in the basket (65 per cent in 1949, 85 per cent in 1955, and almost 100 per cent in 1974, where it has since remained). Although the basket of goods and services is a *sample* of all possible in-scope products, representativeness in the item/commodity selection and the specific details of the product to be priced is maintained by regular reviews of the basket (usually at three-year intervals). Introduction of new goods to the basket of items priced is generally in response to the actual changes in purchasing patterns of households over time. The most recent review of the basket of goods and services was in 2011 (giving the most recent expenditure weights). Although almost all household expenditure is represented in the basket, there are still some omissions. Examples are expenditure on pets, works of art and gambling. As a general and fairly loose guideline, commodities should account for about 0.01 per cent of total household expenditure before they are introduced into the basket of goods. However, decisions about what should be added are also influenced by views on future trends. Some things that are in the current basket have weights that are less than 0.01 per cent, for example Boys' School Uniforms.

The Food group is so important that it is the only CPI commodity group for which an independent monthly index is currently calculated (the Food Price Index or FPI). Originally (1891–1924) there were several groups which could be classified as Food – Groceries, Dairy Products, Meat and Other – growing from 59 commodities in 1907 to 94 in 1914. Today these are all in the Food group, which has five subgroups: Fruit and Vegetables; Meat, Poultry and Fish; Grocery Food; Non-alcoholic Beverages; and Restaurant Meals and Ready-to-eat Food. Most of the subgroups comprise several classes of goods. In total there are 14 classes and 161 commodities within the Food group.

Grocery Food was originally a broad concept, including every kind of food except dairy products and meat. Items like fruit and vegetables later became separate subgroups. The opposite was the case for dairy produce, which is now in the Grocery Food subgroup. Since 2006, the Grocery Food subgroup has been made up of six classes: Bread and Cereal; Milk, Cheese, and Eggs; Oils and Fats; Food Additives and Condiments; Confectionary, Nuts and Snacks; and Other Grocery Food. Not surprisingly, given their importance and long standing in the CPI, food items are discussed in several of the following sections.

2 Stability of items/commodities priced

The war years provide an interesting illustration of some of the practical problems encountered over time in operating the basket. With the efforts of domestic manufacturers fully diverted to meeting the needs of the Armed Forces, there were shortages of some standard household commodities. An extreme example of the fluctuations that have to be accommodated in the CPI over time was the shortage of children's shoes during the war. In response to questions in the House in August 1943, the Minister of Supply and Munitions stated:

> The shortages . . . have been due principally to the decreased supplies available from the United Kingdom during 1941 and 1942 but also to the huge production of military footwear in our local factories. Advice was received however, that New Zealand's quota of footwear from the United Kingdom for the current year would total 450,000 pairs (which is a very satisfactory figure) and together with increased local production of children's footwear, . . . , it is anticipated that the shortage of children's footwear will be overtaken (Baker, 1965, p.467).

Products and services come and go, driven by a range of factors. New products and services have a life cycle, pricing strategies are designed to shift consumption patterns, and technologies introduce services that might have had no obviously comparable counterpart in earlier periods of time. In the midst of all this dynamism the CPI basket attempts to 'freeze' a level of value to the consumer for the period from one CPI revision to the next. The basket is then 'refreshed' and brought up to date by bringing in the new items that make it representative of the current day. This process usually means that the new basket as a whole delivers more value to consumers, reflecting the long-term growth in purchasing power. Certainly a fully representative basket from 100 years ago would look a little 'thin' by today's standards. However, consideration of basket items does give some insight into the changing experiences of the daily lives of New Zealanders.

Details of changes in major categories of expenditure in the CPI between 1914 and 2006 are given by Forbes and colleagues (this volume). Although there have been conceptual changes to price indices, as discussed above and elsewhere in this volume (e.g. Pike), the basket can be used to investigate the stability of some commodities in household purchasing patterns over time. A number of basic goods have been in the CPI from its inception, some have stayed in the CPI since their introduction and others have moved in and out of the basket.

Commodities that have been surveyed in the CPI can, therefore, be categorised into the following three groups:

- Hundred year commodities, that have been surveyed since the inception of price indices in New Zealand (although quantities, etc. may have changed over time).
- Enduring commodities, that have remained in pricing surveys since their introduction into the basket of goods.
- Transient commodities, that have only remained in the basket for short periods of time.

Selected examples in each of these three categories are discussed below.

2.1 Hundred year commodities

There are both more commodities and more groups of commodities in the basket today than there were originally. Table 2 gives the items within each of the seven commodity groups created in 1914 that have been surveyed in some form for the last hundred years.

Table 2. Hundred year commodities

Group	Commodity
1. Groceries	Bread
	Flour
	Tea
	Coffee
	Sugar
	Tomato sauce
	Potatoes
	Onions
	Cabbage
	Apples, eating
2. Dairy Products	Milk
	Butter
	Cheese
	Eggs
3. Meat	Beef
	Bacon
	Sausages
5. Fuel and Light	Firewood
6. Clothing	Men's socks
	Women's underwear
7. Miscellaneous	Train and tram fares
	Newspapers
	Men's haircuts
	Electricity
	House rent

2.1.1 Dairy products: milk and cheese

In terms of expenditure, milk has always been the most important. In 2011, of every $100 a household spent on food, about $5 went on fresh milk. However, over the last century, retail milk sizes and prices have experienced many changes. Initially milk was heavily regulated with, for example, the 1944 Milk Act, local milk authorities and the Milk Board. Both producer and consumer prices were set, with the difference being met by government subsidies. Milk price changes are detailed in Forbes (this volume). The fixing of milk prices was lifted in 1976, government subsidies were removed in 1985 and the milk industry was fully deregulated in 1993 (Statistics New Zealand, 2011).

Cheese accounts for about 2 per cent of New Zealand household expenditure on food (that is, for every $100 New Zealanders spend on food, about $2 is spent on cheese). This percentage has stayed reasonably stable for over three decades since 1980. In 1914 only 1lb blocks of New Zealand (cheddar) cheese were tracked in the CPI, but currently four different types of cheese are tracked: mild cheddar, cottage cheese, gourmet (mainly camembert) and processed slices.

2.1.2 The demise of home baking

According to the American Home Baking Association (cited in Statistics New Zealand, 2009), home baking began to decline in the 1960s as lifestyles became busier and more women took up paid work, reducing the time available for meal preparation. The New Zealand CPI reflects this decline in home baking. The traditional ingredients of flour, sugar, eggs and butter are all hundred year commodities, but their relative importance in the CPI has declined over time. In 1949, when a 25lb (11.3kg) bag of flour was priced, flour accounted for 0.8 per cent of household spending on food. In 1975, the CPI moved to collecting prices for a 1.5kg bag. By this time, flour's relative importance in the household food basket had fallen to 0.5 per cent of household spending on food. Although it has fluctuated slightly in the intervening years, it was again at 0.5 per cent of household expenditure on food in 2011.

Table 3. Relative expenditure weight of baking goods (as a percentage of household spending on food)

Year	Item			
	Flour	Sugar	Eggs	Butter
1949	0.8	4.6	4.0	4.8
1956	0.6	3.0	5.9	4.8
1966	0.5	2.5	3.9	3.2
1975	0.5	2.1	3.3	2.5
1978	0.6	1.7	2.7	2.3
1981	0.6	1.9	2.2	2.3
1984	0.7	1.3	2.1	2.0
1989	0.5	1.2	1.4	1.7
1994	0.6	1.0	1.2	1.3
1999	0.6	0.7	1.0	0.9
2002	0.3	0.4	1.0	0.8
2006	0.3	0.5	0.9	0.6
2008	0.4	0.4	1.1	0.6
2011	0.5	0.6	1.0	0.7

The relative importance of sugar has fallen similarly; in 2011 it accounted for about 0.63 per cent of household spending on food, about 70 per cent lower than in 1975 and 85 per cent lower than in 1949. Likewise, in 1949, eggs accounted for 4 per cent of household food spending, but by 1975, the importance of eggs had fallen to 3.3 per cent, and they now account for just under 1 per cent of household spending on food, 75 per cent lower than in 1949. The relative importance of butter in household food spending has also fallen over time, from 4.8 per cent in 1949 (or £4 and 16 shillings of every £100 spent on food) to only 0.74 per cent in 2011, a fall of about 85 per cent. There has been a shift towards margarine, which was introduced to the basket in 1975. At that time, 79 per cent of spending (in dollar terms) on butter and margarine was on butter, and the remaining 21 per cent was on margarine. The relative importance of spending on butter as a percentage of spending on butter and margarine overall, declined further to 51 per cent in 2011. Table 3 shows the changes in expenditure weights for flour, sugar, butter and eggs within the Food group between 1949 and 2011.

2.1.3 Bread

Bread is considered by many New Zealanders to be the staple of life. While it has indeed been a staple in the New Zealand diet over the last century, both the quantity and the type of bread purchased has changed. In 1914 it was assumed that a typical household consumed about seven 2lb loaves a week. A 2lb loaf was just under four pence (equivalent to about $2.45 in 2014) and bread made up about 10 per cent of a household's weekly food budget. In 1949, bread made up 4.7 per cent of the Food group. It shrank to 2.9 per cent in 1965, then rose again to 5.5 per cent in 1993. Bread's relative importance then decreased again, but has remained at about 4 per cent since 2002. Over time, bread became available in different varieties, sizes and packaging, and more types were included in pricing surveys. In 1955 the standard size for bread tracked in the CPI changed to a 28oz loaf. Only white bread was priced until wholemeal bread, wholegrain bread, and bread rolls were added in 1980, 1989 and 1993 respectively.

2.1.4 Fresh fruit and vegetables

Fresh fruit and vegetables have always been important foods, with apples, potatoes, onions and cabbage all being hundred year commodities. The fruit-eating habits of New Zealanders have been quite changeable and our favourite fruit is now bananas (an enduring commodity introduced in 1949). Before 1974, the estimated value of home-grown fruit and vegetables was included in the CPI weights together with prices of purchased goods. With the introduction of the expenditure-based CPI in 1974, home-grown produce was no longer counted, and the proportion of total spending on fruit and vegetables reduced from 19.6 per cent in 1965 to 15.9 per cent in 1974. Although there have been numerous additions and deletions to the fruit and vegetable basket over the years, reflecting how consumers' tastes and choices have changed over the last three decades, the expenditure weight of this subgroup as a whole has been relatively stable at approximately 14 per cent.

2.1.5 Miscellaneous hundred year commodities

Tobacco, newspapers and men's haircuts are also hundred year commodities. Over time, relative expenditure on cigarettes and tobacco has lessened, with a current weight of 2.13 per cent. The precursors of four of the current major daily newspapers, the *New Zealand Herald*, the *Dominion Post,* the *Press* and the *Otago Daily Times,* were in the first price surveys. At this time newspapers were the dominant (and for many people, the only) form of communication of local and world events. Newspapers and periodicals accounted for almost 3 per cent of total expenditure in 1914 but only 0.56 per cent in 2011.

Men's haircuts are a hundred year commodity but women's haircuts have only been included in the basket since 1949. In 1914, men's haircuts accounted for just under 1 per cent of total expenditure. About sixty years ago in 1951, a man's haircut would have cost about 2 shillings (about $6 in today's terms). Thirty years later, in 1981, it cost about $4, or $15 in today's terms. In 1980, men's haircuts were separated into wet and dry cuts. In the March 2014 quarter, the average cost of the men's wet haircuts sampled in the CPI was about $39.

Train fares are the only one hundred year transport commodity. Rail passenger transport (both tram and train fares) had a weight of about 4 per cent in 1924, although the commodities in the basket were more limited back then. By 1965, the number of commodities in the CPI had expanded, and the weight for rail passenger transport (urban, suburban, and long-distance train fares) was 0.55 per cent. In 2011, the weight for rail passenger transport (urban, suburban, and long-distance train fares) was 0.07 per cent, although there are some conceptual differences between the 1965 and 2011 CPI baskets.

2.2 Enduring commodities

Many of the enduring commodities that have entered the CPI basket reflect our changing lifestyle in the home, with less time being spent on household chores. Section 4.3 details the introduction of household appliances, many of which, such as washing and sewing machines, vacuum cleaners, motorised lawn mowers and refrigerators, became enduring commodities. Other examples of time-saving enduring commodities are the cut bread loaf (introduced in 1965), fried fish (introduced in 1974), disposable nappies (introduced in 1980), frozen mixed vegetables and duvets (introduced in 1993).

Technological advancements have allowed us to communicate with each other in different ways and are reflected in another set of commodities that, once introduced, became enduring, including telephone services (introduced to the basket of goods in 1955) the television (introduced in 1965) the home computer (introduced in 1988) and the cellular phone (introduced in 1999). The evolution of the television, as evidenced in changes in the basket of goods, is discussed in Section 4.2 below. Despite new forms of communication emerging, such as the Internet (introduced into the basket in 1999) and digital downloads (introduced in 2008), postage (first introduced in 1930) remains an enduring commodity.

Some leisure activities, such as going to the cinema, have been enduring commodities. Cinema admission prices were added to the CPI basket in 1949 when a 'trip to the flicks' would have cost about 2 shillings and 10 pence. In the March 2014 quarter, after allowing for general inflation, this was equivalent to about $10, whereas the average 2D cinema admission price was about $16.07 for an adult on a Saturday evening at that point in time. That is, it is relatively more expensive to go to the cinema today than 60 years ago. This may also reflect that over the years, visual entertainment alternatives such as television have emerged.

Women's haircuts and cosmetics, introduced in 1949, are also enduring commodities, but the items priced have changed considerably over time. Roughly 60 years ago, in 1951, a women's haircut would have cost about 3 shillings (almost $9 in today's terms). In 1949, prices were collected for a women's haircut, a women's hair set, and a women's permanent wave (perm). These remained unchanged until 1980, when the hair set was dropped, and 2006, when the perm was replaced by a women's hair colouring (cut and colour), and two beauty therapy services – an eyebrow shape and a half leg wax – were added.

In today's terms, a hair set or a perm would have cost 5 shillings and sixpence or £1 and 15 shillings respectively – about $16 and $105 respectively. Over the last 30 years, prices for hairdressing have risen faster than the CPI, increasing at an average annual rate of 5.2 per cent (compared to an average annual rate of 3.9 per cent for the total CPI). Of the four types of haircut tracked in the CPI today, the women's cut and colour is the most expensive, on average. The next most expensive is the women's haircut, followed by the men's wet cut. The cheapest is the men's dry cut.

Alcohol is also an enduring commodity, first introduced to the basket of goods as 'Beer for consumption on licensed premises' in 1955. Prices for alcoholic beverages in the CPI were initially collected for only one item, a 9oz (approximately 255ml) glass of draught (tap) beer, sold at on-licence premises. In 1955, that single glass of beer would have set you back 6 pence. In today's terms, after allowing for inflation, this is equivalent to about $1.20. The late addition of alcohol to the basket reflects perceptions of what was then deemed to be a basic good. Table 4 lists the major alcohol additions to the CPI basket and shows that wine and spirits were only included in the basket for the first time in 1974.

Whisky, gin, and wine are all enduring commodities, included in the CPI basket today. However, sherry was transient, being removed in 2006. In 1999, the beer items priced included cans of low alcohol beer and 'stubbies' (small bottles of beer). In the most recent review in 2011, an additional off-licence Ready To Drink (RTD) item was added to the basket, to reflect the increase in popularity of this type of beverage. Between 1999 and 2011, the volume of spirits available for consumption containing less than 23 per cent alcohol tripled, from 20.1 million litres to 61.9 million litres. Over the same period, the total volume of alcoholic beverages available for consumption increased by 13 per cent, from 418 million litres to 472 million litres. The Alcoholic Beverages subgroup had a weight of 4.8 per cent in 2011.

Table 4. Alcohol items added to the CPI basket

Item	Date added
Beer for consumption on licensed premises	1955
Beer for consumption off licensed premises	1965
Significant expansion in the range of alcoholic beverages priced – 16 alcohol items added including 4 types of whisky, 3 types of gin, 1 wine and 1 sherry	1974
Expansion to 27 items, the largest number to have appeared in the basket – including coffee-based and whiskey-based liqueurs	1988
25 on- and off-licence items, including 8 beers, 10 spirits and 7 wines	1999

A number of seasonal fruits and vegetables have been enduring since their introduction to the basket in 1949, including tomatoes, lettuce and bananas. New Zealanders love bananas, spending significantly more on them than on any other fruit, with apples being the banana's closest rival. Fresh bananas have been included in the CPI basket since the modern CPI was first published in 1949. Back then, bananas' weight was 0.9 per cent of the Food group, and it has not changed much since – it is currently 1.02 per cent of the Food group. We import about 18kg of bananas for every person each year, or about two bananas each a week, and this has remained reasonably consistent over time. Together, bananas, apples, potatoes, tomatoes and lettuce are the most popular Fruit and Vegetable consumer choices, accounting for more than 30 per cent of this subgroup over the past 60 years.

2.3 Transient commodities

Changing eating habits and fashions mean that some foods that may once have been viewed as enduring have become transient. Examples are marmalade (in the CPI basket from 1949 to 1983) and 'the party favourite', saveloys (in the basket from 1974 to 2008). Table 5 gives an overview of some of the changes in the food basket over the period 1955–2008.

The way we purchase food has also had an impact on the priced commodities, with delivered milk being specified in the basket for 57 years from 1942 to 1999, then disappearing.

Similar fashion changes are apparent in the alcoholic beverages that we drink. For example, wine coolers, made from wine and fruit juice, were briefly popular, being introduced to the basket in 1988, and removed at the next review in 1993.

Fashion dictates many of the items priced in the basket – not just clothing, but also the types of furniture, linen (e.g. continental quilts introduced in 1980 then replaced by duvets in 1993), crockery, and cars that we purchase. Children's toys (teddy bears) first entered the basket in 1955, with tricycles being added in 1965. However, many specific toys are transient in the basket. For example the iconic New Zealand toy, the buzzy bee, was only specifically priced in the basket between 1993 and 2008. The items priced in 2011 were Board Games, Dolls, Soft Toys, Construction Sets (e.g. building blocks, interlocking blocks) and Metal Toys (e.g. toy cars).

Changing technology and changing leisure activities, discussed further in Sections 4.2 and 4.4, have also caused some items to become transient.

Changes have also occurred in forms of communication. Although telegrams were in the basket for 50 years (from 1930 to 1980) they became less important as electronic communication became the norm. In 1999 the New Zealand Post Office stopped offering telegrams. Postage and Telegrams accounted for only a small amount (0.53 per cent) of total expenditure in 1949, but this had further reduced by 2011 with the whole Postal Services class accounting for only 0.17 per cent.

The speed of change of the commodities in the basket is governed to some extent by the periods at which reviews take place. Since 1999 this has been at roughly three-yearly intervals. However, the length of time spent in the basket has tended to decrease over time for some types of commodities such as electronic goods, which have had increasingly short periods in the basket. For example, while records were in the basket for 38 years (between 1955 and 1993), video cassette recorders only remained in the basket for 23 years (between 1983 and 2006) and DVD-Video combos were only in the basket for the two years between 2006 and 2008.

Table 5. Food basket additions and deletions 1955–2008

Year	Added	Removed	Year	Added	Removed
1956	Canned pineapple Frozen peas Beef mince Corned silverside Canned sardines Milk powder Rice Jelly crystals Spaghetti Baked beans	Beetroot Gooseberries Dried peas Corned brisket Golden syrup	1988	Mandarins Broccoli Salami Cheese, exotic Muesli Muesli bars Greater range of takeaway foods	Grapefruit Parsnips Weiner schnitzel Liver, lambs fry Dripping Baking powder Custard powder Jelly crystals Salt
1965	Frozen beans Canned beans Roaster chicken Canned salmon Instant coffee Fruit juice	Runner beans Herrings in tomato sauce	1993	Grapes Frozen vegetables, mixed Mussels Milk, over the counter Infant formula Cottage cheese Peppercorns Ethnic meals	Brussel sprouts Frozen beans Canned meat, corned beef Canned sardines Rolled oats Pepper, white
1974	Kiwifruit Cucumber Saveloys Yoghurt Margarine Cooking oil, vegetable Takeaway foods	Rhubarb Canned peas Canned beans Tripe Sheep's tongue	1999	Avocado Alfalfa sprouts Capsicum Taro Zucchini Fresh pasta Energy drinks	Milk, delivered Milk powder Quiche Baked potatoes
1977	Asparagus Mushrooms Milkshakes	Fruit extract liquid	2002	Two-minute noodles	–
1980	Nectarines Pasta Novelty ice cream	Silverbeet Swedes Ground coffee Cocoa	2006	Green beans Spring onions Parsnips Canned tomatoes Canned soup Soy sauce Dried herbs Ground coffee Bottled water Frozen complete meals	Worcestershire sauce Peppercorns Soup powder Takeaway soup
1983	–	Marmalade	2008	Fresh pineapple Cooked chicken Soy milk Free range eggs Hummus dip Chilled fruit juice	Fresh peaches Saveloys Condensed milk
			2011	Dried apricots Frozen berries Frozen chicken nuggets Flatbread	–

3 Changing purchasing patterns

Societal change is reflected not only in the presence of a commodity in the CPI basket of goods, or in the length of time it remains in the basket, but also in the proportion of the household budget spent on a commodity – its weight. Figure 1 shows the 2011 weights of groups in the CPI over time and demonstrates that the major change over time has been to the Miscellaneous group. Over time this group has been subdivided into a number of groups, including Communication, Credit Services, Education, Recreation, and Personal and Healthcare, as the total average household expenditure on each of these has grown. This demonstrates that households are increasingly purchasing services, such as health and education, rather than commodities. The distinct change in the distribution of the weights in 1974 is the result of the introduction of the modern expenditure-based CPI.

Figure 1. Weights of CPI Groups (1924–2011)

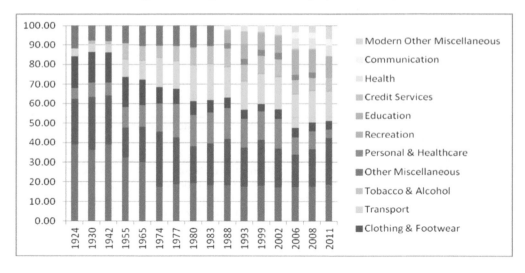

Removal of the Miscellaneous group in Figure 2 shows the changes in weights for the other groups since 1974. The most volatile group is the Housing/Rent group, but much of this is because of the methodological changes in the way housing has been treated in the CPI (see Pike, this volume). The most marked change is in the Housing Operation group, which includes the Household Appliances subgroup, probably because the price of household appliances has dropped in real terms relative to wage earnings, as discussed in Section 3.3 below. There has also been a reduction in expenditure on Clothing and Footwear, reflecting the increasing availability of cheaper imported items.

Although the expenditure weight of the Food group has been relatively stable since 1974, consumers appear to be more sensitive to food prices than to prices of other commodities. This is likely because food is an essential commodity and is directly related to daily living. Because of the narrow scope of the CPI before 1974, the Food group was a large proportion of the CPI, accounting for more than half of the index in 1914. Since 1974, its share of the CPI has dropped dramatically, mainly as the result of the change to an expenditure base rather than a shift in household spending. Since the 1970s, the relative importance of the Food group to total household spending has fluctuated between 17 per cent and 20 per cent, making it the second most significant group in the CPI behind Housing and Household Utilities.

Figure 2. Weights of selected CPI groups (1974–2011)

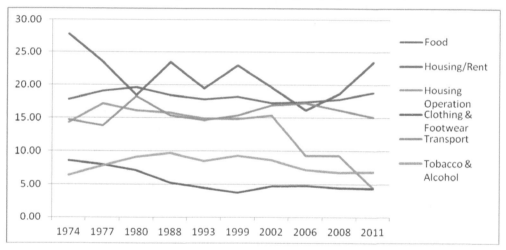

4 Social and political factors related to changes in the basket of goods

As stated earlier, before the expenditure-based CPI of the mid-1970s, the commodities priced in the basket of goods were influenced by political decisions. Since then, changes in the basket have become more frequent and reflect a number of social phenomena, including the availability of a growing variety of goods and services both nationally and internationally, technological changes (such as refrigeration and computing), and growing commercialisation of formerly home-produced goods and services (as a result of, among other things, rural–urban population drift). While the previous section discussed commodities in the basket of goods in terms of their endurance in the basket, this section categorises changes using the following categories, adapted from a draft produced by Brian Easton (private communication, 15 July 2011; some of the material in this section is also extracted from this draft):

- Changes in commodity availability, including reduced significance or obso-lescence, introduction of new commodities and renaming of commodities
- Technology advances
- Automation of household activities
- Growth in leisure activities
- Globalisation

The changing role of government in the economy, and the impact of government policies on prices, is discussed separately in Section 5.

4.1 Changes in commodity availability

4.1.1 Reduced significance of commodities

That some commodities reduce in significance over time is clearly demonstrated by the transient commodities discussed previously. Examples of obsolescent commodities include ironmongery, household goods such as scrubbing boards and clothes wringers, personal items such as plugs of tobacco and laundering of men's stiff collars, and fabric types such as madapolam, Hoyle's prints, Japanese silk and Samarang kapok. Dried peas and clothes wringers were deleted in 1955, silk stockings and LP records in 1965, winceyette infants' pyjamas, boys' caps and hand lawn mowers in 1974, and library subscriptions in 1977. Dressmaking material and equipment was also slowly phased out. There are numerous other examples in early baskets that may be of interest to historians.

A number of other commodities that are not yet obsolescent have reduced in significance over time. For example, tram and train fares have reduced in importance; they accounted for 4 per cent of total expenditure in 1914, but all of Rail Passenger Transport only accounted for 0.09 per cent in 2011.

4.1.2 Introduction of new commodities

There seem to be three major factors influencing the introduction of new commodities: the emergence of new technologies, the rise of leisure activities, and globalisation. These are discussed separately in Sections 4.2, 4.4 and 4.5.

4.1.3 Renaming of commodities

One explicit example of a simple name change is the tree tomato (introduced to the basket in 1955), which was renamed 'tamarillo' in 1974. In the area of clothing in particular, there are instances when the functional purpose of a good has not changed over time, but a change in the style of the good has resulted in a change of name. On occasion there also seems to be a name change without any major change in the style of the good. An example of this is women's underclothes. In 1924 the items surveyed were called "ladies' underwear, longcloth" or "ladies' underwear, woven woollen", and "children's woollen bloomers". In 1930, ladies' underwear was categorised by whether it was silk or woven woollen, then in 1942 there were two classes of bloomers (wool or locknit) and one class of panties (locknit). In 1949, 1955 and 1965 only interlock panties were surveyed, changing to nylon panties in 1974 and 1977. From 1980 through until 2002, a simple "panties" or "women's panties" description was used. In 2006 and 2008 the term used was changed to "women's underpants". Although the function of these items has remained essentially the same, stylistic changes in the early garments are reflected in the name changes from underwear to bloomers to panties. However, the final name change from panties to underpants simply reflects a change in language usage (to a more appropriate term). A similar but less marked language change is observed with brassieres, first included in 1949 and remaining in the basket until 2002, then being renamed as 'bras' from 2006 onwards.

Sanitary towels ('Libertex') entered the basket in 1955, being renamed as sanitary pads and tampons in 1980. Sanitary pads and tampons were identified separately in 1993 and have had relatively similar weights since (between 0.03 per cent and 0.05 per cent of total expenditure). Interestingly, condoms (which have been publicly available as a commodity for the whole of the last century) were not identified as a separate item until 1988 (alongside contraceptive pills). This may, in part, reflect increasing social acceptability rather than increasing purchase.

4.2 Technology advances

While some commodities have been enduring, often the item priced has changed over time with the introduction of new materials, processes and technologies. Cameras are an example where the item priced has changed along with technological improvements. Cameras were introduced to the basket in 1974, with the Instamatic camera appearing in 1980. Analogue cameras were replaced by digital cameras between the CPI basket reviews in 2002 and 2006 for two main reasons: the need to reflect a significant shift by households from purchasing film cameras to digital cameras, and difficulties in collecting prices for film cameras from some retail outlets in the sample. Digital cameras have themselves been subject to rapid change. One of the most important price-determining characteristics of digital cameras is the number of effective megapixels (a measure of how much fine detail a camera can capture). At the

September 2005 quarter, the most common megapixel range in the CPI sample when first selected was '4 and over but under 5'. Since digital cameras were introduced into the CPI, camera technology has evolved considerably, and digital cameras of at least 10 megapixels are now widely available. The pixel distribution of the CPI sample has changed significantly over the years since digital cameras were added to the basket.

Photographic film and developing costs were introduced to the basket in 1955, but the items priced have changed together with processing developments. Both black-and-white and colour printing costs were surveyed from 1965 until 1977 but since then only colour film and printing has been priced.

Television is another example of technology change. Television had its first public transmission in Auckland in 1960 (Ministry for Culture and Heritage, 2012), then in Christchurch and Wellington a year later (Television New Zealand, 2012). Five years after its introduction, nearly 315,000 TV sets were licensed in New Zealand (Department of Statistics, 1965) but the first item priced (also in 1965) was TV hire. It was then very expensive to own a TV – the average price of a 23-inch black-and-white consolette TV set was about £138 in 1965, or $5,210 in today's terms. It was five times as expensive to own as a portable transistor radio at that time, so hiring was an option that many households chose, although this was somewhat expensive as well. In 1965, the average charge for hiring a TV for two years was about £119 ($4,490 in March 2014). In the 1966 Census, 63.3 per cent of households had a TV set, but TV coverage was not nationwide and ownership varied by location, based on availability of reception. The highest density of ownership was in the Auckland and Wellington regions (Department of Statistics, 1966).

In 1975, colour TV sets were added to the basket as well, with the average price of a 26-inch colour set being about $840 ($8,100 in today's terms), a very significant amount for many households. In spite of the cost, TV ownership (colour and/or black and white) reached 93.8 per cent of households, based on the 1976 Census (Department of Statistics, 1980). In 1979, colour TVs had become increasingly popular and black-and-white TV sets were removed from the CPI basket. Then, in 1994, pay TV was added to the basket. Sky, the first pay television service, began broadcasting in 1990 using an ultra-high-frequency network. This progressively spread across the country until 1996. In 1997, Sky introduced a nationwide satellite service (Statistics New Zealand, 2010). In 2006, flat-panel TV sets with LCD and plasma displays were added to the CPI basket. In that year, a 32-inch LCD-display TV cost about $2,750. By comparison, the same sized TV in the September 2012 quarter would have cost about $680. The 2008 review signalled the end of cathode ray tube TV sets; they were removed from the basket and free-to-air digital television receivers were added, reflecting the introduction of Freeview. In 2011, the current CPI pricing specifications for LCD and plasma-display TV sets were expanded to include 3D-display TVs. In the March 2014 quarter, a 40-inch television cost $1,047.

Transport is another area that has experienced significant technological change. The earliest price indices only included tram and train fares. The Transport group was established in 1955 with the addition of the costs of private motoring, and it has a number of enduring commodities such as air travel fares (entering the basket in 1974). In 2011, for every $100 New Zealand households spent on goods and services covered by the CPI, about $15 was spent on transport. Transport had the third-highest expenditure of the 11 CPI groups, after Housing and Household Utilities ($24 of every $100) and Food ($19 of every $100).

In 2011 (compared with 2002), consumers spent relatively more on vehicle supplies and services (that is, petrol and vehicle repairs), and relatively less on purchasing vehicles and public transport. As Figure 3 shows, households spent almost three times as much on private transport supplies and services as they did on either of the other two. The increasing price of petrol is the key contributor to the growth in transport supplies and services. Public transport currently (2011 weights) only accounts for about 20 per cent of household spending on transport.

In vehicle markets, most households buy second-hand cars. As a proportion of total car spending (i.e. excluding motorcycles and bicycles), expenditure on second-hand cars has reduced from 83 per cent in 1999 to 67 per cent in 2011, while relative spending on new cars has doubled over the same period to 33 per cent. Automobile makes are transient, being dictated by fashion. In 2011, Toyota was the most popular medium-sized car brand and Holden and Ford the most popular large car brands.

Figure 3. Relative weights of subgroups within the Transport group: 1999–2011

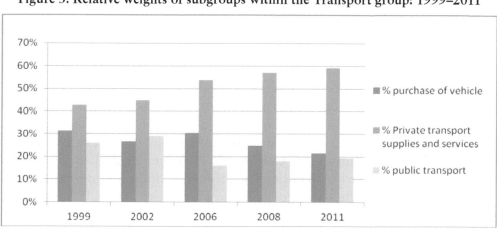

The introduction of new technologies and processes also had an impact on household activities and the type of food we purchased. For example, runner beans were replaced in the basket by frozen green beans in 1965, and dehydrated vegetables were added in 1974. Paper towels and disposable nappies were both introduced to the basket in 1985.

4.3 Automation of household activities

The invention of labour-saving appliances helped make the labour-intensive chores of the early twentieth century easier and quicker. For example, prices were collected for scrubbing boards, hand clothes wringers, and brooms from 1924 until 1949, 1955 and 2008 respectively. Major household appliances, including washing machines, sewing machines, vacuum cleaners and lawn mowers, were introduced into the basket of goods and services in 1949. These innovations changed the nature of housework and have now become part of a normal household. In the 1971 Census, 96 per cent of New Zealand households had refrigerators, while 92 per cent had washing machines (Department of Statistics, 1975). Some of the household appliances discussed below are enduring commodities that have remained in the basket of goods since their introduction, while others are transient, being superseded by new enduring commodities.

Initially, the commercial household appliances discussed below were expensive relative to average weekly earnings. Now, even with more sophisticated features, the prices of household appliances have fallen relative to average earnings, making them more affordable for households. Table 6 shows the price of a selection of appliances at the time they were introduced to the basket, in equivalent 2014 prices and relative to average weekly earnings at the time each appliance was added to the basket.

4.3.1 Washing machines and clothes dryers

In 1949, the average price of a washing machine was about £60, equivalent to about $4,250 in March 2014. It was quite a significant outlay for households in those days, so many did not have a washing machine. The 1956 Census asked about refrigerators and electric washing machines in New Zealand households for the first time. Over 40 per cent of New Zealanders did not have access to an electric washing machine (Department of Statistics, 1956). People without electric washing machines still relied on the old method of 'boiling the copper' to do their laundry (Ministry for Culture and Heritage, 2012). Laundry had to be twisted and squeezed by hand or put through a clothes-wringer to extract water. The manual clothes-wringer was also part of the 1949 CPI basket, and when it cost about £6.10s (about $460 in today's terms).

Table 6: Summary of commercial household appliances in CPI basket

Year added to CPI basket	Appliance	Price at time appliance added to basket	QES average weekly earnings at time appliance added to basket	Original price in today's (2014) terms[1]	Price at March 2014 quarter	QES average weekly earnings at March 2014 quarter
1949	Washing machine	£60	£470 a year[2] (£9 a week)	$4,250	$774	$913
	Vacuum cleaner	£29		$2,075	$374	
	Hand mower	£7		$485	n/a[4]	
	Sewing machine	£34		$2,440	$2,431	
1955	Refrigerator	£98	£715 a year[3] (£14 a week)	$4,860	$1,254	
1965	Motor mower, reel	£47	£17	$1,755	n/a	
	Motor mower, rotary	£67		$2,540	$664	
1988	Microwave oven	$790	$451	$1,450	$264	

1. Price at the time appliance was added to the basket adjusted by the increase in the CPI from then to the December 2012 quarter.
2. Median income for males (estimated) from 1951 Census.
3. Median income for males from 1956 Census.
4. Appliance no longer in the CPI basket.
Source: Statistics New Zealand

More sophisticated washing machine models were introduced over the following decades. They had features like spin-drying, and controls for wash temperature and agitation speed. In 1965, semi-automatic washing machines with spin dryers were added to the CPI basket. Their average price was £109 (about $4,130 in today's terms) whereas the average price of a washing machine with a 5.5-kilogram loading was approximately $774 in the March 2014 quarter. Over the years, washing-machine ownership has gradually increased. By the 1966 Census, 88 per cent of New Zealand households had access to a washing machine (Department of Statistics, 1966).

Clothes dryers were seen as more of a luxury by households, and were not introduced to the CPI until 1974. In the 1976 Census, 38 per cent of households had electric clothes dryers (Department of Statistics, 1980). In this Census, 38 per cent of households also owned a fully-automatic washing machine that required you only to load the dirty laundry at the start and unload the clean laundry after the wash. These were different from the electric washing machines asked about in the 1966 Census that required some manual intervention.

4.3.2 Sewing machines

The sewing machine was invented centuries ago. It became popular in the home by offering women relief from hours of hand sewing, especially at a time when it was more common to make clothes than buy them ready-made. Sewing machines were included in the CPI basket when the modern CPI was first published in 1949. At that time they retailed at an average price of £34 (about $2,440 in March 2014). Sewing machines have evolved over time – from pedal-driven to electric and then to electronic. Today, a machine can come with programmable stitches, embroidery units, and buttonhole functions, with prices varying widely, depending on the available features. In the March 2014 quarter, prices started at just under $500 for those with basic stitch features, and went to almost $8,500 for those with embroidery units, with the average price being $2,431.

Although sewing machines are an enduring commodity, their importance in household work has diminished as cheaper clothing has become widely available. The expenditure weight for a sewing machine was 0.13 per cent in 1949, but only 0.01 per cent in 2011.

4.3.3 Vacuum cleaners

Vacuum cleaners make sweeping and dusting easier. When they were first introduced to the CPI basket in February 1949, their average price was £29 (about $2,075 in today's terms). In the 1966 Census, nearly 90 per cent of New Zealand households owned one (Department of Statistics, 1966). At that time, it took about one-and-a-half weeks' average earnings (before-tax), as measured by Statistics New Zealand's Quarterly Employment Survey (Statistics New Zealand, 2013), to cover the price of a vacuum cleaner (see Table 6 above). Vacuum cleaners continue to be an important appliance in the home to this day, with expenditure weights (0.15 per cent in 1949 and 0.05 per cent in 2011) not decreasing at the same rate as that for sewing machines. Prices have become much cheaper over time, and newer technologies have been introduced, such as retractable power cords, suction controls, and bagless models. In 2014, the average price of a 2,200-watt vacuum cleaner tracked in the CPI was $374. This was less than half the average ordinary time weekly earnings of $913 (Table 6).

Commercialisation of household activities has taken another step, with people becoming increasingly busy and hiring someone else to clean their house. Housekeeping charges were added to the CPI basket in 2008, when the average charge for cleaning a three-bedroom house was $59.

4.3.4 Lawn mowers

Hand lawn mowers that do not use any type of electricity or petrol were included in the 1949 CPI basket. At that time, the price was £7 (about $485 today). A similar type of lawn mower is still available. Prices for both hand mowers and motor mowers were tracked until 1974. However, the popularity of hand mowers was declining, and after 1974, only motor mower prices were tracked. Hand mowers have been a transient commodity in New Zealand's CPI whereas the motor mower is currently an enduring commodity.

Motor mowers were around in New Zealand in the early 1920s, before they became popular. The first New Zealand-made petrol-powered lawn mower was manufactured in 1938, but this was beyond the reach of most New Zealand households until well into the 1950s and 1960s (Envirohistory NZ, 2009). In 1965, motor-powered lawn mowers in 'reel' type and 'rotary' type were added to the CPI basket. At that time, they were £47 and £67 respectively (or $1,755 and $2,540 in today's terms). With average weekly earnings of £17 in 1965, it would have taken three to four weeks' gross earnings to cover the price of a motor mower. Despite this cost, it was quite common for households to own one. In the 1971 Census, nearly two in three households owned a motor mower (Department of Statistics, 1975). Over the years, motor mowers have become cheaper relative to earnings. The average price of a 46cm rotary lawn mower in the March 2014 quarter was $644, less than a week's average gross earnings.

As with housekeeping, it has now become popular for some households to hire someone to mow their lawns. Lawn mowing services were added to the CPI basket in 2008. The average charge for lawn mowing then was $28, which generally included green waste removal, edge trimming, and weed control. By the March 2014 quarter, it had risen to $34.

4.3.5 Refrigerators and freezers

Refrigerators were added to the CPI basket in 1955. Although they had been around for decades, only 54 per cent of New Zealand dwellings had the sole or shared use of a refrigerator in the 1956 Census (Department of Statistics, 1956). Those who did not have access to a refrigerator stored perishables like meat in a food safe – a box with a netting side through which air circulated (Ministry for Culture and Heritage, 2012). The average price of a single cabinet refrigerator in 1955 was £98 (about $4,860 today), which was nearly 60 per cent more expensive than a washing machine at that time (£62). Based on the median income for males of £715 (before-tax) a year in the 1956 Census, it took about seven weeks' (before-tax) income to cover the price of a refrigerator and about five weeks' income to cover the price of a washing machine (Department of Statistics, 1956).

Ten years later, prices had become marginally cheaper in today's terms, and new models and technologies had been introduced, such as the addition of freezer compartments. In 1965, a dual-temperature refrigerator (with separate deep-freeze compartment) was added to the CPI basket. This model had an average price of £119 (about $4,470 in today's terms), while the single-cabinet model was £109 (about $4,125 today). As shown in Table 6, it took more than six weeks' earnings to cover the price of a single-cabinet refrigerator. Prices of refrigerator-freezers have become cheaper over the decades in today's terms. In March 2014, a refrigerator-freezer with 373-litre capacity was about $1,254. This was less than two weeks of the average ordinary time (before-tax) weekly earnings ($913 for the same period).

Stand-alone freezers were added to the CPI basket in 1974. While some modern refrigerators included a separate compartment for freezing food, it was quite common for households to buy a separate freezer. In February 1975, the average price of a 311-litre freezer was $240 ($2,310 today). While refrigerator-freezers continue to be included in the CPI today, and are therefore another enduring commodity, stand-alone freezers and stand-alone refrigerators were dropped from the basket of goods and services after 1988 and 2006 respectively.

4.3.6 Dishwashers

Dishwashers started to become known as a home kitchen appliance in the 1950s. In earlier years, only restaurants, hotels, and wealthy families had dishwashers, as they were large and expensive appliances (Thompson, 2009). Over the following decades, they became smaller, cheaper, and more efficient, which saw them grow in popularity among households. In 1980, dishwashers were added to the CPI basket.

4.3.7 Microwave ovens

Microwave ovens were developed in the 1940s. The first products sold were much larger than we have today, about the size of a refrigerator, and were also mainly sold to restaurants. Microwave ovens became smaller and less expensive in the 1960s, and by the mid-1970s were widespread in homes. The microwave oven was added to the CPI basket in 1988, when the average price was $790 (about $1,450 in today's terms). In the March 2014 quarter, a 32-litre microwave oven had an average price of $264, one-third of its actual average price in 1988.

4.3.8 Electric stoves

Before electricity became widespread, it was common for households to cook food using a coal, wood, or coke range. As electricity generation and gas supply reached more areas in New Zealand, electric ranges and gas ranges became popular. Table 7 gives the percentages of New Zealand dwellings using coal, wood, or coke ranges, electric ranges, gas ranges or other means of cooking, in the 1945 and 1971 Censuses (Department of Statistics, 1945 and 1975) and shows our growing reliance on electricity for cooking.

As the means of cooking was previously considered part of housing, it was not directly included in the CPI basket until the expenditure-based conceptual change was introduced in 1974. The proportion of total household expenditure on electric ranges has remained quite stable over time, with a weight of 0.14 per cent in 1974 and 0.09 per cent in 2011.

Table 7. Fuels used for cooking (percentages)

Type of Stove	1945 Census	1971 Census
Coal, wood, or coke	38	5
Electric	30	87
Gas	24	8
Other, or combination of methods	8	0
Total	100	100

Other forms of what were once normal household activities have also been commercialised. For example, professional exterior and interior decorating was added to the basket in 1965, and delivery charges for online shopping have been included since 2011.

4.4 Growth in leisure activities

Some transient commodities reflect New Zealanders' changing leisure activities. In the late 1800s the piano was an important focus for social gatherings. For example, in 1895, New Zealand and Australia imported more pianos than the United States. Up until the 1970s, one in four homes in New Zealand had a piano, but they have since become less important in our lives (Jan Preston, New Zealand musician, personal communication, 2013). This is reflected in the piano's presence in the basket from 1965 to 1993.

The range of leisure activities priced in the basket has increased over time. One example of the growth in leisure activities is expenditure on restaurant meals and takeaway (ready-to-eat) food, with the relative expenditure, compared to total expenditure on food, increasing from 17.7 per cent in 1980 to 21.1 per cent in 2011. Over the same period, the relative expenditure on non-alcoholic beverages within the Food group increased from 7.1 per cent to 11.3 per cent. Although recreational and cultural services were first introduced to the basket in 1949, recreational items kept being added. Examples include golf green fees and boys' football boots in 1955, concert admission prices and women's swimsuits in 1965, and tramping equipment, sightseeing and scenic tours in 1974.

Other items that would once have been seen as luxuries have also become more widespread, for example, boats, caravans, swimming pools and holiday accommodation costs were introduced to the basket in 1974.

4.5 Globalisation

The impact of increasing globalisation on New Zealand society is possibly best reflected in our changing eating habits, with many new foods becoming popular and enduring in the basket. These include the previously mentioned banana in 1949, canned pineapple in 1955, margarine and yoghurt in 1974, pasta in 1985, pizza in 1988, avocado and taro in 1999, and hummus and soy milk in 2008. The introduction of new foods meant that less was spent on more traditional items. For example, meat was 7.42 per cent of total expenditure in the basket in 1949 but the Meat, Poultry and Fish subgroup only accounted for 2.57 per cent of expenditure in 2011. In addition, the proportion of expenditure on restaurant meals/takeaways, and the diversity of these types of meals, have increased over time.

Increased awareness of global trends has influenced some of the transient, fashion-dictated, transport goods, such as types of vehicles purchased. Private motor cars were introduced in 1955, together with vehicle servicing, petrol, cycles and telephone rentals. Telephone access enabled increasing national and international communication. Air travel also became more important over time, with domestic airfares being included from 1974, international airfares (prepaid in New Zealand) from 1980, and overseas package holidays from 2006 (These had previously been represented by international airfares).

5 Changing role of government in the economy – impact of government policies on prices

Government's role in the economy has changed over time. A century ago, the emphasis was on price control regulation and provision of subsidies, as discussed in the chapter on price changes over the last century (Forbes, this volume). In more recent times, the setting of fees at a national level that affect a large group of the population has resulted in these items of expenditure becoming significant enough to be included in the CPI pricing regime.

Over the last hundred years, the forms of government involvement in the economy that have been reflected in the CPI history have included:

a. Subsidies that aimed to protect consumers from some of the consequences of international events. The history of food subsidies is discussed in 'One Hundred Years of Prices: Food and Transport' (Forbes, this volume).
b. Price controls, rationing and government production. The world wars placed extreme demands on the New Zealand economy and mechanisms were needed to provide tight control on the utilisation of resources and the production activity of the economy.
c. Tariffs and industry regulation. The removal of tariffs and industry regulation throughout the period from 1983 to 1995 had a significant impact on price rises after 1992, as cheaper imported alternative goods became more readily available and industries like telecommunications became subject to a higher degree of competition.
d. Direct charging for services provided by government. This area is reflected more directly in the basket and this section gives examples of some of these charges.

One transient (but long-term) commodity that clearly was a result of government policy was the licence fees paid to fund radio and television services in New Zealand. The radio licence fee was introduced in 1922 and the television licence fee was introduced in 1960 (Statistics New Zealand, 2000). In 1961, about 5,000 television licences were issued. In 1965, this was up to nearly 315,000, including free licences issued to institutions (Department of Statistics, 1965). The cost of a television licence in 1965 was £6.10s a year (about $245 today). Advertisements started screening within a year of television broadcasts starting, providing additional funding. Over the years, advertising gradually increased and became the main funding source for 'free-to-air' channels. The television/radio licence was in the pricing basket for the CPI from 1949 until 1999, when television licensing was abolished (Horrocks, 2009).

There have been a number of changes to the basket that resulted from changes in health policy. For example, X-ray fees were dropped in 1955, and medical insurance and prescription charges introduced in 1983 and 1988 respectively. Public hospital fees included in the basket from 1993 to 1999 were, at least in part, a response to the 'user charges' that were introduced by the Government in 1992 "to discourage free hospital use over primary care, to reduce health expenditure, to improve equity of primary care by making higher income people pay more and to encourage healthy living" (New Zealand Parliament, 2009).

Another area that reflects government charges is education. School books have been included in the basket since 1949 and school examination fees were first introduced to the basket in 1974. University textbooks and university tuition costs have also been included since 1974. The sharing of tertiary education costs between students and government was formalised with the introduction of the Student Loan Scheme in 1992, which enabled students to borrow course fees, course costs and living costs (New Zealand Parliament, 2011). The expenditure weight for the Tertiary and Other Post-school Education class of the CPI increased by 186 per cent between December 1993 (when the series started) and March 2008. It accounted for 0.77 per cent of total household expenditure in 2011. This is consistent with increases in both the volume and price of tertiary education. New Zealand's official yearbooks show that tertiary education consumption has increased significantly since the early 1980s. The number of students attending tertiary education institutions increased by 55 per cent in the decade between 1980 and 1990, by 154 per cent between 1990 and 1999 and by 32 per cent between 1999 and 2008 (Ministry of Education, 2014). Changes to the volumes and prices of primary and secondary education have not been as significant as those of tertiary education.

The reflection of cost increases in the CPI from government-imposed charges is not the same as political interference in the construction of the CPI. The political selection of early CPI baskets of goods was an indirect form of political interference, but in the mid-1970s there was a clear move towards a more objective, expenditure-based index. Since then, New Zealand has been free of political interference in the calculation of the CPI, unlike some other countries such as Argentina (Berumen and Beker, 2011). New Zealand convenes 'independent' CPI Advisory Committees, however these are only advisory and have no statutory powers. This independence does not extend to the policy uses of the CPI. For example, as discussed by Reddell (this volume), since the 1990s a modified version of the CPI has been used to measure inflation in the Reserve Bank's Policy Targets Agreements with the Minister of Finance. Also, a more recent government decision excluded the impact of tobacco tax increases from CPI adjustments to social welfare benefits (The Treasury, 2010) because there have been successive increases in recent years to the tax on tobacco as a disincentive to smoking. Tobacco is part of the current basket of goods and services (currently accounting for 2.13 per cent of the basket). The Treasury (2010) estimated that the increased taxes would "lift the CPI by an estimated 0.6 per cent over the next 2½ years" (p.1) but, in addition to recommending that this be a one-off change, in part of their justification for it they state that "tobacco products are unique in the basket of goods covered by the CPI in being both addictive and extremely harmful".

Summary

Selected commodities in the CPI basket of goods over the last hundred years have been analysed in this chapter from two perspectives: firstly, by their durability within the basket, and secondly, by the type of change that they reflect. However, these are just two of many perspectives from which the rich historical data contained in the basket of goods could be viewed.

It is only in recent years that this data has been produced in a form that is readily available to researchers. While it does have some limitations (for example, it is not particularly useful to look at those clothing and other fashions which change rapidly), there is now an opportunity for it to be used much more widely to enrich other sources documenting New Zealand's social and political history.

References

Baker, J. V. T. (1965). *The New Zealand people at war: war economy* (Vol. 5). Historical Publications Branch, Department of Internal Affairs. Wellington. Available from http://nzetc.victoria.ac.nz/tm/scholarly/tei-WH2Econ.html

Berumen, E. and Beker, V. A. (2011). Recent developments in price and related statistics in Argentina. *Statistical Journal of the IAOS*, 27, 7–11.

Department of Statistics (1945). *Population Census 1945*. Author. Wellington.

Department of Statistics (1956). *Population Census 1956*. Author. Wellington.

Department of Statistics (1965). *The New Zealand Official Year Book, 1965*. Author. Wellington.

Department of Statistics (1966). *Census of Population and Dwellings, 1966*. Author. Wellington.

Department of Statistics (1975). *Census of Population and Dwellings, 1971*. Author. Wellington.

Department of Statistics (1980). *Census of Population and Dwellings, 1976*. Author. Wellington.

Envirohistory NZ (2009). *The lawnmower – The great New Zealand love affair*. Available from http://envirohistorynz.com

Forbes, S. (this volume). One Hundred Years of Prices: Food and Transport. pp. 69–95.

Forbes, S., Keating, J., Roberts, E., and Higgs, C. (this volume). Prescriptivism to Positivism? The Development of the CPI in New Zealand. pp. 1–25.

Horrocks, R. (2009). *A History of Television in New Zealand*. Available from http://www.nzonscreen.com

Ministry for Culture and Heritage (2012). *Overview – NZ in the 1950s*. http://www.nzhistory.net.nz/culture/the-1950s/overview, updated 20-Dec-2012.

Ministry of Education (2014). *Education Counts, Participation*. Available from http://www.educationcounts.govt.nz/publications/tertiary_education

New Zealand Census and Statistics Department (1945). *Population Census 1945*. Author. Wellington.

New Zealand Parliament (2009). *New Zealand Health System Reforms: Parliamentary support*. Research papers. Author. Wellington.

New Zealand Parliament (2011). *Paying for Tertiary Education: Parliamentary support*. Research papers. Author. Wellington. Available from http://www.parliament.nz/en-nz/parl-support/research-papers/00PlibCIP131/paying-for-tertiary-education

Pike, Chris (this volume). CPI Frameworks, 1949–2014. pp.26–39.

Reddell, Michael (this volume). Monetary Policy and the Consumer Price Index: Some Perspectives. pp.130–150.

Statistics New Zealand (2000). *The New Zealand Year Book 2000*. Author. New Zealand.

Statistics New Zealand (2009). The rise and fall of traditional baking. *Price Index News*. Available from http://www.stats.govt.nz/browse_for_stats/economic_indicators/CPI_inflation/baking-goods-in-the-cpi.aspx

Statistics New Zealand (2010). *Fifty years of television in New Zealand*. http://www.stats.govt.nz/browse_for_stats/economic_indicators/CPI_inflation/fifty-years-of-watching-the-box.aspx

Statistics New Zealand (2011). Tracking milk prices in the CPI. *Price Index News*. Available from http://www.stats.govt.nz/browse_for_stats/economic_indicators/prices_indexes/tracking-milk-prices-in-the-cpi.aspx

Statistics New Zealand (2013). *Quarterly Employment Survey – information releases*. Available from http://www.stats.govt.nz/browse_for_stats/income-and-work/employment_and_unemployment/quarterly-employment-survey-info-releases.aspx

Statistics New Zealand (2014a). *Long-term data series*. http://www.stats.govt.nz/browse_for_stats/economic_indicators/NationalAccounts/long-term-data-series.aspx

Statistics New Zealand (2014b). *Price Index News*. Available from http://www.stats.govt.nz/tools_and_services/newsletters/price-index-news.aspx.

Television New Zealand (2012). *About TVNZ: The early years*. http://tvnz.co.nz/tvnz-corporate-comms/early-years-4919779

The Treasury (2010). Aide memoire: excluding the impact of the tobacco excise increase from cpi adjustments. Memorandum for the Minister of Finance. Author. Wellington. http://www.treasury.govt.nz/publications/informationreleases/budget/2010/pdfs/b10-am-tsy-eitei-16apr10.pdf

Thomson, J (2009). *History of the dishwasher*. Available from http://ezinearticles.com

Acknowledgements

This chapter contains material extracted from Statistics New Zealand's online regular newsletter, *Price Index News,* available at http://www.stats.govt.nz/tools_and_services/newsletters/price-index-news.aspx. Special thanks to Chris Pike, Vince Galvin, Nick Martelli, Peter Campion and Alan Bentley of Statistics New Zealand for their expert input, comments and quality assurance of this chapter.

One Hundred Years of Prices: Food and Transport

Sharleen Forbes

Abstract

Price indices have been published in New Zealand for one hundred years, since 1914. Price changes for two groups of commodities, Food and Transport, are examined from two perspectives: firstly by the changes in price in nominal dollars, and secondly by changes in price relative to the overall CPI (as a measure of inflation) over time. Specific commodities from each of the groups are used to illustrate the variety of factors that influence price change.

1 Introduction

There are a number of factors that can affect prices, some of which impact across all groups of commodities, such as supply-and-demand inflationary pressures, global financial crises, natural disasters and government goods-and-services taxes (GST). GST was first introduced at 10 per cent in New Zealand as part of the Labour Government's 'Rogernomics' economic reforms (driven by the Minister of Finance, Roger Douglas). It applied to almost all types of goods and services (some exceptions exist, such as residential rents and financial services). GST has been raised twice, to 12.5 per cent in 1989 and to 15 per cent in 2010 (Ministry for Culture and Heritage, 2014).

Other factors influence only specific commodities, such as government regulations and subsidies, exchange rates, seasonal weather events and changing consumer preferences, including willingness to pay more for perceived superior goods. According to the Ministry for Culture and Heritage (2005), price regulation has had a long history in New Zealand with, for example, wartime price control measures such as the Board of Trade Act 1919 and the Economic Stabilisation Act 1948. In June 1982, the then Prime Minister, Robert Muldoon, imposed a price and wage freeze that he believed would dampen inflation, but the incoming Labour Government in 1984 removed this and repealed price-control statutes in 1986–1987, believing that "too much state intervention in the economy impaired economic performance" (Ministry for Culture and Heritage, 2005). Some regulation of industry (including, among others, electricity, telecommunications, education and insurance) returned after 1999. It is within this complex environment that price indices are collected.

These have been published in New Zealand since 1914 and a number of basic goods and groups of goods have been included in pricing surveys from their inception. As stated in Forbes (this volume) commodities that have been surveyed in price indices fall into three categories:

- Hundred-year commodities that have been surveyed since the inception of price indices in New Zealand (although quantities, etc. may have changed over time).
- Enduring commodities that have remained in pricing surveys since their introduction into the basket of goods.
- Transient commodities that have only remained in the basket for short periods of time.

This chapter discusses a selection of the first two types of commodities from two long-standing groups, Food and Transport, that illustrate some of the factors influencing price change over time. The Food and Transport groups have been included in price indices in some form since 1914 and 1924 respectively, although the commodities within them have changed markedly. Before 1942, there were a number of different Food categories (groups), but since 1942, Food has been a group in its own right. Transport became a group in 1955 but existed before that as either Transport or Fares categories in the Miscellaneous group. Housing has also been in the price indices for this length of time but is not included in this analysis as there have been a number of changes in methodology and commodities within this group (see Pike, this volume).

Price change over time is looked at from two perspectives:

1. Change in prices in nominal dollars over the hundred years, with the Food Price Index (FPI) being used to calculate 'today's' prices for commodities in the Food group, and the CPI being used for commodities in the Transport group.
2. Change in prices relative to changes in the total CPI over time.

The latter enables us to determine which commodities have become cheaper relative to overall inflation as measured by the CPI, and which have become dearer.

As Figure 1 shows, there was a generally increasing trend in inflation as measured by the CPI over the last hundred years. However, this growth was steeper after the introduction of the expenditure-based Consumers Price Index in 1974. The decade with the flattest growth in this latter period was from 1990 to 2000. Although the last few years show an increase, this appears to be at a lesser pace than in some previous years. The sharp growth in 1986, and smaller steps in 1989 and 2010, reflects the introduction of, and increases in, GST.

Figure 1

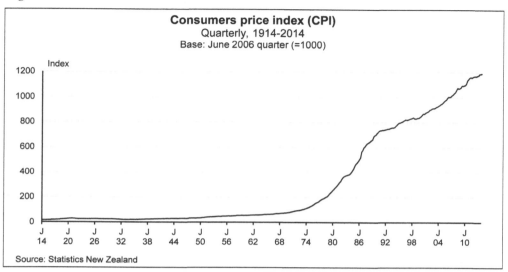

Consumers price index (CPI)
Quarterly, 1914-2014
Base: June 2006 quarter (=1000)

Source: Statistics New Zealand

As summarised in Easton (2012), the history of price change in New Zealand over this time falls into four broad periods:

a. Low inflation with interruptions between 1914 and 1935, where, apart from high inflation after the First World War (driven by the price of imports from Britain) and the disinflation associated with the Depression, prices were flat.
b. Moderate inflation between 1935 and 1966, where inflation averaged about 3 per cent, settling down after a period of inflation following the Second World War.
c. High inflation from 1966 to 1992, when price levels increased more than 11 times, having approximately trebled over the previous 100 years.
d. A period of moderation after 1992.

2 Food group

As food made up a large proportion of the index for its first 50 years, there is almost no difference between food and overall price changes in this period. Figure 2 shows how prices in the Food group of the CPI have moved over the past 50 years in relation to the price movements for the overall CPI. In general food prices have increased in line with the overall CPI, except for some periods when food prices increased more rapidly (and then flattened off).

The first of these more rapid increases began in the June 1979 quarter when food prices increased 9.6 per cent, compared with a 4.5 per cent increase in the CPI. Milk prices doubled between 1980 and 1982. Increases in the Fruit and Vegetables subgroup and the Meat, Poultry and Fish subgroup also contributed to the increase. Higher prices for the Meat, Poultry and Fish subgroup were the main driver of the sharp increases to Food group prices starting in the September 1989 quarter (when both movements were also influenced by an increase in GST from 10 per cent to 12.5 per cent in July 1989), and again for the increase beginning in the March 2001 quarter. During both of these periods, increasing export prices for meat were also recorded. The increase in food prices starting in the June 2006 quarter was initially also due mainly to increases in the Fruit and Vegetables subgroup and the Meat, Poultry, and Fish subgroup. The Grocery Food subgroup contributed to this increase from the December 2007 quarter, with higher prices for dairy products and for bread and cereals. These increases are consistent with increases in export prices for meat and dairy products, and with import prices for cereals and cereal preparations over the same period.

Figure 2

Subsidies are one of the significant influences on food prices over the years, with several basic foodstuffs being among a list of commodities that were subsidised by government between 1942 and 1976. Introduced during the Second World War as part of economic stabilisation policies, subsidies proved a popular way of keeping basic commodities affordable for families. These subsidies began to be removed in 1967 when they were taken off butter, bread and flour. The subsidy on bread was subsequently restored, being finally removed along with eggs and milk in 1976 (Statistics New Zealand, 1990, p.619).

Similarly, short-term events in the wider world can drive local impacts, as illustrated by the events of the 1970s. The seventies began with a worldwide commodity boom, driven by increased demand originating in the Soviet Union and falling supply arising from crop failures in South America. This, alongside the ending of the Bretton Woods currency arrangements, saw increased demand for agricultural production worldwide and rapidly increasing prices. Initially the New Zealand Government used the subsidy schemes to reduce the inflationary pressures but the subsequent ending of New Zealand's preferred access arrangements into the European Union in 1973, and the actions of the Organization of the Petroleum Exporting Countries (OPEC) oil cartel in the same year, eventually made these arrangements unsustainable (Dalziel and Lattimore, 1999). The cost of the food subsidies increased from less than $20 million to nearly $60 million in 1975, and in 1976 the Minister of Finance, Robert Muldoon, stated "the time had come for New Zealanders to take a deliberate cut in our standard of living in the interests of future solvency" (Garlick, 2012, p.97). The result was the significant price increases shown above.

Grocery food price rises have generally moved in line with the overall food group. For example, the Food group of the CPI rose by 9.8 per cent between the March 2008 and June 2009 quarters, and the Grocery Food subgroup increased by 9.5 per cent over the same period. There have been slightly greater differences in recent years, but both the Food group and the Grocery Food subgroup have shown signs of easing.

3 Food subgroups

3.1 Dairy products

Although New Zealand food prices in general are comparable with those in other countries, this is not the case for dairy products. The 23 per cent annual rise in New Zealand's dairy prices (FPI for milk, cheese and eggs) in the year to May 2008 was more than double that of the United States (11.0 per cent) and Australia (10.3 per cent). This was their largest annual increase in dairy prices for almost 30 years. The United Kingdom also showed a lower increase than New Zealand, rising 16.6 per cent over the same period.

In New Zealand the dairy industry has been subject to government regulation and subsidisation, discussed in detail with respect to milk in Section 3.1.1 below. However, since 1999, prices of dairy products have risen and fallen, reaching highs during 2001–02, to a lesser extent in 2005–06, and again since the middle of 2007 (Figure 6). New Zealand's dairy prices in this country are linked to export prices – when export prices rise or fall, domestic prices generally follow. One of the major reasons for the increase in dairy prices during 2001–02 was the low exchange rate for the NZ dollar against the US dollar. Dairy producers export a large amount of their products and get paid in US dollars – this means that US dollars need to be converted back to NZ dollars so they can be spent or invested at home. Over the years, rising dairy prices have been driven by an imbalance in global demand and supply due to rising production costs, increased demand from emerging undeveloped markets, and natural disasters in some of the other major dairy exporting countries.

3.1.1 Milk

Milk prices are a focus of New Zealand media attention, as both social and economic considerations have combined to make it a commodity significantly impacted by public policy. In the early part of the twentieth century milk was heavily regulated and subsidised, but in more recent years the major factor influencing internal price has been rising export prices. Up until the 1980s New Zealand's milk industry was heavily regulated. The New Zealand Milk Board, established in 1953, oversaw 44 district milk authorities that were responsible for, among other things, setting producer and consumer prices. A government subsidy was paid to make up the shortfall between the two prices. From 1937 until 1967, free milk was delivered daily to schools throughout New Zealand. Children received half a pint of milk each. (In 2011, Fonterra announced a 'Milk for Schools' plan, offering all New Zealand primary-aged children a free serving of Anchor Lite UHT milk every school day, which is currently being rolled out to all schools that wish to participate; see https://www.fonterramilkforschools.com/about). Price fixing was removed in 1976, followed by the removal of the subsidy from 1 April 1985 (Gilmour, 1992; Smith and Signal, 2009).

In the 1890s, milk was measured in quarts (equivalent to 1.14 litres) and retailed for just over 3 pence on average (under 3 cents in decimal currency terms). By 1914, the average price of a quart had risen to about 4 pence, and then by June 1950 had doubled to 8 pence. In 1956, the bottle size tracked in the CPI changed from a quart to a pint. At the time of the change, the quart average price was about 9.2 pence, and the pint average price was about 4.6 pence. The pint average price changed very little for the next 11 years until 1967, when decimal currency was introduced. In 1967 a pint cost 4 cents (equivalent to about 66 cents in March 2014 after allowing for general food price inflation). A 2-litre equivalent price would be $2.32.

In 1975, the bottle size tracked in the CPI was formally changed from the imperial pint (equivalent to 568ml) to the metric size of 600ml. At that time, the average price of the 600ml bottle was 4.01 cents (equivalent to 39 cents – or $1.31 for 2 litres – in today's terms). There was a 20-month transition period, starting in 1972, during which both the old 568ml pint bottles and the new 600ml bottles were on the market at the same price. This additional volume for the same price was shown in the CPI as a gradual price drop in seven steps, from 4.01 cents per 568ml pint in September 1972 to 3.79 cents in March 1974 when the transition was completed. The retail price of a pint of milk doubled in February 1976 to 8 cents from 4 cents. Eight cents in January 1976 is equivalent to 68 cents – or $2.25 for 2 litres – in March 2014, after allowing for food price inflation. There were further increases of 3 cents a bottle in February 1980, 3 cents a bottle in November 1980, 4 cents a bottle in August 1981, and 5 cents a bottle in June 1982, which took the price to 30 cents. The price remained at 30 cents a bottle through the 1982–84 wage/price freeze.

Although the changes in the bottle size collected make milk price change comparisons difficult, it is apparent that milk became more expensive. Figure 3 shows the average price of milk in New Zealand during the period from 1956 to 1984.

Figure 3

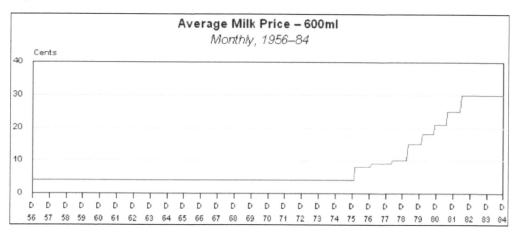

By October 1986, when a goods and services tax (GST) of 10 per cent was introduced, the price of milk had risen to 45 cents (equivalent to 94 cents – or $3.14 for 2 litres – in March 2014). Supermarkets were able to sell milk from 1987. In 1989, changes made to the package sizes tracked in the CPI included dropping the 600ml bottle and adding a 1-litre container. The 600ml price in December 1988 was 55 cents and the average price for the 1-litre container was 98 cents. As can be seen in Figure 4, the 1-litre price rose from $1.07 to $1.10 when GST rose from 10 per cent to 12.5 per cent in July 1989. After full deregulation of the domestic milk industry in 1993 (Moffitt and Sheppard, 1988), milk could be sold at any price. By December 1993, the average price of a 1-litre container had increased to $1.21. At that time, a further change was made to the package size for which average prices were reported and prices were collected for both 1- and 2-litre containers for delivered milk, and milk from supermarkets, service stations and dairies.

In January 1994, the average price of a 2-litre container was $2.37 (equivalent to $3.83 in March 2014). As Figure 5 shows, the average price remained fairly steady until November 1995, when it rose to $2.50. In August 1998, there was a 7 per cent increase, to $2.85.

Figure 4

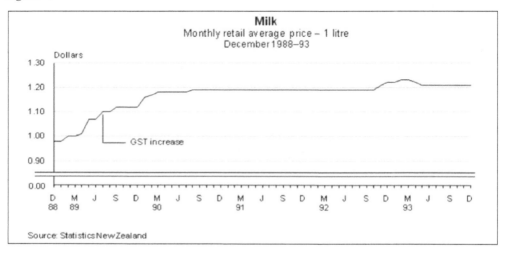

Figure 5

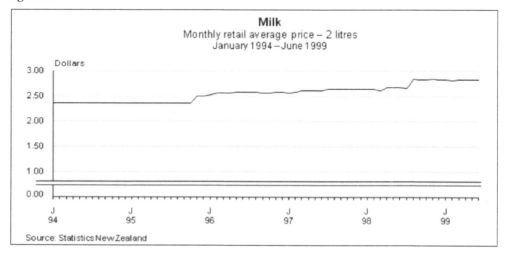

Export prices affected local prices in the early twenty-first century, with the average price reaching $3.20 in January 2002 (a high point for dairy export prices), before falling by about 12 per cent to $2.83 by February 2004

(when dairy export prices reached a low). By June 2006, the average price had increased about 1 per cent to $3.13, but was still below the January 2002 level. The average price fell to $2.60 by June 2007, before rising over the following 15 months to $3.37 in September 2008, reflecting a jump in world dairy prices. Prices then drifted down to $3.16 in November 2009 as world dairy prices fell from their peaks, before turning around and rising again to their highest level of $3.68 by February 2011. The price in February 2011 was 9.5 per cent higher than a year earlier, and 42 per cent higher than in June 2007.

Although the February 2011 average price is the highest recorded in 'nominal' terms, in 'real' terms prices have at times been higher in the past. For example, the average price of $2.37 in January 1994 is equivalent to $3.78 in February 2011, and the average price of $3.20 in January 2002 is equivalent to $4.18 in February 2011, after allowing for food price inflation. High milk prices tend to be cyclical. Twice in the past decade, there have been rises in the price of milk that have been followed by price falls – for example, milk prices fell in 2006–07 and again in 2009–10. In 2013, they were increasing again. Figure 6 gives time series of price changes for the three dairy product commodities, milk, cheese and butter, over the last 15 years.

Figure 6

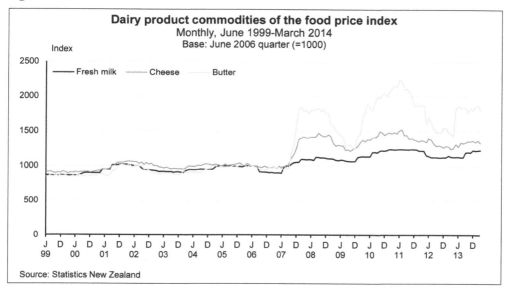

Source: Statistics New Zealand

Fresh milk is the hundred-year commodity, but over time both fresh milk and preserved milk have been included in the basket of goods. Fresh milk has been subject to more price fluctuations than preserved milk, but preserved milk has had bigger price increases over the past decade or so. For example, between March 2000 and December 2010 the price of preserved milk soared by 60 per cent, outpacing the 41 per cent increase of fresh milk.

The price growth of milk products was, to some extent, contributed to by the increasing demand for New Zealand milk products from the international market, particularly China, as consumers' incomes and demand for quality milk products rise. After the 2008 milk scandal in China, China's milk imports from New Zealand surged more than five-fold, hitting 353 million kilograms in 2010 (up from 69 million kilograms in 2008). By 2012, milk powder, butter and cheese amounted to 19 per cent of New Zealand's total exports to China, compared to 4.6 per cent in 2008. The value of dairy products exported to China was $2.2 billion in 2012 compared to $406 million in 2008 (Statistics New Zealand, 2012).

3.1.2 Cheese

As Figure 6 shows, along with other dairy products, retail cheese prices began to rise sharply in August 2007, reflecting the big increases in international dairy product prices.

For the first eight of the last 15 years, cheese prices tracked similarly to milk prices, but in the year to July 2008 they rose much more steeply, a rise of 42.3 per cent. The price of a family (1kg) block of cheddar cheese rose at a considerably greater rate (59.3 per cent) than the price of a 125g round of camembert (10.6 per cent). Increases for cottage cheese (21.5 per cent) and processed cheese slices (24.7 per cent) were between those recorded for cheddar and camembert. Andrew Smith, general manager of marketing at Fonterra Brands, said (personal communication, 12 September, 2008) that the main production input costs vary for different types of cheese. Prices of block cheese – such as cheddars and processed cheese – are linked to international dairy commodity prices. In contrast, gourmet or specialty cheeses, such as camembert, are linked to the price of domestic 'white milk'. Fresh milk prices increased by 10.2 per cent in the year to July 2008, broadly in line with the 10.6 per cent increase for camembert.

The 1980s was the most notable period for cheese price growth, with an increase of 144 per cent between June 1981 and December 1989. Cheese prices were relatively stable in the 1990s, but became more volatile in the 2000s, with sharp increases and decreases following one another. This fluctuation is in sharp contrast with the smoother growth of general food price in the 2000s. For example, between June 1981 and December 2010, cheese prices increased by more than 300 per cent, outpacing the 259 per cent increase of the general food price as measured by the FPI.

3.1.3 Butter

New Zealanders have always had a soft spot for butter as a dairy spread and baking ingredient. Butter is a hundred-year commodity in the CPI basket, but there has been a shift towards margarine (Forbes, this volume). In 1975, butter averaged less than half the price of margarine, costing about 32 cents per pound whereas margarine cost about 67 cents per pound. Equivalent figures today are $3.75 for butter and $2.26 for margarine.

As Figure 6 shows, for eight of the last 15 years, butter prices tracked similarly to milk and cheese prices, but in the year to July 2008 they rose much more steeply than either milk or cheese, a rise of 89.4 per cent. Since 2008, butter prices have been the most volatile of the dairy products.

3.2 Grocery items

3.2.1 Flour and bread

Flour is a hundred-year commodity, but the size of items priced has changed over time. In 1949 a 25lb (11.3kg) bag of flour had an average price (in Auckland) of 4 shillings and 5 pence. Allowing for food price inflation, this is equal to about $16 in today's terms. Bread is also a hundred-year commodity and in 1914, the average price of a 2lb loaf was just under 4 pence (equivalent to about $2.45 in the March 2014 quarter). It rose to 7.5 pence by 1953, dropping in price relative to general food price inflation. Over time, more varieties and sizes have been added to the CPI and, since 1978, bread weights have been measured in grams. Since 1981, bread prices have risen more steeply than the overall FPI (rising 443 per cent in the 30 years from 1981 to 2011 compared to an increase of 280 per cent in the FPI). Much of the bread made in New Zealand is made from imported wheat, so a major factor affecting bread (and flour) prices is adverse weather affecting crop sizes in the main countries we import from.

3.2.2 Sugar

In 1949, a 6lb (2.7kg) bag of sugar cost an average of 3 shillings and 2 pence in each of the four main centres. After allowing for inflation, this is equal to about $11.20 today. Six-pound bags were collected until October 1976, when 3kg bags were introduced. These cost an average of $1.34 (about $10 in today's dollars) throughout New Zealand. In 1981, the size of the bag changed again, falling to 1.5kg, with an average price of $1.28 in January of that year (about $4.90 today). In March 2014 the average price of a 1.5kg bag was $2.76. That is, sugar today is effectively less than half the price it was in 1949.

3.2.3 Eggs

Eggs were (and still are) priced by the dozen and had an average price of 2 shillings and 9 pence in Auckland in January 1949 (about $10 in today's terms, compared with an actual national average price in March 2014 of $3.69). After allowing for general food price inflation, the price of a dozen eggs has also become substantially cheaper over the past 50 years, now costing about 60 per cent less in today's dollars than in 1949.

3.3 Fresh fruit and vegetables

Fresh fruit and vegetables demonstrate the impact of seasonal weather events on prices, with seasonal price changes being greater than year-to-year changes in many cases. Prices for fresh fruit and vegetables tend to change frequently, so these are typically gathered from supermarkets and greengrocers within selected urban areas on a weekly basis. All fresh fruit and vegetables are priced on the basis of cheapest available at the time of price collection, usually with respect to variety, as long as the variety chosen is of suitable quality for most uses (that is, not damaged or spoiled). In-store prices for most fruit and vegetable items are 'per kg', while some are 'per head', such as pineapple, broccoli, cabbage, cauliflower and lettuce. For calculation of the FPI, the price per kilogram for items priced per head is calculated by dividing the shelf price by the weight per head, recorded by Statistics New Zealand price collectors.

The hundred-year commodities in this class are apples, potatoes, onions and cabbages. However, there are also a number of enduring commodities, including lettuce, tomatoes and bananas. Price changes for apples and each of the three enduring commodities given above are discussed below.

Potatoes and onions provide an interesting example of how seasonality and world events can interact to produce significant issues. Prior to the war, supply of these two vegetables was known to be subject to unpredictable surpluses or shortages due to variable weather conditions. The war years exacerbated these conditions considerably. The increased need to provide for the armed forces, (including the American Forces stationed in New Zealand) and some supply problems (speculation at the time was that home vegetable supply was severely disrupted by Home Guard and other war-related community activity) led to the Department of Agriculture starting the Service Vegetable Production Scheme in July 1942 and entering the vegetable-growing business. Demand increased further in 1943 when it became New Zealand's responsibility to service the Allied Forces fighting in the Pacific. It was in this context that the subsidies referred to above were introduced (Statistics New Zealand, 1990).

3.3.1 Apples

According to the 2012/13 Household Economic Survey, households spent an average of $64 a year on apples, now our second most popular fruit, behind bananas. Apple prices are collected for loose apples or bags of up to 3kg but, rather than targeting a specific variety, price collectors track the cheapest available variety of good quality apples at the time of price collection so the variety may vary from week to week or store to store. Collecting the 'cheapest available' prices is done for selected commodities that have little quality difference across different brands or varieties, and for which consumers are unlikely to exhibit much brand or variety loyalty (i.e. are likely to buy the cheapest). While this may not result in an intuitive average transaction price it should adequately represent price movements over time, as well as allowing the published price changes to be representative of consumers' buying patterns.

Apple prices tend to be highest in summer, usually reaching a peak in December or January. Prices fall when the new season's stock becomes available and are typically cheapest in autumn, before gradually becoming more expensive through the rest of the year. While there has been a gradual increase in apple prices since 2006, as shown in Figure 7, the seasonal variation is far greater than the annual change. At the December and January peaks, the two months before the harvesting season starts, prices of the cheapest variety can be as high as double the lowest monthly prices.

Figure 7

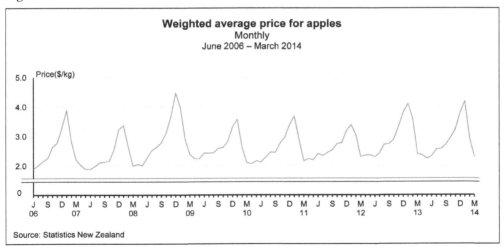

The dominance of an apple variety reflects both its harvesting season and its keeping quality (Figure 8). Royal Gala and its less-common parent variety Gala dominated from February to April in both 2012 and 2013. This reflects its harvesting season (February and March). Braeburn apples are harvested in late March and April but dominate as a variety from May to November because of their excellent storage qualities. Pacific/NZ Rose, the third most commonly collected variety, also stores well. Jazz is a cross between the Royal Gala and Braeburn varieties, harvested in early March to early April. It enjoys a modest but sustained presence until the following January. The harvesting season (April and early May) also plays a part in the popularity of the Granny Smith variety.

Figure 8

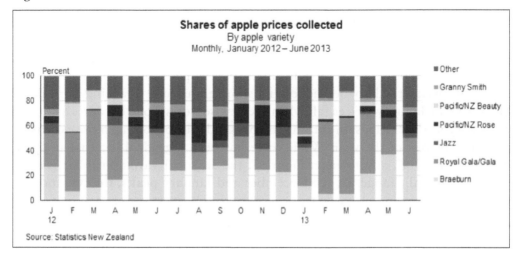

Source: Statistics New Zealand

3.3.2 Bananas

Over the 30 years from 1983 to 2013, bananas doubled in price – from $1.39 to $2.80 per kg. Although the highest average price during this period was in April 2009 ($2.97 per kg), the price in March 1990 was also high ($2.72 per kg), before dropping over the next four years to a low of $1.37 per kg in May 1994. New Zealand imports bananas from overseas to satisfy our demand. Because of this, banana prices are directly influenced by costs such as overseas freight prices, foreign exchange rates, and overseas suppliers' prices. This can cause short-term price fluctuation. However, these fluctuations have been limited as we now have choices about where we source our bananas from. In 1990, Ecuador was almost the sole source of our bananas, but over the next four years we imported heavily from Panama.

Figure 9 shows that banana prices increased at a slower rate than the FPI, which tripled over the 30 years to 2013. Had bananas increased at the same rate as the FPI, we would have paid about $4.50 per kg in March 2013 rather than the $2.80 we actually paid. In real terms, bananas have become cheaper since 1949. Figure 9 also shows the close relationship between the average price of banana imports and the average retail price.

Figure 9

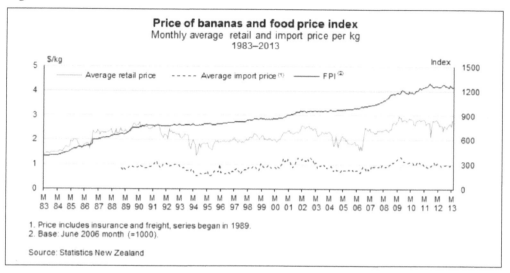

1. Price includes insurance and freight, series began in 1989.
2. Base: June 2006 month (=1000).

Source: Statistics New Zealand

3.3.3 Lettuce

Most fruit and vegetables have seasonal prices, being more expensive in the winter months (June, July and August) but not all demonstrate stable seasonal patterns. As Figure 10 shows, lettuce has prices peaking in either July or August. Once the winter months are over and spring has begun, prices for lettuce and other green vegetables become much cheaper as supply flourishes. Prices for lettuce usually fall sharply from their winter peaks, and are cheapest in either December or November, in time for summer salads.

Inclement weather can impact not only on the shelf price of a head of lettuce, but also on the quality of lettuce heads, notably the size. As lettuce prices per kg are used in the calculation of the FPI, higher lettuce shelf prices and lighter weights have a double impact. Not only do higher shelf prices directly impact on what households pay per head, the smaller size of lettuce heads results in a higher price per kg. There is a strong inverse relationship between shelf prices and weights per head; when shelf prices are low, weights per head are larger, and when shelf prices rise, lettuce heads are smaller. This results in the large swings in prices per kg – seen as the 'saw-tooth' pattern of price change in Figure 10. This unstable seasonality is most extreme in recent years. Not surprisingly, summer months show the best shelf prices and the largest lettuces.

Figure 10

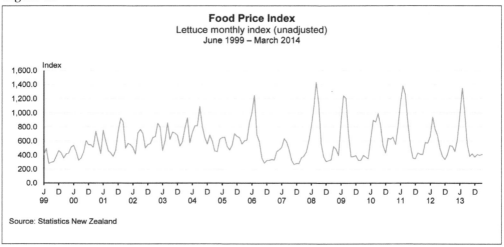

3.3.4 *Tomatoes*

Fresh tomatoes have featured in the CPI basket since 1949, when tomatoes had an average retail price of 1 shilling and 1 penny per pound in the March 1949 quarter (equivalent to about $8.70 per kg today). By comparison, the weighted average retail price in the March 2014 quarter was about $3.40 per kg. In real terms, tomatoes have also become cheaper since 1949.

Although the harvested area for tomatoes is significantly smaller for those grown indoors than outdoors, the volume of tomatoes produced is similar. Indoor tomatoes can be grown all year round, while outdoor tomatoes are only grown at warmer times of the year in New Zealand. In 2010, the estimated volume of fresh indoor tomatoes produced was about 40,000 tonnes, compared with 50,000 tonnes for outdoor tomatoes (Plant & Food Research and Horticulture New Zealand, 2010). Some tomatoes are bought fresh by consumers, and some are further processed. Three processed tomato products are currently tracked in the CPI: canned tomatoes, tomato-based pasta sauce, and tomato sauce.

Tomato sauce retail prices have been tracked since at least 1921. Tomato sauce was tracked in the 1949 CPI basket in a 10oz (283g) bottle at an average price of 1 shilling and 6 pence (equivalent to about $5.44 today). Most tomato sauce prices collected now are for between 560g and 600g (in both cans and bottles). The weighted average retail price in March 2014 was $3.06 for 560g of sauce. It takes 920g of fresh tomatoes to produce a 575g can of Wattie's tomato sauce (Heinz Wattie's Ltd, personal communication, 16 December 2011).

Of the processed tomato products, canned tomatoes are the newest in the CPI basket, introduced in 2006. Tomato-based pasta sauces are the next most recent addition, having been added in 1999, replacing tomato paste, which had been added in 1993. Figure 11 shows price series for the three current processed tomato products between 2006 and 2014. Over this time, canned tomatoes had the largest price increase (up 31.1 per cent), then tomato sauce (up 23.1 per cent), then tomato-based pasta sauces (up 21.1 per cent).

Figure 11

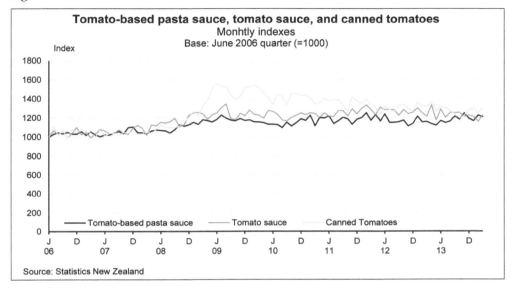

Table 1 shows the average prices of selected food items every decade over the past 50 years and how these have changed relative to today's prices. Prices for each item are given in the fourth column as they were at the time, indexed using the Food group of the CPI to put the prices into current dollars in the fifth column, and expressed in today's dollars and units in the sixth column. Where earlier sizes are significantly smaller or larger, prices will not be strictly comparable.

Table 1. Weighted average retail prices of selected food items

Item	Unit	March quarter	Past price	In today's dollars	In today's dollars and units
Milk	Pint	1959	5d	$0.81	$2.84
		1969	$0.04	$0.62	$2.19
	600ml	1979	$0.10	$0.56	$1.88
	1L	1989	$0.99	$1.84	$3.68
	2L	1999	$2.83	$4.13	$4.13
		2009	$3.29	$3.54	$3.54
		2014	$3.53	$3.53	$3.53

Item	Unit	March quarter	Past price	In today's dollars	In today's dollars and units
Bread, white	28oz	1959	8d	$1.30	$1.14
		1969	$0.12	$1.87	$1.65
	750g	1979	$0.40	$2.25	$2.10
		1989	$1.43	$2.66	$2.48
		1999	$1.84	$2.69	$2.51
	700g	2009	$1.74	$1.87	$1.87
		2014	$1.85	$1.85	$1.85
Apples	1lb	1959	11d	$1.90	$4.20
		1969	$0.17	$2.65	$5.83
	1kg	1979	$0.76	$4.28	$4.28
		1989	$2.19	$4.07	$4.07
		1999	$1.66	$2.42	$2.42
		2009	$3.09	$3.33	$3.33
		2014	$3.15	$3.15	$3.15
Eggs	Dozen	1959	5s 3d	$10.90	$10.90
		1969	$0.58	$9.03	$9.03
		1979	$1.10	$6.20	$6.20
		1989	$2.33	$4.33	$4.33
		1999	$2.74	$4.00	$4.00
		2009	$3.55	$3.82	$3.82
		2014	$3.66	$3.66	$3.66
Sausages	1lb	1959	1s 10d	$3.81	$8.39
		1969	$0.22	$3.42	$7.55
	1kg	1979	$1.48	$8.34	$8.34
		1989	$3.58	$6.65	$6.65
		1999	$4.44	$6.49	$6.49
		2009	$7.03	$7.57	$7.57
		2014	$8.96	$8.96	$8.96
Flour	25lb	1959	6s 5d	$13.33	$1.76
		1969	$1.36	$21.17	$2.80
	1.5kg	1979	$0.58	$3.27	$3.27
		1989	$1.56	$2.90	$2.90
		1999	$1.76	$2.57	$2.57
		2009	$2.12	$2.28	$2.28
		2014	$1.95	$1.95	$1.95
Sugar	6lb	1959	4s 2d	$8.65	$4.77
		1969	$0.37	$5.76	$3.17

Item	Unit	March quarter	Past price	In today's dollars	In today's dollars and units
Sugar	3kg	1979	$1.46	$8.23	$4.11
(continued)	1.5kg	1989	$1.87	$3.47	$3.47
		1999	$1.96	$2.86	$2.86
		2009	$1.98	$2.13	$2.13
		2014	$2.85	$2.85	$2.85
Butter	1lb	1959	2s 0d	$4.15	$4.58
		1969	$0.28	$4.36	$4.80
	500g	1979	$0.53	$2.99	$2.99
		1989	$1.76	$3.27	$3.27
		1999	$1.96	$2.86	$2.86
		2009	$3.41	$3.67	$3.67
		2014	$3.84	$3.84	$3.84

3.4 Premium food products

The FPI contains both standard and premium food products and provides evidence that some shoppers are increasingly prepared to pay significantly more for food products that they perceive to be superior. Examples include standard homogenised versus calcium-enriched milk, white and wholegrain breads, blade and porterhouse steak, etc. Another example is fruit juice. While this has long been available in shelf-stable form, chilled fruit juice has recently grown in popularity and was added to the FPI basket in 2008. In March 2014, shoppers opting for chilled fruit juice or smoothies were prepared to pay an average of $4.20 per litre, 145 per cent more than the average per litre price of $1.36 paid by buyers quenching their thirsts with 3-litre containers of the cheapest available shelf-stable apple-based fruit juice.

Ice cream is an enduring commodity introduced to the CPI basket in 1949, and is an example that demonstrates the impact of consumer choice. New Zealanders are among the highest per capita consumers of ice cream in the world, according to the New Zealand Ice Cream Manufacturers Association (http://www.nzicecream.org.nz/industry.htm). The first item to be priced was a 'slice'. This had an average price of around 3 pence in 1949, equivalent to about 91 cents today. The ice cream item in the CPI basket was changed to a 1-pint block in 1955, showing an average price of 20 pence, equivalent to about $3.77 today. During the 1970s the specification for ice cream in the CPI basket was changed to a metric 2-litre tub, and an ice block was introduced. Following the 1980 CPI review, price movements have been tracked using three separate items: ice cream bought in bulk (2-litre container), novelty ice cream and ice blocks. There have been markedly different patterns of price change for the three items.

The average prices of a 2-litre tub of ice cream in March 2014 were $5.93 at supermarkets, where a range of brands is priced, and $6.64 at convenience stores, where the price of the cheapest available 2-litre tub is collected. The average prices quoted are weighted averages of the selected items priced for the CPI, weighted by store-type expenditure and regional population estimates. The overall average price was around $6.26, compared with an average price of 85 cents in 1975 and $2.10 in 1981. The prices of all three surveyed items rose between the March 1981 and 2014 quarters, with much greater price increases for ice blocks (up 893 per cent) and novelty ice cream (up 656 per cent) compared with the increase for bulk ice cream (up 170 per cent). The annual average price increase was 7.2 per cent for ice blocks, 6.3 per cent for novelty ice cream, and 3.1 per cent for bulk ice cream between 1981 and 2014. Figure 12 shows how prices of each of the three ice cream products have changed relative to the overall food group. Ice block and novelty ice cream prices have risen much faster than the Food group price. In contrast, prices for bulk ice cream have risen by much less than the overall Food group price index. This demonstrates a willingness from some consumers to pay increased prices for a good that is perceived to be superior.

Figure 12

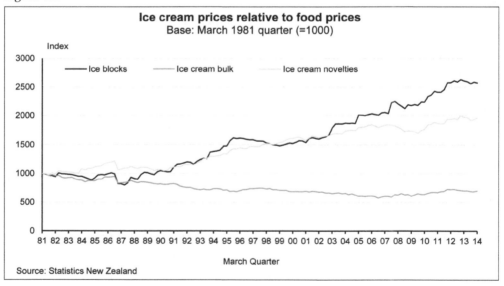

Ice cream prices relative to food prices
Base: March 1981 quarter (=1000)

Source: Statistics New Zealand

4 Transport group

Transport prices have risen 50 per cent over the last 15 years (Figure 13), a slightly greater rise than the overall CPI. Price changes have fluctuated more for transport than for the overall CPI, mainly because of the Private Transport

Supplies and Services subgroup, which is largely driven by rising petrol prices (that are impacted on by international availability of petrol and exchange rates). Price increases have also occurred in the Vehicle Servicing and Repairs and the Vehicle Parts and Accessories classes. If the price of vehicle supplies and services continues to go up and the gap between this and the price of purchasing vehicles continues to expand, consumers may end up spending far more money on services than on the one-off payment of purchasing vehicles.

Wartime rationing of petrol had some extreme effects on prices. New Zealand introduced controls in September 1939, resulting in a week in which petrol consumption was over one million gallons in excess of average weekly consumption as consumers rushed to fill up. The controls were so effective that stocks of petrol were built up and they were removed on 13 November 1939. However, with overseas reserves being short, the restrictions were re-imposed in February 1940 and stayed in force at varying levels of severity for the rest of the war. The war in the Pacific had a particular impact:

> After the news of the outbreak of war in the Pacific became known motorists, evidently expecting restrictions in supply, made an unprecedented rush to petrol stations. Califonts, kegs, kettles, demijohns, vinegar and whisky bottles, tins of all descriptions, and even a dustbin were produced to hold petrol as all available coupons were handed in. However, these activities were curbed to some extent in the afternoon when the Oil Fuel Controller, Mr G. L. Laurenson, banned the use of all receptacles other than fuel tanks. (Baker, 1965, p.418)

Figure 13

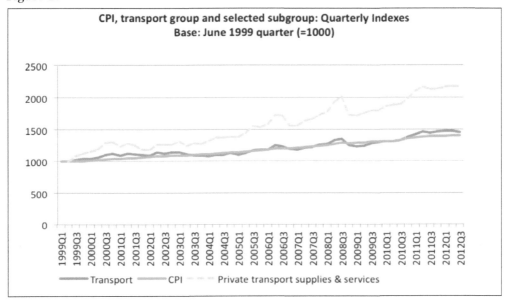

4.1 Public versus private transport

Currently, about 80 per cent of all transport expenditure paid by households is on private transport, including purchasing vehicles and relevant supplies and services, with only 20 per cent being spent on public transport.

4.1.1 Vehicle purchases

The price of vehicles overall has not changed a lot over the last 15 years, apart from a downward movement from 2003 to 2008. Comparing price changes for different types of vehicles (Figure 14), the biggest downward movement was for bicycles (down 20 per cent). Prices of new and used cars had a similar pattern, rebounding after 2009 (the global economic crisis) then remaining flat. The biggest rise in the last 15 years was for motorcycles, which rose in price by up to 18 per cent in the period 1999–2001.

Figure 14

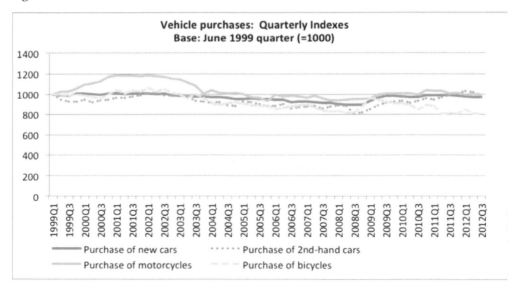

4.1.2 Public transport

As Figure 15 shows, over the last 15 years (from 1999 to 2014), most public transport prices have increased (apart from international airfares). Rail passenger transport increased the most (by 79 per cent), followed by domestic air (60 per cent), road passenger transport (47 per cent) and sea passenger transport (25 per cent). International air travel decreased by 15 per cent.

Figure 15

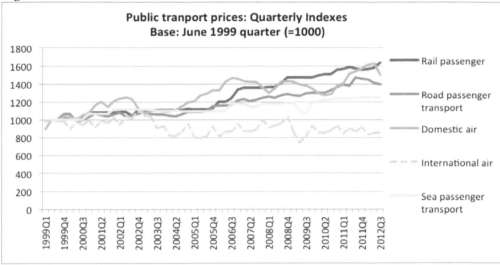

4.2 Domestic and international airfares

Air travel is another example of an industry that has been subject to regulation (and both privatisation and nationalisation). Both domestic and international airfares have been enduring commodities since being added to the basket in 1975 and 1981 respectively. As Figure 16 shows, although they are much more volatile than the overall CPI, domestic airfares have shown a similar trend in price rises in recent years. International airfares are markedly different, being stable or having slightly decreasing price changes over the last 30 years.

4.2.1 Domestic airfares

Since their introduction to the CPI basket, domestic airfares have had an average annual increase of 4.5 per cent compared to an annual average rate of 4.4 per cent for the overall CPI (Figure 17).

Ansett New Zealand began services on New Zealand's main-trunk domestic routes in 1987 and in the next year domestic airfares fell 16.8 per cent. However, they rose sharply from June 1989 to December 1990, increasing 34.9 per cent. During this time, Air New Zealand was privatised by the Government. Over the next decade to the year 2000, domestic airfares continued to increase, but at a lesser rate. The two years to the June 2002 quarter saw domestic airfares climb 24.7 per cent. During this time, Ansett New Zealand was sold to Tasman Pacific Airlines, rebranded as Qantas under a franchise agreement, and then collapsed. Air New Zealand also ran into financial difficulties and was re-nationalised under a rescue plan that involved the Government taking a majority stake. From June 2002 to March 2003, domestic airfares fell 14.7 per cent. Over this period, Jetconnect, flying under the Qantas brand, began servicing main-trunk routes and tourist destinations. Air New Zealand started offering cheaper domestic fares when it introduced an online booking system. Over the following three-and-a-half years, domestic airfares rose 37.6 per cent, reaching a peak in the September 2006 quarter. In 2007, Air New Zealand, followed by Qantas, reduced domestic airfares. These fare cuts, coupled with Pacific Blue's entry into the domestic market, saw airfares fall 11.3 per cent from the September 2006 quarter to the March 2008 quarter. Qantas' low-cost carrier, Jetstar, entered the market in 2009 and domestic airfares fell 13 per cent to levels last seen in 2004. Pacific Blue exited the New Zealand domestic market in mid-October 2010.

Figure 16

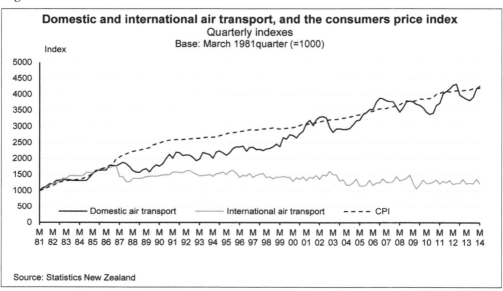

As Figure 17 shows, in real terms, domestic airfares cost much the same now as they did over 30 years ago. However domestic airfares have had some interesting fluctuations in the last few years, for example peaking in the June 2012 quarter and then falling by 11.8 per cent by the June 2013 quarter.

4.2.2 International airfares

Unlike domestic airfares, international airfares are not much more expensive now than when they were added to the CPI basket. International airfares increased a modest 22.2 per cent over the last 33 years, an average annual increase of 0.6 per cent. This is in stark contrast to the overall CPI, which rose 320 per cent over the same time period – an average annual increase of 4.4 per cent. Consequently, international airfares have fallen in price relative to the overall rate of CPI inflation, meaning they have now fallen 70.9 per cent in real terms (as Figure 17 shows).

Figure 17

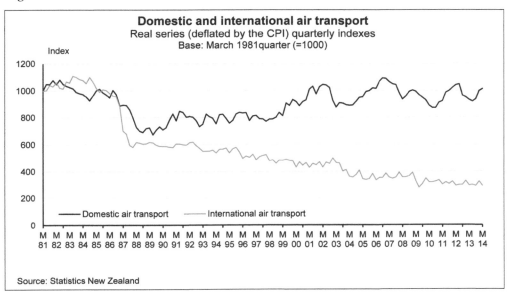

Domestic and international air transport
Real series (deflated by the CPI) quarterly indexes
Base: March 1981quarter (=1000)

Source: Statistics New Zealand

In the five years before the Government relaxed restrictions on foreign investment in domestic airlines in 1986, international airfares rose 69.5 per cent. In the year that followed, airfares fell 28 per cent. However, during the four-and-a-half years to June 1992, international airfares rose 27.8 per cent. During this time, the Government privatised Air New Zealand and further deregulated the airline industry. In 1995, Air New Zealand established a low-cost operator, Freedom Air, in response to the launch of Kiwi Air's discount flights between secondary airports in New Zealand and Australia. Fares fell 10.8 per cent over the next year but Kiwi Air experienced financial difficulties and collapsed later that year.

From 2002 to 2005, international airfares fell 17.5 per cent. This fall coincided with the introduction of online booking systems and revamped fare structures introduced by Air New Zealand, as well as Pacific Blue's entry to the trans-Tasman market. International airfares rose slightly over the next three years, with prices typically showing seasonal peaks in the December quarter of each year. The two quarters following December 2008 saw airfares fall 28.5 per cent to their lowest point since June 1981. This fall was influenced by the global financial crisis and by fuel prices falling from their peak in 2008. While prices for international airfares have risen since then, they are still only at levels seen in March 1982.

5 Summary

While the overall CPI indicates that there has been a steady overall increase in prices (inflation), particularly since the introduction of the expenditure-based index in 1974, this is not the case for all of the commodities priced within the CPI. A number of specific goods, such as sugar, eggs, bananas, tomatoes and international airfares, have decreased in cost in real terms, while others, such as milk, bread and cheese, have increased. Even with seemingly similar goods there can be different patterns of price change. For example, there are different levels of price rise for different types of processed tomatoes and for different modes of public transport. Ice blocks and novelty ice cream are now more expensive in real terms but bulk ice cream is cheaper. For seasonal items, such as fresh fruit and vegetables, the seasonal variation in prices is typically greater than the annual change. As is the case with apples, the dominance of a particular variety is affected by both its harvesting season and its storage qualities. Not all seasonal goods have stable seasonal patterns and lettuce is an example of this.

Some of the changes in prices have been caused by government interventions, such as the regulation and deregulation of the milk and air-travel industries, and the imposition of and changes in goods and services taxes. Imported goods such as bananas and motor vehicles are influenced by global factors such as overseas freight prices, foreign exchange rates, and dependency on suppliers. Bread is an example of a commodity that has prices affected by weather events in the countries we import wheat from. The price of other goods is simply influenced by consumer preference and willingness to pay, as shown by luxury ice creams and chilled fruit drinks. Different types of the same commodity can have different factors influencing prices. Cheese is an example, with the prices of block cheese being impacted on by international dairy commodity prices but specialty cheese prices being linked to the price of domestic 'white milk'.

The published Consumer Price Index is a single figure designed to give an overall estimate of price change but, as these examples demonstrate, it is only at the commodity level that the complexity of the influences on prices can be disentangled.

References

Baker, J. V. T. (1965). *The New Zealand people at war: war economy* (Vol. 5). Historical Publications Branch, Department of Internal Affairs. Wellington. Available from http://nzetc.victoria.ac.nz/tm/scholarly/tei-WH2Econ.html

Dalziel, P., and Lattimore, R. (1999). *The New Zealand macroeconomy: a briefing on the reforms.* Auckland: Oxford University Press.

Easton, B. (2012). *The course of prices: 1860 to today.* Available at http://www.eastonbh.ac.nz/2012/03/the-course-of-prices-1860-to-today/

Forbes, S. (this volume). The Changing Basket of Goods, pp. 40–68.

Garlick, T. (2012). *Social developments. An organisational history of the Ministry of Social Development and its predecessors, 1860–2011.* Ministry of Social Development. Wellington. Available from http://www.msd.govt.nz/documents/about-msd-and-our-work/about-msd/history/social-developments.pdf.

Gilmour, S. (1992). *History of the New Zealand milk board: A study of the corporatist alliance between the state and the domestic milk sector.* Lincoln University. Agribusiness and Economics Research Unit. Available from http://researcharchive.lincoln.ac.nz/dspace/handle/10182/246

Moffitt, R. G. and Sheppard, R. L. (1988). *A review of the deregulation of the New Zealand town milk industry.* (Discussion paper no. 122). Canterbury: Lincoln College, Agribusiness and Economics Research Unit. Available from http://researcharchive.lincoln.ac.nz.

Ministry for Culture and Heritage (2005). *Law and the economy.* Te Ara: The encyclopedia of New Zealand. Available from www.teara.govt.nz.

Ministry for Culture and Heritage (2014). Goods and Services Tax Act comes into force. NZHistory. Available from www.nzhistory.net.nz

Pike, C. (this volume). CPI Frameworks, 1949–2014, pp.26–39.

Smith, M. and Signal, L. (2009). *Global influences on milk purchasing in New Zealand – implications for health and inequalities.* University of Otago. Available from http://www.globalizationandhealth.com/content/5/1/1

Statistics New Zealand (1990). Prices (chapter 13). In *New Zealand Official Yearbook 1990* (pp. 613–615). Wellington: Department of Statistics. Available from http://www3.stats.govt.nz/New_Zealand_Official_Yearbooks/1990/NZOYB_1990.html#idchapter_1_171828

Statistics New Zealand (2012). *New Zealand Official Yearbook 2012.* Wellington. Author. Available from http://www.stats.govt.nz/browse_for_stats/snapshots-of-nz/yearbook/economy/national/trade.aspx

Acknowledgements

This chapter contains material extracted from Statistics New Zealand's online regular newsletter, *Price Index News*, available at http://www.stats.govt.nz/tools_and_services/newsletters/price-index-news.aspx. Special thanks to Chris Pike, Vince Galvin, Nick Martelli and Peter Campion of Statistics New Zealand for their expert input and quality assurance of this chapter.

Making Weights: Family Budget Studies in New Zealand, 1893–1937

Evan Roberts

Abstract

Consumer price indices, by combining the price of different goods into a single index, require each item to be weighted within the index. Both international statistical agencies and academic scholars generally prefer to obtain expenditure weights using surveys of household or family expenditure. But budget surveys are challenging to obtain, requiring large samples and placing a heavy burden on respondents. This chapter shows how New Zealand dealt with these challenges before World War II.

1 Introduction

Price indices, by definition, combine the changing prices for multiple goods into a single index whose value changes over time as prices change. Fundamental to constructing price indices, then, is a decision about the relative worth of different commodities in the index. For example, should changes in the price of beer account for a greater proportion of the value of the index than changes in the price of newspapers? Questions like this extend across the range of commodities in the index. Price indices would still perform a valid function if the importance of different commodities were assigned arbitrarily. Mathematically, the index would still be measuring changes in a vector of prices. Yet inherent in the idea of a consumer price index is that the relative importance of commodities in the index should reflect something about consumer behaviour. That is, the importance of commodities in a consumer price index should be based on what consumers spend money on. For example, if consumers spend half their income on food, half the value of the price index should reflect food prices. Within that broad category, more specific types of food such as milk, bread and meat can be allocated smaller fractions of the index, and the process repeated for other categories of expenditure such as housing costs, transportation and recreational expenditures. Following standard statistical terminology, the share of a consumer price index allocated to particular commodities is often called the commodities' 'weight' in the index.

A substantial amount of the pure economic and statistical theory of price indices is concerned with the observation that consumers change expenditure patterns in response to price changes. That is, the weight of each item in consumers' spending patterns changes when prices change. For example, when the price of movie tickets goes up, people will tend to purchase fewer movie tickets and redirect their expenditure onto something else. Whether movie tickets account for a larger or smaller share of consumers' expenditure depends on the strength of people's desires for movie tickets relative to other goods at a particular level of income. The theory and observation that consumers change their behaviour in response to price changes might imply that the price index needs to be continually updated in response to price changes. In practice, however, the weights for items in consumer price indices are updated infrequently.

A key reason consumer price index weights are infrequently updated is that obtaining the weights is itself a costly activity. Obtaining reliable weights requires knowing what the average household spends its money on. Historically, these surveys were called family or household budget studies. Budget studies require a large sample of households willing to accurately document and decompose their expenditures over a period of between a week and a year – a heavier demand on households than participating in most other social surveys. Long survey periods are required because many consumer expenditures vary seasonally (e.g. food prices or use of home heating) or are 'lumpy', occurring only several times a year or less than annually (e.g. clothing, appliances and cars). Survey size and sample length are partial substitutes in budget studies. If you sample a large enough number of households for a week, you will find a small number of people purchasing clothes, appliances and cars, even though in most weeks most households buy neither appliances nor cars.

Because budget studies demand a lot of the households participating in them, statisticians in New Zealand found that many people dropped out of the surveys, making the surveys less representative of the average consumer. The conscientious households that remained in the survey were atypical in ways that might have affected their expenditure. In historical studies, the families that tended to remain in budget studies typically had a well-educated and numerate wife who kept good records of expenditure; or the family had fewer children and thus a little extra time to participate in a survey of family budgets (May, 1984). The Index Committee that redesigned the New Zealand CPI after World War II archly commented that:

> . . . the probability is that those completing the budgets will represent not the community as a whole, nor any section of it other than the most careful, painstaking, economical, and admirably virtuous section. The weaker members fall by the wayside when it comes to filling in a detailed account of household

expenses over an extended period. Yet, if the results of the budget inquiry are to be regarded as typical, the sample of households covered must include a proper proportion of all types of spending habits (Index Committee, 1948).

At a conceptual level, budget studies are like any other statistical survey: a target population and variables are defined, and a sample drawn, taken, and analysed. At a practical level, the challenges of finding a sufficiently large representative sample of households to provide accurate information were great enough that until after World War II, New Zealand's "experience in family budget inquiries [was] uniformly disappointing" (Index Committee, 1948).

Despite the uniformly disappointing results, New Zealand's early history of family budget studies, from 1893 to World War II, shows serious attempts to grapple with the inherent challenges of the genre. Nor was New Zealand's experience especially disappointing in international perspective. Neither Australia nor Canada, the countries with whom New Zealand can most fairly be compared, made large or successful family budget studies before World War II (Williams and Zimmerman, 1935). This chapter shows that New Zealand's disappointing family budget studies were not from a lack of effort. The first survey of 'workingmen's budgets' was made in 1893. Subsequent surveys of household expenditure were carried out in 1911, 1919, 1930, and 1938. While the results of New Zealand's family budget studies may have seemed "uniformly disappointing", the reasons they were disappointing differed, and comparison with peer countries showed that New Zealand's disappointments were not unique, but perhaps endemic to the four British Dominions. Each successive survey was either methodologically innovative, or attempted to remedy the most serious problems in the previous survey. The final survey in the pre-World War II series, while not conducted by the Department of Statistics and never published because of the war, in fact showed that New Zealand could conduct a high quality budget study, informed by both its own experiences and international developments.

2 International background

The background to New Zealand's own family budget studies is the history of family budget studies in the United Kingdom, United States, and Australia. In most areas of official statistics, including the organisation of censuses and vital statistics, and the collection of economic data, New Zealand was influenced nearly entirely by Britain and Australia. Peripheral interaction with the other Dominions – Canada and South Africa – came at imperial statistical conferences (Nowell et al., 1875; Knibbs, 1920; Heyde, 1988; Beaud and Prévost, 2005). Unusually there was a relatively strong American influence on how New Zealand carried out family budget studies, whereas in other areas of official statistics American experiences had little impact. The relatively strong

American influence on family budget studies was in part due to the various federal and state labour statistics agencies providing a range of examples of how to conduct budget studies (Wright and Bureau of Labor Statistics, 1893; Wright and Bureau of Labor Statistics, 1902; Williams and Zimmerman, 1935). The federal government used trained agents to interview households in person, and obtained samples of 8–60,000 families in pre-World War II budget studies (Stapleford, 2012). Taking a different approach with more limited budgets, many American state labour statistics agencies distributed surveys through unions, employers and random mailings, that respondents were expected to return by prepaid mail. Using these methods some state labour statistics agencies had collected surveys of up to 9,000, but more commonly several hundred, working-class family expenditures in the late nineteenth century (Carter et al., 1991). Thus, using different approaches American statistical agencies had managed to collect large samples of family budgets, far exceeding the numbers collected in any budget studies before the 1870s.

Although the differences in consumption and income between rich and poor had exercised the minds of religious and social theorists alike for centuries, the first recorded statistical study of family budgets was not undertaken until the late eighteenth century in England. Rising concern about the well-being of agricultural labourers and migration to industrial jobs independently prompted a clergymen, David Davies, and a socially concerned aristocrat, Frederick Morton Eden, to collect budgets from over 200 poor families. Both men found that poor families headed by agricultural labourers spent around 70 per cent of their annual income on food. This statistic – the proportion of income spent on food – would become central to assessing and comparing living standards in Europe during the mid- and late-nineteenth century (Stigler, 1954).

Just as the earliest budget studies in England were motivated by political concerns about the well-being of agricultural labourers at the onset of industrialisation, significant developments in family budget studies were made in continental Europe from the mid-nineteenth century when industrialisation in France, Germany and Belgium raised similar political questions about the living standards of wage workers. The focus on urban workers was widespread internationally. Underlying the need to study family budgets was concern that industrial workers in urban areas were not earning enough to feed themselves adequately. The European studies made two important developments. The first, pioneered by Frenchman Frederic Le Play, was to collect accurate records of family expenditures over a long period of time. Le Play and his followers achieved this with frequent – sometimes daily, and at least weekly – visits to families to collect expenditure data over several months or a year (Brooke, 1997; Périer, 1998). As this description implies the method was highly costly, but it obtained high quality data.

Scholars influenced by Le Play collected hundreds of European family budgets in this manner from around 1850 to World War I. Yet the wealth of information in these studies was rarely compiled into a larger statistical profile of averages and variation in expenditure. Contemporary, as well as retrospective, critics of these methods have also emphasised that families agreeing to have a scholar visit frequently may be even more atypical than families keeping good records of their own expenditure. Le Play's methods were rarely applied in English-speaking countries. The second major European development came from the German economist Ernst Engel. After studying a collection of budgets from 153 Belgian families, Engel proposed a law of consumption: "The poorer a family, the greater the proportion of its total expenditure that must be devoted to the provision of food" (Engel, 1857). Testing this hypothesis, and related hypotheses about clothing and heating expenditures, became the major analytical concern of late-nineteenth century studies of family budgets.

Testing Engel's law required larger statistical samples of budgets than scholars influenced by Le Play had collected. Here, American governments made a major contribution. From 1870 to World War I, American state bureaus of labor statistics made more than 300 family budget studies (Wright and Bureau of Labor Statistics, 1893; Wright and Bureau of Labor Statistics, 1902; Williams and Zimmerman, 1935). The studies varied from Le Play-like studies of 22 families to massive surveys of more than 9,000 families, with the median study having 336 families. The state agencies had limited analytical capacity, and many studies were summarised merely as average expenditures within particular places or occupations. Realising that the valuable information overwhelmed their capacity and seeing value in presenting a testimony of individual families' lives, 151 studies published the detailed individual returns of each study. Thirty-eight of these studies are now available electronically, and have been widely used by scholars in the last twenty years (Carter et al., 1991). At the state level, the American studies were able to collect large numbers of budgets by limiting the amount of information asked. A typical survey in this series asked retrospective annual questions about income and expenditure. The more families studied, the coarser the information. Smaller studies gave greater detail about the cost and quantity of specific items such as potatoes or milk.

The proliferation of budget studies in the United States can be traced in large part to the influence of Carroll Wright. After heading the Massachusetts Bureau of Labor Statistics from 1873 to 1878, Wright became the first federal Commissioner of Labor in 1885 and served until 1905. Under Wright's direction, a large budget study of 6,809 American families and 1,735 European families (1,024 from Britain) was carried out in 1889. As with many of the state studies, the individual returns from this survey were published, and have become a significant resource for modern scholars (Commissioner of Labor, 1891a;

Commissioner of Labor, 1891b; Haines, 1979; Gratton and Rotondo, 1991). The 1889 study inaugurated a new era of British and American budget studies that collected detailed income and expenditure information for thousands of families. The American government made further large family budget studies in 1900, 1918 and 1935 (Stapleford, 2009). In Britain, the Board of Trade carried out a survey of British families in 1904, and American families in 1909 (Great Britain Board of Trade 1904, Great Britain Board of Trade 1911). Independent investigators, including Charles Booth and Seebohm Rowntree, made their own budget studies of thousands of British families in London and York around the turn of the century (Rowntree, 1901; Booth, 1903). In both Britain and the United States, studies done by academics and social workers surveying 50 to several thousand families complemented the government studies (Dundee Social Union, 1905; Chapin, 1909; Jones, 1928). Though much smaller than the government studies, they were sufficient for limited statistical analysis.

The international development of budget studies showed the significant challenges in answering a relatively simple question: how did people spend the money they earned? Acquiring a sufficient sample at reasonable cost was the first challenge. In Europe and the United States, where there were more large firms than in New Zealand, many investigators used contacts with employers to find reliable respondents. Government investigators from labour departments often had prior contact with employers, and would ask employers for a list of employees to contact. Selecting respondents through employers allowed verification of occupations and income. Surveys conducted via employers also allowed investigators to know they would be surveying workers from a variety of occupations and industries. Studies that distributed large numbers of survey forms via the postal service or canvassing households, and then relied on households to return the survey, suffered from low response rates and selective samples. The concern of New Zealand's 1948 CPI revision committee that the most "virtuous section" of the community participated in budget studies was grounded in decades of international evidence. Higher response rates, and more detailed and reliable information, could be collected by visiting households, but at much greater expense (Stapleford, 2012). These international experiences informed the way in which New Zealand carried out its own family budget studies starting in 1893.

3 New Zealand family budget studies

Despite its international reputation for progressive politics and state action to improve the conditions of the working class, there were no large-scale surveys of New Zealand working-class families before World War II. Yet the history of budget studies in other countries shows that they were often carried out because the level and distribution of income was a highly pressing political question.

While earnings and inequality were important political issues in New Zealand, the average standard of living was high and inequality relatively low (Nolan, 2009; Inwood et al., 2010). There was simply not sufficient political pressure to study the distribution of income. Statistics of earnings collected by surveying employers about ruling wage rates provided a more easily collected source of regular information on wage levels in New Zealand, and were published in the annual reports of the Department of Labour in the *Appendices to the Journals of the House of Representatives*. These surveys of payrolls lacked the information on what workers spent their money on, but addressed the political need to measure workers' earnings.

However, the Court of Arbitration and other government agencies required occasional updates on the adequacy of wages that could only be obtained by surveying households about both earnings and expenditure. Thus the Departments of Labour and Statistics, and the Social Science Research Bureau, made periodic attempts to collect family budget studies, beginning in 1893. Subsequent surveys were carried out in 1911, 1919, 1930 and 1938. Although none of the studies met contemporary expectations, they all made serious attempts at grappling with issues inherent in conducting a family budget study and not completely solved in any jurisdiction. Tracing the history of these surveys is hampered by the destruction of many of the records of the Department of Labour in a 1956 fire at Wellington's Hope Gibbons buildings (Strachan, 1979).

New Zealand's first family budget study, conducted in 1893, was explicitly motivated by a desire to compare earnings and expenditures with international norms. The report on the study, published as part of the Department of Labour's annual report to Parliament, noted that "similar tables have been published in Great Britain" (Department of Labour, 1893). Yet the way in which the results were presented, tabulating annual summaries of expenditure for 104 families, has closer parallels to the format in which American agencies presented many of their reports. Few British studies presented detailed information for individual families. Some reports from American federal and state labour statistics agencies were received in New Zealand before the 1893 report, as several Department of Labour publications from the 1880s and 1890s refer to results from American studies. Thus the New Zealand survey was informed by recent international experience in carrying out family budget studies.

The 1893 survey was of a similar quality to studies done around the same time in other countries. Although 146 schedules returned from 800 distributed sounds poor, the response rate was similar to those obtained by American state bureaus of labour statistics using similar methods. Schedules were distributed through factory inspectors, labour bureau agents, and trade union secretaries, who were instructed to give the survey to "working-men . . . likely to make bonâ fide returns".

The survey asked families to estimate expenditures on housing, fixtures and clothing on an annual basis, or weekly if rents were paid weekly. Heating costs were estimated on a weekly basis, differentiating between summer and winter. Respondents were meant to recall food expenditures on a weekly basis, with no seasonal variation specified. Again, this was similar to common international practice. Recalling expenditures over the past week was more accurate than asking families to recall expenditures over the year. Showing a sensitivity to measurement issues, the report dwelled on the inconsistencies induced by some families growing their own vegetables, catching their own fish, and owning cows (6 of 103 families).

A far larger problem was measurement of housing costs. Thirty per cent of the 103 families whose returns were printed in the report owned their house, and provided no information on mortgage payments they might have been making on their housing. Rents made up 14 per cent of total expenditure for the remaining families, suggesting the omission of mortgage payments was a significant bias. However, the New Zealand survey was not atypical for its time in neglecting mortgage payments. American and British surveys of the same time often made the same omission, and it was not until after 1900 that international budget studies routinely asked about mortgage payments.

The report on the 1893 survey noted that New Zealand families "almost invariably show a surplus unaccounted for", and commented that some expenditures were "sure to dribble away by unnoticed channels". The wage and earnings information in the 1893 survey appears accurate. The printed responses list the occupation and area the person lived in, and can be compared with wage rates collected by the Department of Labour in surveys of employers. Similarly, the weekly food expenditure reports also appear to be accurate, and show New Zealand wage-earners spending 47 per cent of their income on food. While the omission of housing expenses appears to be the most significant 'dribbling away' of expenditures from the returns, the returns for clothing and recreation also appear to have been understated. The request for annual expenditures on these items likely contributed to underestimates of expenditure. Yet, despite some shortcomings compared to modern practice, the 1893 budget study was well conducted for its time, drawing on international experience, and its omissions were similar to contemporary studies done overseas.

Despite the promising start in collecting family budget studies, it was 18 years before another survey was conducted. Although the results had been published in a report to Parliament, institutional memory about the study was limited. A long-time Statistics Department employee claimed the 1911 survey was the first family budget study in New Zealand (Wood, 1976). Reports on the early twentieth-century studies neglected comparisons with the 1893 survey (Collins, 1912; Fraser, 1915; New Zealand Census and Statistics Office, 1920; New Zealand

Census and Statistics Office, 1930; Index Committee, 1948). The shortcomings of the 1911 and 1919 surveys are likely the main reason later statisticians judged New Zealand's family budget studies to be so disappointing. While the motivation for the 1893 survey (beyond international comparison) was unclear, in 1911 the rising cost of living in New Zealand was a major political concern. The 1911 survey contributed in a limited and indirect way to a 1912 Royal Commission on the rising cost of living (Royal Commission on the Cost of Living, 1912).

Like American, British and Australian surveys of the time, the 1911 survey was targeted at "bona fide workers only". Following the practice of a recent Australian survey, it was proposed to sample nuclear family households where only the father/husband was working (Knibbs, 1911; Royal Commission on the Cost of Living, 1912; Saunders, 2006). Because many New Zealand children left school in their early teens and began working while still living at home, this necessitated a focus on families with children younger than 14. Like in the United States, New Zealand officials were also concerned to exclude families with non-kin boarders who could similarly distort results. While the criteria may appear restrictive to modern readers, they were common in family budget studies conducted before World War I (Williams and Zimmerman, 1935).

The focus on nuclear families with children and a husband earning enough to support them had both moral and practical supports. The moral support for the focus on nuclear families came from broad cultural disapproval of both married women's employment, and boarding and lodging in private houses (Nolan, 2000). While boarding and lodging in private houses was not as common in New Zealand as in the United Kingdom or United States, it was still frowned upon by the middle class (Modell and Hareven, 1973; Fairburn, 1989; Ferguson, 1994). Boarders and lodgers were mostly single men, and had a reputation for excessive alcohol consumption and anti-social behaviour. Their presence in homes with children was potentially dangerous. The practical reason to exclude families with boarders and lodgers from a family budget study was to keep the household composition of the sample more homogeneous. The aim of budget studies was to estimate what an average family spent on various commodities. Families with boarders or lodgers – extra adults – would have different expenditure patterns than families composed of a husband, wife and children. While modern statistical methods allow analysts to easily adjust for differences like this, in the early twentieth century the calculations were done by hand. Selecting households with a similar demographic composition was a practical method of statistical control.

The 1911 survey was more ambitious than the forgotten 1893 survey in both size and methodology, and thus proved the greatest disappointment to its creators of any of the surveys. New Zealand's 1893 survey had asked households merely to recall their annual expenditures on larger items, record regular expenses such as food, rent and fuel for the past week, and record relatively small expenses on items such as education, health, and periodical subscriptions over whatever period the respondent felt it easiest to recall. In the international terminology the 1893 survey had used the schedule method, which taxed respondents' memories and tended to bias expenditure estimates downward. By contrast the account method adopted for the 1911 survey asked respondents to keep a prospective record of their expenditure for months or weeks at a time. It was known internationally to tax respondents' time, and either lead to samples of the unusually conscientious, or to alter respondents' expenditures by making them more aware of what they were spending money on (Lamale, 1959). Indeed, in the late nineteenth and early twentieth century there was substantial encouragement for housewives in Britain, Australasia and North America to keep good accounts, precisely because it could alter decisions. Good household accounts had moral virtues of their own, and potentially good moral consequences (Frederick, 1911; Walker, 1998; Nolan, 2000; Carnegie and Walker, 2007).

In 1911 the New Zealand Department of Labour distributed 2,000 account books that required households to keep a weekly record of expenditures (Collins, 1912). The heavy burden on untrained and unsupported households was apparent when the books were returned after a year. The first disappointment was that only 1,800 surveys had been distributed, as potential respondents learned what they had to do. From the 1,800 distributed, just 69 usable account books were returned to the Department of Labour. Many of the others had entries that were abandoned after several weeks. The usable returns came from what the report called "the more careful and thrifty members of the community". Most notably, 39 of the 69 families reported themselves to be teetotallers. Despite receiving one third fewer usable returns than the 1893 survey, the report on the 1911 survey included 33 summary tables over a 29-page report. Yet unfortunately the report did not include the individual-level summaries of annual earnings and expenditure that had been published in 1893. The 1911 report was a disappointment to its creators who concluded on the hopeful note that "the publication of these returns [might lead] to the creation of a wider public interest in the question" which might be investigated by "some more simple method . . . so that the work entailed on householders will not be so great".

Dramatic rises in consumer prices during World War I motivated New Zealand's next official family budget study in 1919 (New Zealand Census and Statistics Office, 1920). The two earlier surveys had been carried out by the Department of Labour, who had a network of inspectors and agents in contact with employers and trade union officials. In theory, this put the Department of Labour in a better position to carry out the study, but practice had proved otherwise.

Unlike the Department of Labour, who had passed surveys to trade unionists, the Statistics Department aimed to place the surveys with a wider general public. Recognising that the 1911 survey had asked respondents to keep detailed accounts for a year for no greater reward than public understanding, the Statistics Department planned to compensate respondents. The method was innovative, with 19 households from each of the North and South Islands eligible to share in a £100 prize pool.[1] Appealing to the Minister of Internal Affairs to allow the expenditure, the Government Statistician, Malcolm Fraser, noted that the Department of Labour's previous surveys had "proved only partially successful".[2] Moreover, the survey would only ask households to keep accounts for three months. Weekly budgets were to be kept from March to June, a time period long enough to capture less frequent expenditures like clothing, and encompass most of the seasonal variation in food and heating costs encountered in New Zealand.

Unfortunately, the Statistics Department proved little better at collecting a reliable survey. Just 109 reliable account books were returned, from 20,000 distributed. The major deficiency of the 1893 survey – not measuring housing costs properly – was repeated (Wood, 1976). The results were so poor that the Department did not even disburse all of the prize money it had planned, with the first prize being reduced to £10 from a promised £20.[3] As with the 1893 survey, the inclusion of home-owners who did not completely specify their housing costs biased the results of the survey. In 1911, with the sampling frame carefully specified to include only renters, the survey found households spending around 20 per cent of their income on housing, in line with international figures (Bureau of Labor Statistics, 2006). The 1919 survey found households spending an improbably low 13 per cent of their income on housing. Indeed, the problems with the survey were so severe that while its results were eventually published in the *Monthly Abstract of Statistics*, the weights from the survey were not used to update the Consumer Price Index. The slightly less-flawed 1911 results continued to be used (Wood, 1976).

Thus by 1930, New Zealand's consumer price index was based on weights nearly 20 years old. At the instigation of the International Labour Office there was a worldwide effort to standardise price indices with expenditure weights from 1930. New Zealand authorities were highly supportive of international efforts like this, and willingly complied (New Zealand Census and Statistics Office, 1930; Hughes and Haworth, 2013). Despite the poor number of returns

1   Household Budgets, *Evening Post*, 22 February 1919, p.6.
2   Malcolm Fraser to Minister of Internal Affairs, 23 July 1918, Stats 22/1/22. Collection of Household Budgets. Archives NZ.
3   "Household Budget Enquiry, Government Prize Competition" Stats 22/1/22. Collection of Household Budgets. Archives NZ.

from the 1919 survey, the Government Statistician viewed the award of prizes for completing budgets as a successful aspect of the previous survey, and the approach was repeated. Less documentation survives in the Statistics Department archives about the 1930 survey. Thus, it is unclear why repeating methods that had proved unsatisfactory 11 years earlier led to a far more successful survey in 1930. The report on the 1930 survey described the account books as being distributed via "various channels to householders," suggesting that again the Statistics Department attempted to achieve a broader distribution of surveys than would be obtained though contacting employers and trade unionists (New Zealand Census and Statistics Office, 1930). The survey was so successful that it gathered more responses (318) than all the previous surveys combined. The distribution of the survey was geographically balanced, and included responses from smaller cities as well as the four main centres. Demographically, the households matched up well with the New Zealand population. Households in the survey averaged 4.4 people per household, compared to 4.3 in the country as a whole in 1926. The only notable imbalance in the composition of the survey was that 44 per cent of respondents were white-collar workers. While the survey was motivated by concerns about substantial change in expenditure shares over time, the 1930 survey showed remarkably little change from 1911 in the share of money spent on broad categories of goods (Table 1).

The deficiencies of the 1893 and 1919 surveys can be seen in the under-representation of housing in expenditure shares in those years. A major cause of the low housing share in the 1893 and 1919 surveys was under-reporting of housing expenditures by home-owners. Yet renters in the 1893 survey also appear to have under-reported rents. Rents for farm labourers were commonly included in wages. Even after excluding farm labourers from the analysis, 14 of the 75 renters in the 1893 survey did not report rents at all. Recalculating the expenditure shares for the smaller group of people who rented and reported their rent shows more realistic expenditure shares for New Zealand families. The rents reported by these families are within the range of house rents in New Zealand cities collected in other surveys. The expenditure shares from this apparently accurate subset of 1893 households are close to expenditure shares observed internationally at the same time. The necessities of life – food, shelter, heat and clothing – made up more than 80 per cent of family budgets in 1893. Despite the difficulties New Zealand authorities had in obtaining a large sample of family budgets, the overall picture painted by the data collected is similar to that seen abroad in the United States and Australia, countries with a similar level of per-capita income before World War II (Crafts, 2002). Until the early twentieth century most working class families spent most of their money on the necessities of life. Yet, even for these families whose income was below the national average, the majority were able to afford regular purchases of books and newspapers. In the first half of the twentieth century as the nation and families got richer, they spent less of their money on food and more on 'sundries', the growing 'other items' category in Table 1.

Table 1. Expenditure shares in New Zealand family budgets, 1893–1937

Expenditure Group	1893	1893 renters	1911	1919	1930	1937
Food	50.9	48.0	34.1	38.3	29.5	35.3
Housing	6.1	16.0	20.3	13.1	21.9	19.9
Clothing, drapery, footwear	18.9	16.1	13.9	15.9	12.6	10.2
Fuel and light	6.9	7.3	5.2	6.1	6.2	5.6
Miscellaneous items						
Tobacco	–	–	1.1	1.1	1.3	1.6
Tram fares	–	–	2.8	2.7	3.5	2.0
Insurance	2.3	1.7	2.5	2.9	3.8	4.8
Recreation	1.2	1.2	1.6	1.8	2.2	2.5
Other items	13.7	9.7	18.5	18.2	19.0	27.4
Total	100.0	100.0	100.0	100.0	100.0	100.0
Cases	106	61	69	109	318	247

However, the weights for a consumer price index must do more than represent broad expenditure categories. People do not just eat "food". They combine different foodstuffs in different proportions depending on relative prices. Despite the plethora of tables published from the 1911 survey, the report did not include more detailed expenditure shares than "food" and "clothing". More detailed information is only available from the 1893 and 1930 surveys. While the individual returns from the 1930 survey are not available, the food returns from 1893 appear reliable. Comparing the reported weekly expenditures with information on food prices allows estimates of the quantities of food purchased by different families. Overall, the reported expenditures comport with a plausible level of consumption of the various food groups for families of the size reported. The share of food expenditure on different food groups is summarized in Table 2. Again, the story revealed by the expenditure shares is one of material progress. In 1893, starches, butchers' meats, tea and sugar dominated food expenditure. Just a small proportion of food expenditure went to fresh fruit and vegetables. These patterns of food purchases are consistent with British and American studies of how workers with physically intense jobs but limited incomes got enough calories – they ate a plain diet high in fat and sugar (Pearson, 1913; International Labour Office, 1939; Oddy, 1970; Dirks,

2003). By 1930 the New Zealand diet had diversified substantially, with people obtaining more protein and fat from dairy products, and 30 per cent of food expenses going to fruit, vegetables and a variety of other foods.

Table 2. Share of food groups within food expenditures, 1893–1937

Food group	1893	1930
Bread and flour	20.5	13.9
Butchers' meat	23.3	19.0
Bacon	2.9	3.0
Milk	7.4	12.1
Butter	9.0	12.1
Sugar	8.0	3.9
Tea, coffee and cocoa	10.2	4.5
Fresh vegetables and fruit	4.2	11.7
Other food	14.5	19.8
Overall food share	48.0%	29.5%

The 1930 study showed that the Statistics Department was capable of conducting a well-organised family budget study. It would prove a useful baseline for comparing living standards before and during the Great Depression. When the First Labour Government took office in 1935 it made major changes to industrial relations legislation and economic policy. Leading into the 1938 election the Government was anxious to show that its policies had, in fact, benefited the working-class electorate that had supported it. These needs motivated the final pre-World War II family budget survey in New Zealand. Somewhat suspicious of the existing bureaucracy, the new government established a Social Science Research Bureau inside the Department of Scientific and Industrial Research. The Bureau, headed by Terence Doig, was asked to conduct a cost-of-living study of tramway and boot-and-shoe workers.

International influences again played a part in the motivation and design of the survey. The Institute of Pacific Relations, an American-based non-governmental organisation, was interested in sponsoring research that compared living standards in developed countries around the Pacific Rim (Hooper, 1988). Starting in 1932 they began planning a comparative series of family-budget studies in Japan, the United States, New Zealand and Australia (Huntingdon et al., 1937). In all four countries the studies were meant to encompass a group of wage-earners whose industry was exposed to international trade, and a comparison group of workers whose industries were not exposed to trade. The grand ambitions of the study were not quite realised, with only the American and New Zealand surveys reaching the field. The breakdown of American relations with Japan in the late 1930s derailed the survey in Japan, and it is unclear why the Australian survey was not completed (Eggleston et al., 1939).

The American studies were carried out in the San Francisco Bay area, and the New Zealand studies in Wellington and Christchurch. In both countries, tramway workers were chosen as the group not exposed to international trade. New Zealand's trade-exposed group were boot-and-shoe workers. Extensive archives of correspondence and technical documentation survive from the New Zealand surveys at Archives New Zealand. All of the individual surveys and much technical documentation survives for the San Francisco families at the University of California, Berkeley.[4] While 250 New Zealand families were surveyed across the two industries, forms for just 92 families survive, documenting such items as family composition, residence during the year, social isolation, and reading habits, among others. Just 68 forms from the budget study carried out with the same families have survived to the present.

Despite the selective survival of the original survey forms, the 1937 study was probably the best budget study carried out in New Zealand. Following correspondence with the Heller Committee at the University of California, Berkeley, which carried out the American studies, the New Zealand study used survey forms that were almost identical. As in San Francisco, professional enumerators were employed to visit families, conduct the extensive household interview, and explain the way in which expenditures were to be recorded. Whereas the three previous New Zealand studies had asked for summarised weekly accounts over a 3–12-month period, the 1937 study asked for itemised accounts on a daily basis for a month. Thus, in 1911, 1919 or 1930, families were meant to report at the end of a week they had spent, for example, 1 shilling on bacon. The next week they would report expenditure on bacon again. In 1937, each day's quantities and expenditure were to be recorded. Thus, an individual entry in the 1937 survey would appear as "bacon, 1 shilling, 1lb". The detailed information on quantities purchased allowed the 1937 study to support the first ever scientific survey of New Zealand diets (Jackson, 1937).

Despite the high quality of the research for the 1937 study, political controversy over the draft findings meant that its influence was limited (Wood, 1976). The Labour Government wanted the study to show that restoration of wage cuts and other policies had improved living standards among urban workers. The draft report on the survey suggested to officials that progress in improving living standards had not been fast enough, and the Minister of Internal Affairs halted the writing and publication of the report. Terence Doig, the head of the Social Science Research Bureau, resigned and took his

---

4   Records of the Heller Committee for Research in Social Economics, University of California-Berkeley Libraries, CU-47.

criticisms public, before taking his own career to Australia (Wood, 1976). Despite the unfortunate ending to the promising study, the 1937 study data were eventually used in a 1942 re-weighting of the Consumer Price Index (Economic Stabilisation Commission, 1944).

4 Conclusions

Reviewing the 44-year history of family budget studies in New Zealand, the 1948 committee appointed to revise the Consumer Price Index decided that the "uniformly disappointing" results dictated a different approach (Index Committee, 1948). Instead of surveying households to obtain expenditure weights, the government would use its new macro-economic data collection on aggregate expenditure to create weights. This approach required deciding, for example, that certain categories of expenditure were, in the aggregate, consumed entirely by households and not by firms or government. While this assumption is not entirely correct, in the circumstances it was a defensible decision.

Using aggregate expenditures was also somewhat distinctive when compared to post-war international practices. Official American and British price indices had been based on family budgets from their inception in the early twentieth century. In the United States there was strong trade union support for using weights derived from family budgets obtained from the working class, as it meant that the consumer price index tracked price changes for lower-income households. Economic theory also shows that aggregate expenditure methods weigh the purchases of higher-income households more heavily than lower-income households (Deaton, 1998). For this reason, aggregate expenditure methods of constructing price indices have been called "plutocratic" (Prais, 1959). Moreover the government's collection of budget data was supported by American businesses and social scientists, who were able to use the data to study the dynamics of consumer demand (Stapleford, 2007). Among New Zealand's peer countries, Australia and South Africa had used the aggregate expenditure method to provide weights for consumer price indices. Australia's family budget studies before World War II had been, like New Zealand's, small-scale with low response rates (International Labour Office, 1937b; Bambrick, 1968). Surveys of international practice by the International Labour Office in the 1930s also found Latvia, the Netherlands, Poland, and Czechoslovakia using the aggregate expenditure method to weight consumer price indices (International Labour Office, 1933).

New Zealand's family budget studies had been disappointing, but not "uniformly" so as the committee opined. One repeated disappointment was that housing expenditures were poorly measured on two occasions. The other disappointments were often the unforseen outcome of trying to overcome inherent challenges in conducting family budget studies. That is, the disappointing results were not for a lack of trying. New Zealand family budget studies were of comparable quality to many done overseas, and their particular problems reflected particularities of the New Zealand industrial and political environment.

New Zealand statistical officials worked almost entirely on their own without a supporting community of social scientists in universities and social reform organisations. In continental Europe, Britain and the United States, non-governmental studies had demonstrated how house-to-house collection of family budget studies could obtain high quality results. This approach was labour-intensive, and beyond the capability of New Zealand's government agencies on their own. Moreover, New Zealand studies could not take advantage of the numerous large workplaces that American and British officials used to find respondents.

Thus, the New Zealand studies attempted to recruit a cross-section of the community by advertising widely and providing prizes for timely and apparently accurate completion. While the response rates to these methods were lower than officials hoped for, the approach was innovative. Compensating respondents for their time has become accepted in survey research since World War II, but it is rare in both historical and modern government surveys (Bevis, 1948; Yu and Cooper, 1983). The New Zealand surveys also attempted to collect detailed itemised expenditure reports in the 1911, 1919 and 1930 surveys. In attempting to collect itemised expenditure the New Zealand authorities responded to the problems in asking aggregate retrospective questions about expenditure seen abroad and in New Zealand's 1893 survey. Aggregate and retrospective questions led respondents to state expenditures in round numbers, and miss seasonal or irregular purchases.

Despite the various disappointments in New Zealand's pre-World War II family budget studies, the overall picture they give of New Zealand living standards is consistent with other evidence on economic development. Expenditure shares in the New Zealand family budget studies are similar to those found in American and Australian surveys – countries with a similar culture (and thus consumer tastes) and level of overall national income. In the long run, the disappointment of New Zealand's family budget studies is their small size and the destruction of most of the original surveys. The small size of the surveys frustrated contemporaries and is frustrating for historians, because little can be said from the surveys about inequality or distribution in the New Zealand past. The destruction of most of the original surveys compounds this problem, leaving historians dependent on the tabulations made at the time.

Comparison with other countries of a similar size or history places New Zealand's history of family budget studies in perspective. In comparison to small European countries, such as Denmark (International Labour Office, 1937a), Finland (International Labour Office, 1934), Norway, and Sweden (International Labour Office, 1935), New Zealand's achievements in collecting family budgets were limited. From around 1910 and through the 1920s, the Scandinavian countries took regular family budget studies with 500–1,500 families (Williams and Zimmerman, 1935). Thus, it was clearly possible for small countries to initiate and maintain regular high-quality surveys of household expenditures.

Comparison with other British Dominions is more apt, and shows the New Zealand history was not unique. Like New Zealand, the Australian statistical authorities managed to collect few family budget studies before World War II. Indeed, all the major Australian budget studies before World War II were taken between 1911 and 1921 (Williams and Zimmerman, 1935), and Australian economists of the era decried their country's lack of data on household expenditures (Sawkins, 1928; Eggleston et al., 1939). Despite their proximity to the family budget work being done in the United States, and concerns about the living conditions of immigrant wage-earners in Toronto and Montréal, there are no statistical studies of family budgets for urban workers in Canada before World War II (Williams and Zimmerman, 1935). In South Africa, just three surveys of family budgets were made in this era, in 1914, 1925 and 1936 (International Labour Office, 1937b). In this light, New Zealand's five studies of varying quality are creditable. Moreover, two (1893 and 1937) of the New Zealand studies have surviving micro-level data, and a third (1930) was sufficiently large and well-conducted that its tabulated results provide a valuable record of household expenditure patterns on the eve of the Great Depression. Thus, New Zealand's "experience in family budget inquiries" was not nearly as "uniformly disappointing" as its own statistical authorities had lamented. The individual inquiries had their own distinctive strengths as well as disappointments, and the overall record of family budget inquiries was comparable, and often better, than in the other British settler colonies to which New Zealand is traditionally and fairly compared.

References

Bambrick, S. (1968). Australian Price Indexes from Federation to the Present. *Australian Journal of Politics & History* 14(2), 219–232.

Beaud, J.-P. and J.-G. Prévost (2005). Statistics as the science of government: The stillborn British Empire statistical bureau, 1918–20. *The Journal of Imperial and Commonwealth History* 33(3), 369–391.

Bevis, J. C. (1948). Economical Incentive Used for Mail Questionnaire. *The Public Opinion Quarterly* 12(3), 492–493.

Booth, C. (1903). *Life and Labour of the People in London*. New York: Macmillan.

Brooke, M. Z. (1997). *Le Play: engineer and social scientist.* New Brunswick, New Jersey: Transaction Publishers.

Bureau of Labor Statistics (2006). *100 Years of U.S. Consumer Spending: Data for the Nation, New York City, and Boston.* Washington, D.C.

Carnegie, G. D. and S. P. Walker (2007). Household accounting in Australia: Prescription and practice from the 1820s to the 1960s. *Accounting, Auditing and Accountability Journal* 20(1), 41–73.

Carter, S. B., R. L. Ransom and R. Sutch (1991). The Historical Labor Statistics Project at the University of California. *Historical Methods* 24(2), 52–65.

Chapin, R. C. (1909). *The standard of living among workingmen's families in New York city.* New York: Charities publication committee.

Collins, J. W. (1912). *Inquiry into the Cost of Living in New Zealand, 1910–11.* Wellington: Government Printer.

Commissioner of Labor (1891a). *Sixth Annual Report of the Commissioner Of Labor, 1890. Cost of Production: Iron, Steel, Coal, Etc.* Washington, D.C.: Government Printing Office.

Commissioner of Labor (1891b). *Seventh Annual Report of the Commissioner Of Labor, 1891. Cost of Production: Textiles, Glass.* Washington, D.C.: Government Printing Office.

Crafts, N. F. R. (2002). The Human Development Index, 1870–1999: Some revised estimates. *European Review of Economic History* 6(3), 395–405.

Deaton, A. (1998). Getting Prices Right: What Should Be Done? *Journal of Economic Perspectives* 12(1), 37–46.

Department of Labour (1893). Report of the Department of Labour. *Appendices to the Journals of the House of Representatives.* Wellington. H-10.

Dirks, R. (2003). Diet And Nutrition in Poor And Minority Communities in the United States 100 Years Ago. *Annual Review of Nutrition* 23(1), 81–100.

Dundee Social Union (1905). *Report on Housing and Industrial Conditions in Dundee.* Dundee: Dundee Social Union.

Economic Stabilisation Commission (1944). Report on the New Zealand Wartime Prices Index. *Appendices to the Journals of the House of Representatives.* Wellington. H-43.

Eggleston, F. W., E. R. Walker, George Anderson, J. F. Nimmo and G. L. Wood (1939). *Australian standards of living.* New York: Australian Institute of International Affairs and Institute of Pacific Relations.

Engel, E. (1857). *Die Productions – und Consumptionsverhaeltnisse des Koenigsreichs Sachsen.* Zeitschrift des Statistischen Bureaus des Koniglich Sachsischen Ministeriums des Innere 8 and 9.

Fairburn, M. (1989). *The ideal society and its enemies: the foundations of modern New Zealand society, 1850–1900.* Auckland: Auckland University Press.

Ferguson, G. (1994). *Building the New Zealand Dream.* Palmerston North: Dunmore Press.

Fraser, M. (1915). *Report on the Cost of Living in New Zealand, 1891–1914.* Wellington: Government Printer.

Frederick, C. (1911). *The new housekeeping: efficiency studies in home management.* New York: Doubleday.

Gratton, B. and F. M. Rotondo (1991). Industrialization, the Family Economy, and the Economic Status of the American Elderly. *Social Science History* 15(3), 337–362.

Great Britain Board of Trade (1904). Consumption and the Cost of Food in Workmen's Families in Urban Districts of the United Kingdom. British Parliamentary Papers. London. Cd2337.

Great Britain Board of Trade (1911). Cost of Living in American Towns. British Parliamentary Papers. London.

Haines, M. R. (1979). Industrial Work and the Family Life Cycle, 1889–1890. *Research in Economic History* 4, 289–356.

Heyde, C. (1988). Official statistics in the late colonial period leading on to the work of the first Commonwealth Statistician, GH Knibbs. *Australian Journal of Statistics* 30(1), 23–43.

Hooper, P. F. (1988). The Institute of Pacific Relations and the Origins of Asian and Pacific Studies. *Pacific Affairs* 61(1), 98–121.

Hughes, S. and N. Haworth (2013). Foundations for longevity: the ILO, New Zealand and the strategies of autonomy, relevance and presence. *Labor History* 54(3), 286–300.

Huntingdon, E. H., B. Lasker and M. G. Luck (1937). *Living on a Moderate Income: the incomes and expenditures of street-car men's and clerks' families in the San Francisco Bay region.* Berkeley: University of California Press.

Index Committee (1948). Report of Index Committee. *Appendices to the Journals of the House of Representatives.* Wellington. H-48.

International Labour Office (1933). Index Numbers of the Cost of Living and Retail Prices. *International Labour Review* 27(4), 539–557.

International Labour Office (1934). Recent Family Budget Enquiries: The Finnish Family Budget Enquiry of 1928. *International Labour Review* 30(2), 236–242.

International Labour Office (1935). Recent Family Budget Enquiries: The Swedish Family Budget Enquiry of 1933. *International Labour Review* 31(6), 869–880.

International Labour Office (1937a). Recent Family Budget Enquiries: The Danish Family Budget Enquiry of 1931. *International Labour Review* 36(5), 688–699.

International Labour Office (1937b). Recent Family Budget Enquiries: The South African Family Budget Enquiry of 1936. *International Labour Review* 37(2), 250–261.

International Labour Office (1939). An International Survey of Recent Family Living Studies: II. Food Expenditure and Consumption Habits. *International Labour Review* 39(6), 814–846.

Inwood, K., L. Oxley and E. Roberts (2010). Physical stature in nineteenth century New Zealand – a preliminary interpretation. *Australian Economic History Review* 50(3), 262–283.

Jackson, P. R. (1937). A study of eighty New Zealand dietaries. MA, University of Otago.

Jones, D. C. (1928). The Cost of Living of a Sample of Middle-Class Families. *Journal of the Royal Statistical Society*, 463–518.

Knibbs, G. (1920). The organisation of imperial statistics. *Journal of the Royal Statistical Society*, 201–224.

Knibbs, G. H. (1911). *Inquiry Into the Cost of Living in Australia, 1910–11*. Melbourne: Commonwealth Bureau of Census and Statistics.

Lamale, H. H. (1959). *Methodology of the survey of consumer expenditures in 1950*. Philadelphia: University of Pennsylvania.

May, M. (1984). The "Good Managers": Married Working Class Women and Family Budget Studies, 1895–1915. *Labor History* 25(3), 351–372.

Modell, J. and T. K. Hareven (1973). Urbanization and the Malleable Household: An Examination of Boarding and Lodging in American Families. *Journal of Marriage and the Family* 35(3), 467–479.

New Zealand Census and Statistics Office (1920). *Prices: An Enquiry into Prices in New Zealand*. Wellington: Government Printer.

New Zealand Census and Statistics Office (1930). A Study of Family Budgets in New Zealand. *Monthly Abstract of Statistics*, November 1930.

Nolan, M. (2000). *Breadwinning: New Zealand Women and the State*. Christchurch: Canterbury University Press.

Nolan, M. (2009). Constantly on the Move, but Going Nowhere? Work, Community and Social Mobility. In G. Byrnes (ed.) *The New Oxford History of New Zealand*. Auckland: Oxford University Press, 357–388.

Nowell, E. C., E. G. Ward, H. H. Hayter and J. Boothby (1875). Conference of Government Statistics. *Journal of the Statistical Society of London* 38(2), 252–257.

Oddy, D. J. (1970). Working-Class Diets in Late Nineteenth-Century Britain. *The Economic History Review* 23(2), 314–323.

Pearson, K. (1913). The Statistical Study of Dietaries. *Biometrika*, 530–533.

Périer, P. (1998). Le Play and his followers: over a century of achievement. *International Social Science Journal* 50(157), 343–348.

Prais, S. J. (1959). Whose cost of living? *The Review of Economic Studies* 26(2), 126–134.

Rowntree, B. S. (1901). *Poverty: a study of town life*. New York: Macmillan.

Royal Commission on the Cost of Living (1912). Cost of Living in New Zealand. *Appendices to the Journals of the House of Representatives*. Wellington. H-18.

Saunders, P. (2006). The Historical Development of Budget Standards for Australian Working Families. *Journal of Industrial Relations* 48(2), 155–173.

Sawkins, D. T. (1928). The Australian Standard of Living. In P. Campbell, R. C. Mills and G. V. Portus (eds) *Studies in Australian Affairs*. Melbourne: Melbourne University Press.

Stapleford, T. A. (2007). Market Visions: Expenditure Surveys, Market Research, and Economic Planning in the New Deal. *Journal of American History* 94(2), 418–444.

Stapleford, T. A. (2009). *Cost of Living in America: A Political History of Economic Statistics, 1880–2000*. Cambridge: Cambridge University Press.

Stapleford, T. A. (2012). Navigating the Shoals of Self-Reporting: Data Collection in US Expenditure Surveys since 1920. *History of Political Economy* 44 (suppl. 1), 160–182.

Stigler, G. J. (1954). The early history of empirical studies of consumer behavior. *The Journal of Political Economy*, 95–113.

Strachan, S. R. (1979). Archives for New Zealand Social History. *New Zealand Journal of History* 13(1), 89–95.

Walker, S. P. (1998). How to secure your husband's esteem. Accounting and private patriarchy in the British middle class household during the nineteenth century. *Accounting, Organizations and Society* 23(5–6), 485–514.

Williams, F. M. and C. C. Zimmerman (1935). *Studies of Family Living in the United States and Other Countries*. Washington, D.C.: United States Department of Agriculture Miscellaneous Publication No. 223.

Wood, G. (1976). *Progress in Official Statistics, 1840–1957*. Wellington: Department of Statistics.

Wright, C. D. and Bureau of Labor Statistics (1893). *Analysis and index of all reports issued by bureaus of labor statistics in the United States prior to November 1, 1892*. Washington, D.C.: Government Printing Office.

Wright, C. D. and Bureau of Labor Statistics (1902). *Index of All Reports Issued by Bureaus of Labor Statistics in the United States, Prior to March 1, 1902*. Washington, D.C.: Government Printing Office.

Yu, J. and H. Cooper (1983). A Quantitative Review of Research Design Effects on Response Rates to Questionnaires. *Journal of Marketing Research* 20(1), 36–44.

Acknowledgements

I thank Corin Higgs and James Keating for superb research assistance. This chapter is part of a programme of research on the history of the New Zealand Consumer Price Index, initiated by Sharleen Forbes, and funded by a Victoria University of Wellington University Research Fund grant. The research for this chapter was initiated while the author taught at Victoria University. Sharleen Forbes, Chris Pike, Grant Scobie, Les Oxley, Kris Inwood and Thomas Stapleford provided helpful comments on drafts of this chapter. I thank the Minnesota Population Center (NIH R24 HD041023) for additional support.

A Political Economy of the CPI

Brian Easton[1]

Abstract

The Consumers Price Index (CPI) occurs in an economic, political and social context. That does not mean that the statistic lacks authority, nor that its compiler (today, Statistics New Zealand) lacks independence. But, as we shall see, the history and development of the index (or indeed, any social statistic) has to be seen in a broader setting.

1 Introduction

Two or three apparently independent events occurred in the latter end of the first decade of the 1900s, which led to the establishment of the CPI. This suggests that there was some underlying driver. Almost certainly that was the end of the Long Depression, about a decade earlier.

There were no good measures of economic output in those days, and periods of stagnation were identified by falling prices. British prices had been falling from about 1875 and bottomed around 1895, indicating that the New Zealand Long Depression was part of an international phenomenon. By the end of the nineteenth century, prices had begun to rise. A similar pattern is evident in the available New Zealand series, although the fall had begun at least a decade earlier. Perhaps that reflected the ending of supply shortages from the boom caused by the alluvial gold in the south and the war in the north; possibly, too, international transport costs were falling. The implication is that the British price level was an important influence on the New Zealand price level; there was, after all, a full monetary union.

2 Early development of the CPI

Presumably these were the factors which led James Hight, lecturer in economics and history at Canterbury University College from 1901 and professor from 1909, to suggest to James McIlraith that he investigate the course of prices for his doctorate. The resulting thesis, *The Course of Prices in New Zealand: An*

1   Economic and Social Trust of New Zealand; www.eastonbh.ac.nz.

Inquiry into the Nature and Causes of the Variations in the Standard of Value in New Zealand, was published by the Government Printer in 1911 because, as Hight explains in the introduction, "there [was] no University Press" in New Zealand.[2] (The Introduction is interestingly defensive about the use of indices at all: "The index number is now regarded as an indispensable instrument in an inquiry into questions affected by changes in the power of money", pointing out that they have been "available for some time . . . in England and America".) McIlraith (1911) averaged the wholesale prices he gathered to get his index; he does not seem to have had access to expenditure weights from, say, a representative household budget survey.

Back in 1840 the New Zealand Government had been instructed by the Colonial Secretary in London to collect data on prices, presumably reflecting the Victorian appetite for 'facts', as the resulting statistics seem to have been published but were otherwise unused until McIlraith's thesis. He constructed a variety of indices from 1861 to 1910, later extending the series to 1913 (McIlraith, 1913, pp.348–54; McIlraith, 1914, pp.341–2.) It is noteworthy in the context of this chapter that McIlraith is interested in general price levels, and does not specifically estimate a consumer price index, although there is some material there towards the construction of one (if expenditure weights were available).

In his 1911 introduction Hight mentions the "recent rise in the cost of living". This was the second event. Prices seemed to be rising. This was an international phenomenon, but the usual local suspects were blamed, including, unsurprisingly, wages; especially blamed was the Industrial Conciliation and Arbitration (IC&A) Act established in 1894. It is true that about that year (more or less) prices bottomed, but the coincidence of two events does not prove causation, nor that New Zealand's IC&A Act caused English prices to start rising too.

There seems to have been a sufficient public outcry for John Findlay, the Minister of Internal Affairs (at the time his department included the Registrar General's Office, which was responsible for official statistics), to offer a public rebuttal in 1908. Findlay pointed out that between 1895 and 1907 an index of wages rose 23 (actually 23.7) per cent and the price of provisions "on the bare necessaries of life" rose 22.0 (actually 22.5) per cent, concluding that "wages and prices for necessary foods had advanced at nearly equal rates in thirteen years".[3] Despite the price index covering only food (and probably beverages),

2   My much valued personal copy was given to Hight by McIlraith "With the Author's Compliments". Wolf Rosenberg subsequently acquired it and in the course of time gifted it to me. From various handwritten additions to the tables, Hight may have had my copy with him during the sittings of the 1912 Royal Commission on the Cost of Living.

3   Reported in the *Wanganui Herald*, 23 May 1908, p.4. I am grateful to Sharleen Forbes, Corin Higgs, James Keating and Evan Roberts for drawing my attention to this. See also the *New Zealand Official Year Book 1908*, pp.541–5.

this may be the first occasion that a (fledgling and incomplete) consumer price index appeared officially in New Zealand.[4]

The third event, possibly related to the second, but also with independent roots, was initiated by the 'Harvester' decision, in which the Australian Court of Arbitration attempted to fix a wage specifically designed to guarantee to a worker a certain standard of living (Woods, 1963, p.95). The New Zealand Court of Arbitration was aware of the decision, and its judge even said he thought it was the Court's duty to establish a minimum living wage for the lowest paid workers (Rowley, 1931). However, except in 1908 when it wrote "We think that anything less than 7s per day is not a living wage where the worker has to maintain a wife and children", the Court itself said nothing significant about a living wage prior to the First World War (Woods, 1963, pp.95–6).

Perhaps one other event contributed to the development of the official index. In 1910 the Census and Statistics Act created the Office of the Government Statistician. Within a couple of years the 1912 Royal Commission on the Cost of Living was established, chaired by Edward Tregear, previously Secretary of Labour. Hight was one of its members, and McIlraith, described as its principal witness, was closely and intelligently cross-examined by his mentor. It reported within the year. The 13 questions posed to the Commission suggest there was a wider remit (perhaps even a review of the economy) but whoever drew them up was obviously not an economist.

3 The official series gets underway

At the head of the Commission's list of recommendations was that official statistics needed to be greatly improved. Apparently the government responded with additional funding, and a 'mini-boom' in the production of statistics followed. Indeed, in 1914 the office may have been at its peak of brilliance, with Douglas Copland working on price statistics and John Condliffe working on external statistics; both were economics students of Hight and both went on to distinguished international careers. It was Copland who began the official development of what was to become the Consumers Price Index, although he was limited by available data and covered only food, fuel, lighting and housing (about 60 per cent of household expenditure), omitting apparel and services, among other things.

There are various versions of the aphorism that "experience is what you get just after you need it". It is usual to get statistics long after they are needed. But in the case of the CPI, the 'Copland and successors' data series soon proved relevant. Its origins had reflected a change in the world view; after decades of

4   Unless otherwise sourced, all statistics used in this chapter come from New Zealand Official Year Books.

falling in the late nineteenth century, consumer prices began perceptibly rising towards its end. While the rises may have been a calamity in terms of what was considered the declining norm, they were small; according to Margaret Arnold-Galt's consumer price series (Arnold, 1983) they rose by only 28 per cent (about 1.3 per cent p.a.) from their nadir in 1895 to 1914. There was a barely noticeable acceleration towards the end of the period (1.9 per cent p.a. in the last five years).

But in the next five years, to 1919, the rise was 8.4 per cent p.a. – an aggregate increase of 50 per cent. Marvellously, the official statisticians already had underway a framework (albeit incomplete) to monitor the change.

The inflation was, of course, a consequence of financing the First World War, here and offshore, through monetarisation. It disturbed traditional relativities. Much of that story belongs elsewhere, but one of the pressures was on wages (complicated at first by awards only being able to be updated every three years). The Court of Arbitration had begun to place some reliance upon the fragmentary price base as early as 1912 (Woods, 1963, p.97). Following a change in legislation, the Court announced in April 1919 that, in addition to basic wages, "the Court will grant to workers a bonus by way of compensation in the cost-of-living and this bonus will be varied from time to time according to the rise or fall in the cost-of-living as ascertained by the Dominion [sic]" (Woods, 1963, p.101).

4 The 1920s and 1930s

This led to a famous incident in 1920 (explored in detail by George Wood) in which the Court awarded a 9s-a-week cost-of-living bonus and then shortly after replaced it with a bonus of 3s a week (almost 1d an hour when an unskilled wage was 1s.32d an hour) because of an "erroneous" misunderstanding of the data presented by the acting Government Statistician (Wood, 1976, pp.63–72). The essence of the problem (it appeared again in the double-digit inflation era of the late 1970s, but in political squabbles) was that increases can be measured point on point or period average on period average. Under low inflation the difference may not matter much, but when there is high and variable inflation, it does.

Focusing on the kerfuffle obscures a creeping structural change. The Court was no longer primarily concerned with a fair wage but was increasingly concerned with the impact of price increases, despite the insertion of the expression "fair standard of living" briefly in the IC&A Act in 1921–2. The focus then was some notion of "real wages" or, more precisely, "real consumption wages".

Wage fixing was under considerable pressure following the disruption from inflation during the First World War and the stagnation of the 1920s.

Meanwhile the statistics office was improving, as best it could, the quality of its measurement of consumer prices. The implication (often overlooked) is that earlier parts of any continuous Consumers Price Index series are far inferior to later ones in terms of quality, coverage, comprehensiveness and accuracy. Those who use the series over the long term as if it were statistically consistent do so at some peril. An indicator of the problem is the expression 'Consumers Price Index', introduced in 1948; previously it had been called the Retail Prices Index, although it included items not sold by retailers.[5]

However, there is a practical political economy issue, especially around the treatment of housing, which Arnold-Galt observes has been revised every time the overall regimen has been reviewed (Arnold, 198?). The difference may not be trivial; while the prices of most items in the regimen follow the median and, in any case, their weighting is too small for a different path to matter much, housing outlays are both a large part of consumer spending and tend to rise markedly faster than any median. Hence the treatment of housing can markedly affect the course of the index. For instance, following the 1955 revision, the owner-occupied housing component included the going price of a house (which, not incidentally, is an asset price). Had that approach been used in the CPI of the first decade of the 2000s, the CPI might well have been increasing at 0.5 or more per cent p.a. than was reported. (At which point the counterfactual becomes unclear, because the Reserve Bank might have been forced to maintain a more restrictive monetary stance in order to keep within the target zone specified in the Policy Targets Agreement.)

More generally, illustrative of the ambiguity arising from the lack of rigorous underpinning, there was a tendency to use interchangeably, or prefer, the expression 'cost-of-living' over 'consumers price index', a practice which persisted long after the Government Statistician had eschewed the former term as meaningless.[6] Ironically, the first statutory reference to the CPI in the IC&A Act is in a 1936 amendment introducing General Wage Orders, in which the Court was required "to have regard to the general and financial conditions then affecting trade and industry in New Zealand, the cost of living, and any fluctuations in the cost of living since the last order". Previously the Court had taken it into consideration, but now there was a statutory direction.[7]

---

5   An additional complication is a deeply technical one: what exactly is the underlying conceptual basis of a Consumers Price Index? Unravelling the issue belongs to a paper yet to be written.

6   A view strongly conveyed by Jack Baker in his second-year statistics lectures.

7   IC&A Amendment Act 1936, Section 3. The next subclause introduces the requirement that the rate would be sufficient to enable a man in receipt of it to maintain a wife and three children in a fair and reasonable standard of comfort, codifying earlier Court decisions (although they were often involving two children), and the Harvester decision of 1907.

5 The Second World War

The legislation was suspended in December 1942, when the government introduced a comprehensive plan for economic stabilisation (lurking in its background surely was the memory of the inflation during the First World War). Key to the scheme was a Wartime Prices Index, with the requirement that if it rose by more than 22 per cent, there would be a corresponding increase in wages. It consisted of 238 items whose prices were provided by Department of Statistics, but the compilation was done within the Economic Stabilisation Commission. The Department continued to compile the Retail Prices Index, but it was not published until after the war.

The temptation to manipulate the Wartime Prices Index was irresistible. It rose less than 2.5 per cent between March 1943 and September 1947, while the Retail Prices Index rose by 7.4 per cent – three times as much.

There were at least three ways by which the manipulation could occur. The Price Tribunals controlling prices could resist increases in the designated items, allowing cost recovery in the non-designated ones. Items could be subsidised; by 1945–6, subsidies on essential clothing and foodstuffs amounted to $3.0 million, or over 1 per cent of consumer spending, and there were additional subsidies on the inputs of shipping transport, coal production and distribution, and wheat, amounting to another $2.5 million. Meanwhile, the tax on items outside the regimen could be raised; for example, beer duty went up in May 1942.

If these options failed, there were more direct responses. Bernard Ashwin, chairman of the Stabilisation Commission, later recounted:

> I remember on one occasion the statistician's report recorded that prices had in fact increased by more than [the threshold]. I immediately called the Government Statistician and it turned out he had included the price of onions (which couldn't be bought anyway) in his price calculations. I told him the country's economy was not going to be upset by the price of onions and so we withdrew the item and got below the [threshold] again. The country was saved![8]

George Wood (1976, p.94) noted that the more general practice was "when a commodity went off a the market temporarily (and this happened quite often) the price [in the schedule] was held until supplies became available again . . . This meant that the more frequently shortages occurred the easier it was to maintain the index at a stable level."

Certainly, compared to the First World War, price rises in the Second World

---

8   B. C. Ashwin interviewed by John Henderson, March 1970 (Ashwin papers); the details may not be precisely correct.

War were modest; between 1939 and 1946 the increase was 21.5 per cent, a fraction less than 2.9 per cent p.a. Open inflation became a more pressing issue after the war ended.

6 Post-war developments

The Wartime Prices Index included tobacco, but not beer, which was also omitted from the Retail Prices Index. During the review of the regimen in 1949, Wood, now Government Statistician, was contacted by F. P. (Jack) Walsh on behalf of Prime Minister Peter Fraser, who had reacted with horror when an earlier minute mentioned the possibility of including beer. (Fraser consumed vast quantities of weak tea and buttered bread.) "So beer was out." The Committee, which Walsh had stitched up, explained that only Britain included beer prices in its index, while four other English-speaking countries did not (Wood, 1976, p.96)

Wood was greatly hurt by this political intervention. Fraser was still thinking in terms of the index being a measure of the cost of living, which would contain only 'approved' items. Despite its decision on beer, the 1949 Committee recommended "not [to] exclude . . . any group of commodities or services because that particular class of living expenditure was regarded as non-essential or socially undesirable".[9] By the 1955 revision, Fraser had passed on and beer was included.

In 1949 the regulations went a step further: when making a standard wage pronouncement or a general wage order, the Court of Arbitration was required to take into account, among other things, "[any] rise or fall in retail prices as indicated by any index published by the Government Statistician".[10] The term 'cost-of-living' had been replaced by the more specific 'retail prices', reflecting the title of the official index (even though it covered non-retail consumer prices, such as rents). It is also significant that here, and indeed in other legislative examples, a specific index such as the 'Retail Prices Index' or the 'Consumers Price Index' is not named in the legislation.

So, for the first time since 1920, the Government Statistician was a witness in the Court, interpreting and defending the quality and integrity of the Consumers Price Index.

Steadily the public came to trust the CPI, although there have always been outbreaks of distrust and misunderstanding. I recall in the double-digit inflation period of the 1970s people seriously (I think) arguing along the lines that since bread had gone up 10 per cent, butter had gone up 10 per cent and jam had gone up 10 per cent, inflation must have gone up at least 30 per cent.

9   Ibid.
10   Amendment No 14, gazetted on 17 February 1949.

A more valid criticism was that the average regimen did not always reflect the spending patterns of a particular group. A particularly vociferous lobby were superannuitants; eventually an index specific to their needs was constructed, but to their shock it rose more slowly than the CPI, which was not surprising: while as a general rule prices move together, the major exception is housing prices, which rise faster than the rest. Because they had their own housing without a mortgage or were living in subsidised rental housing, their spending underweighted housing expenditure relative to the average household and their price index rose more slowly. Eventually the Superannuitants Price Index was dropped.[11]

Even when Arbitration Court hearings were abandoned, the CPI continued to be used in award wage determination. Typically the union negotiators would make a demand which began with the CPI increase and then added other factors; meanwhile the employers would reluctantly concede the CPI increase while their other factors would suggest a less generous wage increase. Rarely was the veracity of the CPI challenged, even though in the double-digit 1970s and 1980s it was by far the largest element in any negotiation. (There was an associated dispute about the extent to which wage increases caused price increases, the "wage-price spiral".)

A consequence of its perceived trustworthiness was that the CPI has been frequently used in situations where a different deflator might be have been more appropriate (although never, to my knowledge, by the national statistics office). For instance, in the double-digit inflation era, construction contract payments were indexed to inflation. Perhaps it was judged that a specific index would have been too expensive to construct, with the possibility that there could be subsequent litigation over it.

Another misuse has been to use the CPI to deflate nominal aggregates, the components of which have little to do with, or a quite different relationship with, the CPI regimen. For example, deflating nominal GDP by the CPI is either brave or reflects a misunderstanding of both measures. (Conceptually it is equivalent to analysing a single commodity economy which requires only one price; it is rare that economies can be treated so simply.) Yet deflations like this happen too often.

Another problematic use is the conversion of a past nominal price to an equivalent price today using an inflation calculator. Statisticians are well aware of the difficulties (not least the introduction of new products which were unimaginable then – a motor car in 1870?). The changed construction of the measures adds to the difficulties. (Personally I am inclined to compare the price

---

11   I was once asked to criticise the index as biased. Those who contacted me had no evidence
     for this, but believed that if it reported slower rises it must be.

with the wage of an unskilled labourer, which has been well recorded since 1894, or a value with, I am afraid much shakier, aggregate nominal GDP.)

7 Recent developments

The CPI's role in wage fixing has diminished in a low inflation regime where other factors become more important (although outcomes are still checked against it). However, such is the public's acceptance of the CPI's veracity, it became used as a target for monetary management.

Again the statute, in this case the Reserve Bank Act, does not specify a particular index requiring the Bank to maintain "price stability". However, thus far, the Policy Targets Agreement between the Governor of the Reserve Bank and the Government sets limits within which the CPI is to track.

The recommendations from the 1997 CPI Revision Advisory Committee began:

- The Consumers Price Index should continue to be a price index of goods and services purchased by private New Zealand resident households and should be constructed within a conceptual framework consistent with this aim.
- Statistics New Zealand should publish a set of three measures of consumer price change, and the Consumers Price Index should be an acquisitions measure which does not include interest.

   The other two indexes will be an index of the price change of household outlays and an index of the price change of household consumption. To maintain public confidence in the measurement of price changes affecting households, the new measures will be introduced when a suite of real disposable income indexes is also available (Statistics New Zealand, 1997).

Only the first paragraph of the second recommendation has been implemented. (Ha and Mohan, 2004). Thus, interest has been omitted from the CPI even though it is a cost to (many) households. This change reflects a changing role of the index. No longer does it have a central role in wage fixing where ability to pay rather than fairness is increasingly important and inflation is low. Now the most public use of the CPI (with some minor modifications) is as a target range set out in the Policy Targets Agreement between the Governor of the Reserve Bank and the Minister of Finance. The Reserve Bank Act does not specify a particular index, instead requiring the Bank to maintain "price stability". Including interest in the Reserve Bank target (as had occurred in the past) means that actions by the Bank to reduce inflation will increase interest rates, which will, at least temporarily, increase the very measure it is trying to reduce.

One surmises that the change was strongly contested within the advisory committee, with the two further proposed indices being a sensible technical compromise, although arguably the public could have been confused by having three separate measures. The additional recommendation of a suite of real disposable income indices would have involved adding direct taxes into the measurement. Again, it would have been a useful technical addition, but the politicians apparently did not think it a priority.[12]

It could easily be argued that the choice of consumer prices in the target agreement follows neither economic logic nor common sense. After all, private consumption is only about three fifths of (non-financial) market economic activity, and about 40 per cent of that consumption is imports, with prices over which New Zealanders have little influence (other than via the exchange rate).

There may be two major reasons for the CPI being chosen as a target. The first is that the index is still considered important in wage setting, and there remains a belief that the wage path has the potential to disrupt price stability (but that is true for other mechanisms, such as those involving asset prices, the exchange rate and business mark-ups).

The second is that the CPI is so built into the public's psyche about inflation, and the public has so much trust in the index, that it is natural to use it to anchor the price path of the economy. I have argued that a better anchor would be a price index which is more comprehensive of production in the economy and less influenced by the exchange rate. But whatever the weaknesses of the CPI, it is the price measure that the public trusts, and that consideration is probably decisive, although a 'snake' of various price indices might be worth considering if the objective is to improve macro-economic performance.

8 Conclusion

In order to increase the integrity of the database, the Government Statistician is one of a handful of public officials who is given specific statutory independence. Trust is vital for the collection of data, most notably but not exclusively the census, as well as when it is used. Were there less public trust in the CPI, its provision to the same standard of excellence would be considerably more fiscally expensive.

Even so, government spending can influence the Government Statistician's actions. The CPI is probably protected because of its public reputation, although of course there is a constant effort to reduce the cost of collection; the prospect of collecting from electronic price bases looms on the horizon. However, demands for other statistics have often been unfortunately delayed by fiscal considerations; a set of comprehensive national balance sheets is a

12   A de facto suite for households is published by the Ministry of Social Development, but with a lag (e.g. Perry, 2013).

classic example of a database that will turn up sometime after it is desperately needed, like yesterday.

What this chapter has shown is that, while the statutory independence is important, the trust (in the specific case of the Consumers Price Index, anyway) has been accumulated over the years by a myriad of practical decisions. Not all of them have been ideal, and sometimes they have been deficient. Even more importantly, past decisions have reflected particular circumstances, ranging from need (amazingly, not always a retrospective need but sometimes a prospective one) to availability.

Such challenges will not go away. Statistics New Zealand's preoccupation with maintaining the trust of the public, and the independence that is a part of that, will continue to be pressured in the future by factors similar to those it has met in the past.

References

Arnold, M. N. (1983) *Consumer Prices: 1870–1919.* Department of Economics, Victoria University of Wellington.

Arnold, M. N. (198?) *The Treatment of Housing in New Zealand Consumer Price Indices: 1919–1981.*

Department of Statistics (various years), *New Zealand Official Year Books.* Government Printing Office, Wellington.

Ha, Y. and P. Mohan (2004) *Progress on the 1997 Revision Advisory Committee Recommendations.* Statistics New Zealand, Wellington.

McIlraith J. W. (1911) *The Course of Prices in New Zealand: An Inquiry into the Nature and Causes of the Variations in the Standard of Value in New Zealand.* Government Printing Office, Wellington.

McIlraith, J. W. (1913) Price Variations in New Zealand. *Economic Journal,* 23(91) (September 1913).

McIlraith, J. W. (1914) Contribution to Current Topics. *Economic Journal,* 24(94) (June 1914).

Perry, B. (2013) *Household Incomes in New Zealand: Trends in Indicators of Inequality and Hardship 1982 to 2012.* Ministry of Social Development, Wellington.

Rowley, F. W. (1931) *The Industrial Situation in New Zealand.* H. H. Tombs, Wellington.

Statistics New Zealand (1997) *Report of the Consumers Price Index Revision Advisory Committee.* Statistics New Zealand, Wellington.

Wood, G. A. (1976) *Progress in Official Statistics: 1840–1957: A Personal History.* Department of Statistics, Wellington.

Woods, N. S. (1963) *Industrial Conciliation and Arbitration in New Zealand.* Government Printer, Wellington.

Acknowledgements

I should like to dedicate this chapter to J. V. T. (Jack) Baker (1913–2009), the Government Statistician who introduced me to the CPI in his second-year statistics lecture in 1964. I also acknowledge funding from the Reserve Bank of New Zealand and comments from Len Cook and Sharleen Forbes, none of whom, of course, are responsible for any views in this chapter, especially the wrong ones.

Monetary Policy and the CPI:
Some Perspectives

Michael Reddell[1]

Abstract

The Consumers Price Index (CPI) currently plays a central role in New Zealand's monetary policy framework. This chapter explains how that role developed and how it has evolved over the last 25 years. There is nothing inevitable about the current significance of the CPI. Measures of consumer prices had a much less important role in monetary management and analysis in earlier decades, and the CPI could be less important in plausible alternative monetary regimes, without jeopardising medium-term stability in the general level of prices.

1 Introduction

New Zealand's monetary policy has been characterised as "inflation targeting" since the late 1980s. That model was pioneered in New Zealand, but has become a mainstay of the way monetary policy is spoken of, and conducted, in an increasing number of advanced and emerging economies. Some inflation targeting regimes are more formalised than others and New Zealand's is at the formal end of the spectrum.[2] A Policy Targets Agreement, required by statute, contains a numerical target, expressed in terms of CPI inflation, typically covering periods up to five years ahead, formally agreed between the Minister of Finance and the Governor of the Reserve Bank. That target is supported with formal legislated monitoring and accountability structures.

Inflation targeting has now proved to be a moderately durable monetary regime. The Reserve Bank of New Zealand itself has only existed for 80 years, and inflation targeting has been the centerpiece of New Zealand's monetary policy for almost a third of that time. It is easy for younger generations of economists and policy analysts to lose sight of the fact that there is nothing

---

1   Views expressed are those of the author only, and should not be ascribed to the Reserve Bank of New Zealand.
2   The United Kingdom is also somewhat towards the formalised end of the spectrum. For a treatment of some of the statistical issues associated with inflation targeting in the United Kingdom see Baldwin (2013).

130

inevitable about a central role for the CPI, or any other price index, in the conduct of monetary policy – it was different in the past, and it seems quite likely that, at some point in the future, the role will be different again.

In this chapter, I review the central, but evolving, role that measures of consumer price inflation have played in New Zealand monetary policy over the last 25 years, informed in part by my own experiences as an active participant in the process. As context, the chapter looks back at how monetary management in New Zealand was done in earlier decades, and the role that measures of inflation played (or did not play) then. The chapter concludes with some thoughts on possible future regimes, which might involve rather less emphasis on direct measures of consumer price inflation. None of these approaches appears likely to be adopted in the near future – and they may never prove to be appropriate – but the range of options helps illustrate that there is nothing inevitable or unalterable about the current prominent role that the CPI plays in New Zealand's system of monetary policy.

2 Some history of New Zealand's monetary policy

Until at least the 1970s, and perhaps even later, monetary management in New Zealand primarily involved maintaining a fixed exchange rate.

Until 1934, New Zealand had no central bank, and so nothing akin to today's discretionary monetary policy. Until 1914, New Zealand had simply been on the international Gold Standard – notes issued by New Zealand commercial banks were required to be convertible into gold at the same parity as prevailed in the United Kingdom. Banks had to manage their liquidity to ensure this continuous convertibility. The value of money was maintained through the convertibility of bank notes (and, at one step removed, deposits) into something real and tangible. The relative price of gold might change, but sustained or high inflation was largely impossible so long as convertibility (at a constant pre-specified rate) was maintained.

The convertibility of New Zealand banks' notes into gold was suspended, and was never subsequently resumed, when World War I broke out. After 1914, the exchange rate into sterling of New Zealand banks' notes was managed by the banks themselves, acting collectively. Lending policies were altered as required to maintain an exchange rate near parity to sterling. The exchange rate was, however, allowed to depreciate during the Great Depression, and was actively devalued by the banks, at the initiative of the government, in 1933.

Throughout this period, the domestic price level was substantially determined by international events: prices of tradables were largely determined in world markets, although real domestic factors (including the ability to raise foreign capital) influenced the prices of non-tradable goods and services. Maintaining access to international funding markets for the government, and ensuring continued convertibility of the currency, were the focus of what we might today think of as macro-economic policy. The domestic price level mattered in wage-setting, and in the centralised determinations of the Court of Arbitration, but the rate of increase in domestic prices was not directly influenced by domestic policy.

During the Great Depression of the 1930s the unexpected sharp fall in the price level – here and abroad – led to some very substantial redistributions of real wealth. Those with outstanding debts (notably including the Crown) faced a much heavier servicing burden than they had expected, and those holding financial assets received a considerable windfall (see Reddell, 2012). Thus, in the depths of the Depression, one aim of policymakers was often expressed as lifting the price level. But the precise measure, or the size of any desired adjustment, was not something that appears to have been particularly focused on.

The first Reserve Bank of New Zealand Act was passed in 1933. It was a fairly typical, or orthodox, piece of central banking legislation of its day. The 1933 Act does not mention inflation or the price level. In establishing an autonomous central bank, the Act stated that the primary function of the institution would be "to exercise control . . . over monetary circulation and credit in New Zealand that the economic welfare of the Dominion may be promoted and maintained". Following the election of the first Labour government in 1935, amendments to the Reserve Bank Act asserted a clearly pre-eminent role for the government of the day (and in particular for the Minister of Finance), but the general end of policy remained largely unchanged – to promote the "economic and social welfare of New Zealand".[3]

Amendments to the Reserve Bank Act in 1950 in some respects anticipated later developments. In the wake of several years of high inflation immediately after World War II, the Act was amended to require the Bank to "do all such things within the limits of its powers as it deems necessary and desirable to promote and safeguard a stable internal price level and the highest degree of production, trade, and employment that can be achieved by monetary action". As the Minister of Finance noted in speaking to the proposed amendments, "we should at all times avoid the creation of money without a comparable creation of goods – we should avoid it as we should avoid the plague".[4]

In practice, however, adjusting credit conditions and exchange and import restrictions to maintain the fixed exchange rate remained at the heart of policy – the exchange rate was, in fact, to remain unchanged from 1948 until 1967. Successfully managing demand in this way kept inflation broadly under control,

3 See Graham and Smith (2012) for a fuller discussion of the changing legislative mandate.
4 Rt Hon S. G. Holland, *New Zealand Parliamentary Debates*, 1950, Vol. 290, p. 1269.

but there is little sense in contemporary accounts that inflation (let alone any particular measure of inflation) was more important than external imbalances. Both were symptoms of excess demand, and put constraints on what might be done to keep the rate of employment as high as possible. Of the two constraints, the external balance (available foreign reserves, in a world with limited capital flows) was usually the more binding.

Through successive subsequent changes to the statutory objectives for monetary policy during these decades the focus for the conduct of monetary policy changed relatively little. Inflation was not remotely a matter towards which the public or politicians were indifferent, but it was an outcome of all else that was going on, including globally, rather than something directly managed by domestic government agencies.

Inflation became higher, more volatile, and a more central and direct focus of economic policy, in New Zealand and abroad, from the late 1960s. Globally, the anchor that had been provided by the post-war Gold Standard weakened, and finally broke when the United States ended the convertibility of other nations' foreign exchange reserves into gold in the early 1970s.

Domestically, the Reserve Bank had no independent role in New Zealand's policy around inflation – its role was to advise on, and then implement, the monetary policy of the government, as part of the suite of policy instruments being used to manage overall growth in demand. Government policy involved juggling a variety of economic goals, using a range of instruments (often with quite limited use of monetary policy), but the tensions between those goals were becoming increasingly apparent.

Inflation became increasingly central in the domestic, public, political and economic debate – as early as 1972, Labour Party leader Norman Kirk launched his election campaign with a pledge to "knock inflation [then around 5 per cent] for a six". But as inflation rose, and became more volatile, it did not matter greatly which price index measure one looked at, or how precisely that index was constructed: whichever measure one preferred, they were all uncomfortably high and volatile.

A considerable amount of material has been published over the years by the Reserve Bank, and other agencies, on monetary policy and related matters. One way of seeing the shift in emphasis is to look at what was being written and published in the earlier period.

In 1955, for example, the Reserve Bank published *Monetary and Fiscal Policy in New Zealand*, a 250-page book, which has two references to "inflation" in the index, and a couple of pages of very general text. The 1963 book *Money and Banking in New Zealand* is a little more specific but also fairly brief, and the rather longer *Overseas Trade and Finance* (1966) has no references to inflation at all in the index. Governor Low gave a major set-piece speech on

New Zealand monetary policy to an Australian audience in 1968, and while inflation is discussed it is only as one among a variety of undesirable outcomes, and there is no mention of any specific measures of inflation (Low, 1968).

The official Monetary and Economic Council played an important role in economic analysis and debate in New Zealand in the 1960s and 1970s. It produced two major reports on monetary issues, 'The New Zealand Financial System' in 1966, and 'Monetary Policy and the Financial System' in 1972. The Council was at the forefront of efforts to encourage a more modern approach to monetary management, and yet in neither document is there much specific discussion of inflation. The 1966 report (p. 174) notes that "monetary policy is one among several means by which Governments seek to influence the level of expenditures in an economy in order to achieve desired economic and social objectives", while the 1972 report (p. 67) notes that "if the nation is to maintain reasonable economic stability, it must aim to keep the growth of both spending and incomes more or less in step with its capacity to increase production".

Returning to Reserve Bank material, Hawke (1973) wrote an authorised history of the Reserve Bank. Inflation is mentioned in the text in a few places, but there is nothing substantial enough to warrant a reference in the index. Perhaps tellingly, in 1978, the Reserve Bank published a compendium *Long-term Statistical Series*, drawn from the Reserve Bank *Bulletin,* which has no series for prices or inflation at all.

Even very late in the piece, it is striking how patchy the coverage of inflation is. The 1983 second edition of the Reserve Bank's *Monetary Policy and the New Zealand Financial System* had a reasonably substantive discussion of inflation and inflation expectations, but the Bank's 1984 *Post-election Briefing* to the incoming government has a surprisingly limited discussion of inflation.[5] The Reserve Bank's 1986 book, *Financial Policy Reform,* was published at a time when thinking about reforming the Reserve Bank Act was already underway, but it has ten times as many references to the exchange rate as to inflation, and five times as many references to the monetary aggregates.

By late in the pre-reform period, the Reserve Bank's own thinking was clearly shaped by the vertical Phillips-curve approach pioneered by Milton Friedman. In that conception, there were no long-run adverse trade-offs between inflation and real economic activity. But even this 'monetarist' style of thinking, here or abroad, did not lead to a focus on inflation goals directly. Instead it assumed that if a central bank managed the rate of money growth, or of domestic

5   All of this squares with my own memories as a very junior analyst in the Monetary Policy section of the Reserve Bank's Economic Department from 1983 to 1985. We spent a lot of time analysing monetary base developments, sources of injections to liquidity, and sterilisation techniques, and very little time talking about or analysing inflation itself. No doubt others did.

credit expansion in systems with a fixed exchange rate, the (highly important and relevant) outcomes such as inflation and the external balance would, as it were, take care of themselves. Those outcomes were subject to all sorts of other short-term influences, and there were often quite long lags from monetary policy actions to these outcomes, especially in a more market-oriented financial system. Accordingly, they were generally not seen as goals that a central bank – even an independent central bank – would directly target.

3 The Reserve Bank of New Zealand Act 1989

On 1 February 1990, the new, completely rewritten, Reserve Bank of New Zealand Act took effect. The Act was the culmination of several years of development[6] and was passed amid intense political controversy and debate. It gave day-to-day responsibility for monetary policy to the Reserve Bank.

Section 8 of the Act stated that the primary function of the Reserve Bank was to conduct monetary policy to achieve and maintain a stable general level of prices. By international standards, that was an unusually clear ultimate statutory objective. But in practical policy terms, perhaps more important was section 9, which required that targets be agreed between the Minister and the Governor for achieving the section 8 objective. Those targets – inflation targets – became, in effect, performance criteria for the Governor. Failure to achieve the targets became a key element of the grounds on which the Governor could be dismissed: by contrast, in most countries with an operationally independent central bank the Governor cannot be removed for policy failures.

It was quite late in the process of reshaping the Reserve Bank legislation that the notion of inflation targeting as the day-to-day centerpiece of policy took form.[7] Since the change of government in July 1984, and more particularly since the exchange rate was floated in March 1985, the focus for monetary policy – decisions on which were still taken, formally, by the Minister of Finance – had been on reversing New Zealand's poor track record on inflation. Over the previous 15 or so years, New Zealand's inflation rate had, on average, been among the highest in any OECD country. That high inflation was one of the most visible, easily understood, presenting symptoms of New Zealand's economic difficulties.

As was typical internationally at the time, the end goal was not tightly specified. Documents and speeches through this period refer to goals such a "low single figure inflation", or "inflation around that of our trading partners". Either specification would have represented a material improvement on New Zealand's inflation record in the previous decade, or on the outlook in the immediate post-

6   See, for example, Singleton et al (2006).
7   For a fuller account of the origins of inflation targeting see Reddell (1999).

liberalisation period. During the previous few years, the United States and the United Kingdom in particular had markedly reduced their inflation rates – in the United States' case, with an independent central bank, and in the United Kingdom with a central bank that had no independent powers over monetary policy.

Central banks had, typically, argued that the relationship between monetary policy actions and inflation outcomes was often quite long and imprecise, particularly as greater emphasis was placed on more market-oriented instruments. And in the short-term, many things other than monetary policy actions affected measured inflation. Partly as a result, there was a quest for more measureable benchmarks, which could be used to indicate to firms and households, and to financial markets, that monetary policy was (or was not) on course. In particular, in the monetarist thinking that influenced many central banks, measures of the money supply (monetary aggregates) were seen as both fairly directly controllable and likely to bear a reasonably stable medium-term relationship to inflation and/or nominal GDP. Monetary targets played a direct role in the setting and communication of monetary policy in various countries, including the United Kingdom, Australia, Canada, Germany and Japan, in the late 1970s and early 1980s.

The Reserve Bank had been influenced by this thinking and had initially hoped that in a more liberalised environment such monetary targets would provide a useful centrepiece for New Zealand's monetary policy. However, by the time of our liberalisation in 1984/85, both the disappointing experience in other countries, and the severe problems in interpreting our own monetary aggregates as the far-reaching financial controls were removed, meant that the use of monetary aggregate targets was eschewed for the time being. Financial market prices, notably interest rates and the exchange rate, were also thought to be too slender a reed on which to rest the management of monetary conditions. Instead, it was hoped that directly controlling the base level of liquidity in the banking system would, over time, help to deliver the lower and generally more stable inflation rate that was the key ultimate focus of macro-economic policy. As Reddell (1999) records, this optimism did not last long.

The new Reserve Bank of New Zealand Act was forged from a variety of different intellectual influences. On the one hand, the central bank independence literature emphasised a belief that taking day-to-day management of monetary policy out of political hands would lead to lower inflation and/or a price level that was more stable through time. The examples of (then) West Germany and Switzerland, as well as the longer-term experience of advanced economies in the nineteenth century, were adduced to support this line of argument. The newer time-inconsistency literature reinforced this approach, arguing that if day-to-day responsibility for setting monetary policy was left with politicians, they would be unable to credibly pre-commit to low inflation. An independent central bank, not facing re-election incentives, might provide a better option.

But if this strand of literature argued for central bank independence, at least as important were the ideas that underpinned wider state sector reform in New Zealand – in particular, a principal-agent approach to governance issues that was instrumental in the design of the State Sector Act 1988. In this model there was certainly considerable merit in providing operational autonomy for executive agencies, but only within a framework in which the principal – a minister, or Parliament directly – set out measurable and directly achievable goals ('outputs' in the jargon), all within a framework that provided for clear and explicit accountability for non-performance. In the core public sector in New Zealand, chief executives were to be appointed for fixed, renewable, terms, subject to clear performance agreements reached with the relevant Minister. In this model, officials cannot be relied on to pursue the public interest, but need to be kept on a relatively short leash by politicians.

The design of the Reserve Bank of New Zealand Act (and particularly its monetary policy portions) was heavily influenced by thinking around the design and governance of public agencies more generally, even if the final form was a somewhat uneasy (or perhaps 'elegant') mix of the independence (high trust of central bankers) and accountability (low trust) modes of thinking.

The Policy Targets Agreement is the practical centrepiece for the conduct of monetary policy under the Act. Section 9 requires that policy targets must be agreed between the Minister and a potential new (or reappointed) Governor, before that person is (re)appointed. Those policy targets are "for the carrying out" of the Reserve Bank's primary function: "achieving and maintaining stability in the general level of prices".

The requirement for a Policy Targets Agreement does not stand in isolation. It is buttressed by several other key features of the Act. For example:

- The Bank is required to publish *Monetary Policy Statements* at least every six months, in which the Governor must state how and why he plans to conduct policy to achieve the policy targets.
- The Bank's Board – acting, essentially, as monitoring agents for the Minister of Finance – is required to "constantly review" the performance of the Governor in ensuring that the policy targets are met (and that the *Monetary Policy Statements* are consistent with those policy targets).
- The Bank's Board must advise the Minister of Finance if the performance of the Governor in pursuing the policy targets is inadequate, and may recommend dismissal.
- The Governor-General can (through Order in Council, on the advice of the Minister of Finance) dismiss the Governor for inadequate performance in

ensuring that the Bank achieves the policy targets.

Legislative provisions of that sort always envisaged, even if they did not strictly require, targets that were specific and measureable. Few, if any, of the other inflation-targeting countries have anything remotely as formal in their central banking legislation, encompassing both target setting and accountability.

The Act did not, and does not, require that the policy targets be expressed in terms of a price series (levels or rates of change). Indeed, the Treasury had remained somewhat uneasy about inflation targets even after the new legislation had been enacted. There was nothing in the legislation to prevent the use of money or credit targets, nominal GDP targets, money base targets, or perhaps even exchange rate targets, provided they were judged consistent with some conception of "stability in the general level of prices". In some respects, the formalised targets and accountability framework would have fitted most naturally a world in which, say, money base targets had been feasible: the money base is something over which the central bank can have direct control.

CPI inflation targets were used in the Policy Targets Agreement for largely pragmatic reasons. On the one hand, the CPI was timely, not subject to revision, and well-accepted among the wider public; on the other hand, money and credit relationships weren't regarded as sufficiently stable to allow an intermediate targets approach to be taken. But if the Governor's job was to be on the line, it was important to specify the target in a sensible way, which provided as much clarity as possible, while also minimising any incentive on the Governor to pursue economically undesirable outcomes simply to safeguard his or her own job.

4 The first Policy Targets Agreement

On 2 March 1990, the Governor of the Reserve Bank, Don Brash, and the Minister of Finance, David Caygill, signed the first Policy Targets Agreement (PTA).[8] Measurement issues are very clearly to the fore in this document. The CPI remained less than ideal for the purpose. In addition to its deficiencies in the treatment of housing (discussed further below), the CPI was subject to index bias, and it included GST and a wide range of indirect taxes and administered prices (which most accept as something monetary policy should not try to offset). And unlike CPIs in most OECD countries, it was only available quarterly (rather than monthly).

The PTA notes that, while the Bank should monitor a range of price indices, "it is considered that the primary measure of prices used to calculate the inflation rate for the purpose of these targets should relate to the prices of goods and

8   Copies of this, and each subsequent, Policy Targets Agreement are available at http://www.rbnz.govt.nz/monpol/pta/

services currently consumed by households", thus consciously steering away from the GDP deflator, the Producers Price Indices, and asset prices.

The March 1990 PTA went on to note, however, that the CPI itself was "not an entirely suitable measure of these prices", because of the household expenditure-based approach used in construction of the index. In particular, at the time the CPI included the purchase price of existing houses, the prices of new residential sections, and mortgage interest rates themselves.

The Reserve Bank had a clear preference for the CPI to be constructed on a use basis (imputed rents rather than purchases of owner-occupied housing). However, it was the inclusion of interest costs directly in the CPI that had been most problematic for a central bank Governor facing the possibility of dismissal if he failed to meet his inflation target. Taking monetary actions that pushed up official interest rates would, over the medium term, tend to lower inflation. However, as the CPI was then constructed, such actions would have boosted the CPI inflation rate further in the short run, potentially pushing the CPI inflation rate above the top of the target range. Absent formal targets, it would have been easy enough for a central bank to 'look through' this short-term quirk, focusing on the medium term, but in the new legal framework the issue has to be addressed directly.

Accordingly, the PTA stresses that, while "for practical purposes" the CPI would be "the measure of inflation used in setting the targets", the Bank was also required to construct and publish "an alternative measure of consumer prices based on an internationally comparable approach", replacing the official measure of housing costs in the CPI with a measure based on actual and imputed housing rentals. This housing-adjusted price index (or the HAPI as it came to be known) was actually the more important basis for the conduct of monetary policy, since in the event of a forecast deviation between the CPI and HAPI annual inflation rates of at least half a percentage point, the Governor "may choose to renegotiate new policy targets so as to take account of the effect of the deficiencies in the construction of the CPI".

The Policy Targets Agreement also provided for an automatic renegotiation if either a large change in indirect taxes, or a significant change in the terms of trade,[9] would have a significant *direct* impact on the annual inflation rate. The threshold envisaged was an annual inflation effect of at least 0.5 per cent. Whereas in the previous couple of decades (with inflation averaging 10 to 15 per cent per annum) the Bank would have put little weight on fluctuations in the inflation rate of that magnitude,[10] the low and stable range within

---

9   Or "some other crisis situation, such as a natural disaster or a major disease-induced fall in livestock numbers".

10   Not unrelatedly, the Bank did not begin doing detailed quarterly forecasts of the CPI inflation rate at the individual component level until late 1987.

which inflation was now to be targeted, combined with the apparently stiff formal accountability provisions, gave the Bank a considerably greater interest in the details of the construction of the CPI and the behaviour of individual components.

5 Subsequent experience

The first Policy Targets Agreement did not last long. A change of government at the end of 1990 led to an agreement to defer by one year the target date for achieving 0 to 2 per cent inflation. This and other successive changes are outlined in Table 1.

However, the parties also took the opportunity to simplify the document, and to move somewhat away from the low-trust model, in which any of these sorts of material price surprises, discussed in the previous section, could be accommodated only through a formal renegotiation of the targets. Events of this sort had been initially thought of as "exceptional",[11] but experience quickly suggested they might be rather more common (the Iraqi invasion of Kuwait in August 1990, for example, had increased oil prices sharply, and given rise to significant volatility in those prices).

The new PTA formally recognised a variety of types of external shocks to prices which either could not be directly offset or would be too economically costly to offset. But instead of requiring the Bank to come back to the Minister to renegotiate the targets, the December 1990 PTA set out an agreed expectation that "the Bank shall generally react to such shifts in relative prices in a manner which prevents general inflation pressures emerging". The Bank was required to "detail fully its estimate of the direct price impact of any such shock" and set out what measures it was taking to ensure that the effects of such price-level shocks on the inflation rate itself were transitory. The focus shifted to one of transparency in the handling of price shocks.

The Reserve Bank continued to be required to report the HAPI, and deviations between the inflation rates in the HAPI and in the CPI continued to provide a basis on which CPI inflation might legitimately deviate from the 0 to 2 per cent target range. (These provisions were discontinued when the PTA was renegotiated in December 1992, when Don Brash was reappointed as Governor. While the Bank continued to prefer the use of imputed rentals in the CPI, material deviations between the all groups CPI and the CPI ex-interest were now to be the focus for the purposes of the PTA.)

Over the remainder of the 1990s both the construction of the CPI and the

---

11   The wording used in the first (April 1990) *Monetary Policy Statement*. However, even that document reports an explicit estimate of the impact on the CPI of a sharp rise in meat and dairy prices during 1989.

Table 1. Key measurement features in successive Policy Targets Agreements

Period	Formal inflation target range	Official target index	Other indices referred to	Comments
March to December 1990	0 to 2 per cent per annum	All Groups Consumers Price Index	Reserve Bank to develop a verifiable alternative measure using an imputed rentals measure of housing costs.	A significant deviation between the CPI inflation rate and that of the alternative index is a basis for renegotiating the CPI inflation target.
December 1990 to December 1992	0 to 2 per cent per annum	All Groups Consumers Price Index	Required to continue to produce alternative index (the HAPI).	Significant deviations between CPI and HAPI inflation rate is one circumstance in which CPI inflation rate might be expected to move outside the target range.
December 1992 to December 1996	0 to 2 per cent per annum	All Groups Consumers Price Index	Requirement to publish HAPI discontinued. Reserve Bank moved to publish more formally its own "underlying inflation" estimate.	"Underlying inflation" was based on the published CPI inflation rate adjusted for the one-off factors which might legitimately take headline inflation outside the target range.
December 1996 to December 1997	0 to 3 per cent per annum	All Groups Consumers Price Index		
December 1997 to December 1999	0 to 3 per cent per annum	All Groups Consumers Price Index excluding credit services (CPIX)	Publication of "underlying inflation" series discontinued.	Noted the intention of Statistics New Zealand to remove interest rates from the CPI regimen during the planned life of the agreement.
December 1999 to September 2002	0 to 3 per cent per annum	All Groups Consumers Price Index		
September 2002 to present	1 to 3 per cent per annum	All Groups Consumers Price Index		

wording of the PTA evolved. In 1997, on the occasion of the next reappointment of Dr Brash, the target was restated to be expressed in terms of the CPI excluding credit services (CPIX). On the one hand, this dealt directly with the largest and most frequent source of deviation between the target measure itself, and a measure that better captured the appropriate focus of policy and the agreed intent of successive Policy Targets Agreements. However, it also foreshadowed the stated "intention of Statistics New Zealand to remove credit services from the official CPI in 1999".

By the time the next PTA was negotiated in late 1999, those changes to the CPI regimen had been made, and since then the target has simply been expressed in terms of inflation in the CPI itself. In the same review of the CPI, the treatment of housing was also substantially altered: section prices and the purchase price of existing dwellings were replaced by the 'acquisitions approach', based on the construction costs of new dwellings. Since asset prices (e.g. house and land prices) are often more variable than prices of goods and services (e.g. building costs), that change was also seen by the Reserve Bank as likely to reduce the 'noise' in the CPI, relative to the medium-term focus that underpinned the Policy Targets Agreement.

Despite these changes in the composition of the formal CPI, each of them improvements from the perspective of monetary policy, the Reserve Bank has faced a consistent challenge over the years of inflation targeting as to how best to represent the medium-term trend elements of inflation, stripping away the 'one-off' price-level effects that are either beyond the control of monetary policy (for example, indirect taxes or retail petrol prices, which change very quickly as global oil prices fluctuate), or are unlikely to become embedded in the general process of inflation.

Successive PTAs typically required the Bank to detail the effects of individual large shocks, but the Bank was also constantly striving towards a good summary measure. In doing so, the Reserve Bank had two related, but separable, purposes.

Firstly, the framework was built around a formal accountability process, and so a summary measure that gave the Bank's Board and the Minister of Finance a sense of what had happened to the inflation that the Bank 'was supposed' to have been targeting was regarded as useful. No one wanted to dismiss a Governor because oil prices had risen sharply, but equally the monitors wanted a sense of what components of inflation the Bank could reasonably have been expected to have controlled.

In addition, keeping medium-term inflation on track is easier and less costly when business and household expectations of future inflation remain close to the target. Being able to clearly distinguish the 'noise' from the underlying trend in inflation could help to secure stable expectations of future inflation even when the headline measure of CPI inflation was being tossed around by lots of one-off factors.

Policy Targets Agreements have long required the Bank to "monitor prices as measured by a range of price indices", consistent with a view that the CPI itself would rarely be a fully adequate summary of the inflation that monetary policy was supposed to focus on. The requirement to calculate the HAPI was consistent with that approach to the issue.

For some years, the Reserve Bank attempted to supplement these measures by calculating and publishing an estimate of "underlying [CPI] inflation". Starting from the official CPI inflation rate, this measure stripped out the effect of interest rate changes, and, as required, adjusted for the effects of "significant" terms-of-trade changes or "significant" changes in general government charges or indirect taxes. This approach proved useful over a number of years.

However, because the Bank itself did the calculations, there were some concerns that it could be seen to be able to manipulate a measure that was a key part of the accountability process. In practice, "significant" came to be defined as a threshold of a 0.25 percentage point impact on the CPI over 12 months. That was perhaps a reasonable benchmark but it gave rise to anomalies in which a price shock worth 0.24 percentage points was not adjusted for, but one worth 0.26 percentage points was. There was no difference of economic substance, but in some circumstances the arbitrary threshold could make the difference between underlying inflation being inside or outside the target range. In some cases also, there could be material uncertainty about just how large the direct price effects of some of these price shocks were, and about where one drew the line in calculating indirect effects (e.g. the impact of petrol price change on, say, courier delivery fees).

In practice, the largest single adjustment most years had been for interest rates, and once CPIX was adopted as the target the Bank discontinued publishing (or calculating) the underlying inflation series.

But scrapping that series did not change the wish to be able to communicate the underlying trend in inflation. From the early 1990s, the Bank had used Statistics New Zealand price index components to calculate separate CPI series for tradable and non-tradable items for analytical purposes. Later, the Bank began to calculate and publish trimmed mean and weighted median CPI series.[12] Later still, each of these analytical series were picked up by Statistics New Zealand and are now routinely published by them as part of the quarterly CPI release. More recently still, more of the Bank's analytical energies have

---

12   For some time, the 57th percentile series assumed considerable prominence internally, as the measure which had had the same historical mean as the CPI inflation rate itself.

been focused on factor model estimates of the underlying trend in CPI inflation. These measures were reviewed recently in Ranchhod (2013).

With time, there has been considerable evolution in everyone's understanding of how the accountability dimensions of the system should work, in ways that respect both the uncertainty and imprecision around monetary policy and inflation on the one hand, and the statutory focus on accountability on the other.

From a period of initial unease as to just how feasible it would prove to tightly target inflation, the experience of the first few years after price stability was achieved – when all measures of inflation were low and very stable – probably induced an inappropriate degree of complacency and a rather mechanical tone to some of the rhetoric around the framework. This was perhaps captured best in a radio interview with the then Governor in 1993, which the Bank reproduced in its *Bulletin*. In the course of the interview, Dr Brash noted that the Bank had been concerned about the risk of CPI inflation rising above 2 per cent, "which is the top of our target". The interviewer responded "And then you'd lose your job", to which Dr Brash responded, without qualification, "Exactly right" (Brash, 1993).

In fact, two years later when some one-off events took CPI inflation well above 2 per cent (and even the underlying measure moved very close to 2 per cent), there was a reassessment all round, including a recognition that forecasting, and the implementation of monetary policy, were imprecise arts at best. Recent past inflation was by no means irrelevant, and ex post analysis of what had driven recent inflation outcomes remained important, but what really mattered in assessing the Governor's performance in conducting monetary policy was that the Bank should be "constantly aiming" to keep future inflation outcomes within the range, and hence the quality of the analysis and decisions used in support of those efforts should be high. Reddell (2006) discusses the accountability framework more generally.

Thus, there is no one measure now that always and everywhere best represents the sort of underlying inflation the Reserve Bank should focus on, even though the formal target is expressed in terms of CPI inflation. No one measure is best-suited to adjust for each type of shock that can affect the CPI.

And even when all the information from the various cuts of the CPI itself has been taken into account, there is still often useful information about behavior in the "general level of prices" to be gained from looking at other measures, such as the Producers Price Indices, or the Gross Domestic Product, Gross National Expenditure or private consumption deflators (the latter, for example, is the basis for the Federal Reserve's conduct of monetary policy in the United States). There can be persistent differences in the inflation rates across these different measures, which are important to understand (for example, the use of imputed rentals in the private consumption deflator has resulted in a materially lower average inflation rate in that measure than in the CPI over the last decade or so). A recent addition to the Policy Targets Agreement in 2012 is an explicit reminder that asset prices should be among the price indices that the central bank is monitoring.

What started from a quite mechanical vision – perhaps well-suited to other types of (infeasible) monetary policy – has evolved into something that is immensely data-hungry but also requires considerably more judgement.

On paper, the New Zealand system remains quite unusual by international standards. The CPI inflation targets in the PTA are directly tied to the employment (and potential dismissal) of the Governor in a way not seen in any other inflation-targeting country.[13] The role of the Reserve Bank's Board, primarily acting as a monitoring agent on behalf of the principal, the Minister of Finance, is also unusual. But in practice there has been a very substantial degree of convergence in the way in which monetary policy is thought about and conducted. For practical purposes – at least when the near-zero lower bound on nominal interest rates is not operative – New Zealand's monetary policy looks a great deal like that of most other floating exchange rate advanced economies such as Australia, Canada, the United States, the United Kingdom, Sweden and Norway.

Formal accountability through institutional channels remains an important dimension of the system, but the accountability that arises through financial markets and the continuous process of media and public scrutiny is probably more important than was recognised in the late 1980s when the Act was being designed. As ever, the focus is first and foremost on ensuring that monetary policy makes its best contribution to good economic outcomes, not on formal measurement and accountability for its own sake.

If what is formally measured (or even measureable) is given too high a place in any assessment and monitoring framework, it can mean losing sight of some of the key dimensions of what matters economically and what the public cares about (in authorising, through Parliament, an independent central bank). The CPI continues to provide a useful starting point for conversations about the effective conduct of monetary policy, but it can only sensibly be treated as a starting point. Many of the quarterly *Monetary Policy Statements* devote considerable space to articulating why the current headline CPI inflation number is not representative of the medium-term trend in inflation (which is "the focus of the policy target" according to the Policy Targets Agreement).

---

13   Even in Canada, the one other OECD country with (formally) a single decision-maker for monetary policy. Aldridge and Wood (2014) provide some cross-country comparisons of monetary policy governance and accountability arrangements.

6 *What of the future?*

As noted earlier in this chapter, for a long time specific measures of inflation had quite a modest role in New Zealand's monetary policy and excited little interest from the Reserve Bank. By contrast, the most recent Consumers Price Index Advisory Committee (2013) report begins by recommending "that the principal use of the CPI remains to inform monetary policy setting". In some respects, that could be seen as an oddity – shaping a major macro-economic statistic, used in practice for all sorts of purposes, primarily around the current accountability arrangements for a single government agency. In principle, however, there should be a reasonable alignment between those accountability and communications needs, and a good measure of general consumer prices for wider public use.

A new Policy Targets Agreement was signed as recently as 2012, and in that process the incoming Governor and the current Minister of Finance (supported by the professional staff of the Reserve Bank and The Treasury) reaffirmed that inflation targeting, centred on the CPI, continued to serve New Zealand well. The main international economic agencies have also supported the continuing relevance of inflation targeting globally, and there have been further moves towards inflation targeting by Japan and the United States (both at the less formalised end of the spectrum) in the last couple of years. Kendall and Ng (2013) review the new PTA in this wider context.

Indeed, the CPI could yet acquire a little more prominence. The CPI Advisory Committee recently recommended, rather belatedly, that a high-quality monthly CPI be introduced in New Zealand. In most countries, one advantage of CPI-type measures is that they are available not just sooner, but also more frequently, than deflators from the (typically) quarterly national accounts.[14] For a central bank attempting to avoid unnecessary variability, missing out on timely information on the first two months of each quarter's CPI puts monetary policy at more of a disadvantage than it needs to be. Falling costs of electronic data collection should make this overdue initiative more feasible.

However, we cannot simply assume that the CPI will always play such a central role in monetary policy deliberations and decisions. Nothing in the statutory framework requires it (and of course the statutory framework itself has undergone many amendments).

---

14   It is sometimes argued that the fact that CPI data are not revised is a further advantage. I think this is a questionable claim: we simply do not know with certainty how "the general level of prices" (the goal Parliament set for the Reserve Bank's monetary policy) is evolving. That underlying reality is not changed simply because we do not revise the CPI – itself only one approximation to a measure of the general level of prices. The uncertainty is one of the factors that policymakers, and firms and households, need to take into account in their planning (and in devising suitable accountability arrangements).

The desired economic outcome, reflected in section 8 of the Reserve Bank Act, of a "stable general level of prices" can be achieved in a number of different ways. The Act is not specific about the timeframe that needs to be focused on – and of course, is worded in terms of price levels, not of inflation rates. In the past, there were strong arguments made in some parts of the theoretical literature for the superiority of nominal GDP targets, especially in an economy exposed to significant "supply shocks" (such as fluctuations in the terms of trade). In the wake of the global recession of 2008/09 and the sluggish recovery in many economies, there has been a new interest in some circles in the possibility of nominal GDP targeting. It could be argued that such approaches may be slightly less reliant on judgement and less model-intensive if, for example, there is less need to separately identify potential real GDP and the output gap than in inflation-targeting monetary policy regimes.

An argument could also be mounted that expressing the policy target in terms of a wage inflation index might be less prone to many of the one-off factors that affect the CPI, and might be a more appropriate focus for trying to stabilise expectations (since, for example, many more people enter into discretionary wage contracts than set prices, and wages are not only the main source of household income but also the largest single business cost). Perhaps it could be shown to be preferable to let productivity shocks flow into the CPI inflation while keeping nominal wage inflation – a critical component, for example, in the ability to meet debt-service comments (almost all of which are expressed in nominal terms) – more stable. A fixed exchange rate – with a currency of a similar country, with similar neutral interest rates – could also be consistent with a stable general level of prices, as perhaps might some composite index that gave some explicit weight to the importance of asset prices.

It is also plausible that continuing improvements in the National Accounts could lead to the private consumption deflator, or even the GDP deflator, being given a greater role in analysis and communication. In such a world, the central bank might be less interested in, or concerned about, details about the composition or publication of the CPI.

To mention these possibilities is to act neither as advocate nor as prophet. Inflation targeting centred on the CPI is not a perfect monetary system, or even a perfect way of managing a fiat money system. But there probably is no perfect monetary system, or even a single 'end of history' system that will always work best for New Zealand. Inflation targeting itself is a recent innovation by historical standards, and has faced significant challenges in recent years. Perhaps at some point people will look back, remarking in some wonder on the prominent place the CPI once had in monetary policy, in the same way that younger economists are often surprised at how little attention the CPI received in monetary policy discussion in decades past. Perhaps the principal use of the CPI at some point in the future will be for adjusting welfare benefits and deflating historical series, while receiving occasional passing reference in monetary policy documents.

Of course, any change in the orientation of monetary policy would involve some significant transitions. So much, including analysts' frameworks for thinking about the nominal economy, is currently built around a CPI-based inflation targeting system. But change is only ever likely to be made for good reasons, emerging from some growing sense of the possibility of a preferable route. With the current panoply of measures of core inflation derived from the CPI, none of which we can consistently represent as always and everywhere telling us *the* underlying story of inflation, or accurately depicting its medium-term trend, the difficulty of the transitions that might be required should not be overstated.

Private initiatives could also improve the range of data on prices that are available to analysts and policymakers, potentially reducing the relative importance of the CPI. The Billion Prices Project is one example,[15] an academic initiative that uses prices collected from hundreds of online retailers around the world (including New Zealand) on a daily basis. Such measures might not provide a strong basis for a formalised central bank accountability measure, but experience suggests that robust accountability for monetary policy inevitably involves considerable judgement, rather than a single number. The timeliness of such private data could become very valuable to private and central banks' economic analysis.

7 Conclusion

Public sector reform in New Zealand in the late 1980s, with its focus on measureable accountability and lifting performance, combined with the failure of a direct focus on monetary aggregates to provide a practicable guide for the conduct of monetary policy and a 15-year track record of a demonstrably poor inflation performance to give the CPI inflation rate a degree of prominence and formal importance in monetary policy that it had rarely, if ever, had previously.

Over the succeeding couple of decades, the global trend towards adopting inflation targeting, in slightly different forms in each country, has reinforced the prominence of CPI-based measures of inflation in New Zealand policy. The CPI itself remains less than perfect. There is no consistently constructed long-term historical series, undermining efforts to advance our understanding of inflation, there is a consistent upward bias in it relative to even 'true' consumer prices – albeit probably materially less than estimated by Gibson and Scobie

---

15   See http://bpp.mit.edu/

(2010) – and it is thrown around by many developments (some in markets, some in the corridors of government) that should be of little concern to monetary policymakers or to private wage and price setters.

But the CPI is not used mechanically – either within the Reserve Bank or by those charged with holding the Bank to account. Even once the limitations of the index are recognised, the CPI – which has longstanding historical resonance – remains a useful starting point for conversations about pricing behaviour, and about how monetary policy is, and should be, influencing the nominal economy. Information on other price, wage, and nominal income series cannot safely be ignored, and there is a danger that any institution will put too much weight on a specific index if its performance is being measured against it, even if the accountability is not mechanical. But conversations have to start from somewhere, and an increasingly good quality, timely (if less frequent than would be preferred) CPI has served well in that role over the last 25 years.

References

Aldridge, T. and A. Wood (2014). Monetary policy decision-making and accountability structures: some cross-country comparisons, Reserve Bank of New Zealand *Bulletin* Vol. 77, No. 1. March 2014, pp. 15–30

Baldwin, A. (2013). Twenty years of inflation targeting by the Bank of England, Paper presented at the University of Ottawa, mimeo

Brash, D. (1993). Interview with Dr. Don Brash, Reserve Bank of New Zealand *Bulletin*, Vol. 56, No. 3. September 1993, pp. 284–290

Consumers Price Index Advisory Committee (2013). *Report of the Consumers Price Index Advisory Committee 2013*. Available from www.stats.govt.nz.

Dean, R. S. and P. W. E. Nicholl (1983). *Monetary Policy and the New Zealand Financial System*, 2nd edn, Reserve Bank of New Zealand, Wellington

Graham, J. and C. Smith (2012). A brief history of monetary policy objectives and independence in New Zealand, Reserve Bank of New Zealand *Bulletin*, Vol. 75, No. 1. March 2012, pp. 28–37

Hawke, G. (1973), *Between Governments and Banks: A History of the Reserve Bank of New Zealand*, Government Printer, Wellington

Kendall, R. and T. Ng (2013). The 2012 Policy Targets Agreement: an evolution in flexible inflation targeting in New Zealand, Reserve Bank of New Zealand *Bulletin*, Vol. 76, No. 4. December 2013, pp. 3–12

Low, A. (1968). Monetary policy – A New Zealand review, *New Zealand Economic Papers*, Vol. 2, No. 2. pp. 5–14

Monetary and Economic Council (1966). *The New Zealand Financial System*, Government Printer, Wellington

Monetary and Economic Council ((1972). *Monetary Policy and the Financial System*, Government Printer, Wellington

Ranchhod, S. (2013). Measures of New Zealand core inflation, Reserve Bank of New Zealand *Bulletin,* Vol. 76, No. 1. March 2013, pp. 3–11

Reddell, M. (1999). Origins and early development of the inflation target, Reserve Bank of New Zealand *Bulletin*, Vol. 62, No. 3. September 1999, pp. 63–71

Reddell, M. (2006). Monetary policy accountability and monitoring, http://www.rbnz. govt.nz/monpol/about/2851362.html

Reddell, M. (2012). The New Zealand Debt Conversion Act 1933: A case study in coercive domestic public debt restructuring, Reserve Bank of New Zealand *Bulletin*, Vol. 75, No. 1. March 2012, pp. 38–45

Reserve Bank of New Zealand (1963). *Money and Banking in New Zealand*, Reserve Bank of New Zealand, Wellington

Reserve Bank of New Zealand (1966). *Overseas Trade and Finance*, Reserve Bank of New Zealand, Wellington

Reserve Bank of New Zealand (1986). *Financial Policy Reform*, Reserve Bank of New Zealand, Wellington

Reserve Bank of New Zealand (1997). Background note for journalists and analysts on the new Policy Targets Agreement, and the consequential decision to discontinue the calculation and publication of "underlying inflation", http://www.rbnz.govt.nz/monpol/pta/0055243.html

Reserve Bank of New Zealand et al. (1955). *Monetary and Fiscal Policy in New Zealand*, Reserve Bank of New Zealand, Wellington

Gibson, J. and G. Scobie (2010). Using Engel curves to estimate CPI bias in a small, open, inflation-targeting economy, *Applied Financial Economics*, Vol. 20, No. 17. pp. 1327–1335

Singleton, J. et al. (2006). *Innovation and Independence: The Reserve Bank of New Zealand 1973–2002*, Auckland University Press, Auckland

The CPI versus a Cost-of-Living Index: Some Sources of Bias

Antong Victorio

Abstract

The consumers price index (CPI) should ideally be a reliable measure of changes in consumer satisfaction, but because of the way it is calculated, it may diverge from this ideal. This divergence is known as CPI bias. In this chapter, the various types of CPI bias are explained, with examples.

1 Introduction

The consumers price index (CPI) is commonly understood to be a good measure of inflation. Because inflation is assumed to erode a given standard of living, the CPI is also assumed to be a good measure for maintaining such a standard of living. This assumption is not always valid. A living standard may change with or without inflation; it may also remain unchanged despite inflation. The CPI is adequate if a living standard is defined as the continued ability of consumers to purchase the same quantities of a representative market basket of goods. It is not adequate if a living standard is instead defined as consumers being as *satisfied* with the same market basket of goods as they were previously.

The CPI was not initially intended to be such an indicator of consumer satisfaction. This began to change in 1995, when the United States Senate formed an advisory committee to study the CPI, a committee eventually known as the Boskin Commission (Boskin et al., 1997). The Commission recommended that the CPI become more like a cost-of-living index (COLI), measuring consumer satisfaction as well as inflation. As a COLI, the CPI ought to have quantified the satisfaction from a market basket purchased in the past, and it ought to have proceeded by estimating how much income consumers would have needed to achieve that same level of satisfaction with current prices.

Thus the CPI was alleged to differ in important ways from an ideal COLI, a divergence known as a CPI bias. There would be no bias if there happened to be an equality between measured inflation and the required change in minimum income to achieve a previous level of consumer satisfaction. There would be an upward bias if the measured inflation exceeded the required change, and a downward bias if the measured inflation was less than the required change.

The Boskin Commission suggested that the CPI was biased upward by 1.1 percentage points in the year 1996, and possibly by more prior to 1996 (Boskin et al., 1997). This meant that future projections concerning US government budget deficits would have been grossly exaggerated. For example, if the CPI were upwardly biased by just 1 per cent a year, the associated adjustments to welfare payments would have ended up 22 per cent higher than they should have been after a period of 20 years. The Commission's findings also suggested that many COLI policy considerations were being neglected when measuring real incomes, setting monetary policies, defining poverty thresholds, indexing welfare payments and considering changes to the tax code.

This chapter begins by describing CPI bias in the context of an example in standard economic theory.

2 Price-substitution bias

In a COLI, the consumer is envisioned to maximise total satisfaction or utility according to some utility function that depends upon the quantities of the components of the market basket. This results in a minimum level of expenditure that is needed to achieve the maximised utility. This minimum is adjusted to achieve the same utility whenever prices change, while allowing for the quantities to be changed in order to reflect consumer substitution towards cheaper goods and services.

If the CPI is calculated in such a way that the quantities are assumed to be unchanged, the CPI diverges from a COLI according to what is known as a price-substitution bias. The Boskin Commission estimated this bias to be around 0.4 percentage points of its total estimated bias of 1.1 per cent.

To illustrate hypothetically using variables, suppose that the preferences of consumers could be described as a relationship between total satisfaction, as a utility function with satisfaction measured in utils (U), and the quantities (x and y) of two varieties of meat in the CPI market basket (beef and lamb respectively). The relationship is such that total satisfaction depends upon the quantities in a multiplicative way, $U = x\,y$. Preferences are stable in the sense that this relationship does not change over time. If the unit price of beef was $10 per kilo, that of lamb was $30 per kilo, and the consumers' budget for both varieties was $240, total satisfaction would be maximised by the consumers choosing x = 12 kilos of beef and y = 4 kilos of lamb. This combination yields a total satisfaction of (12)(4) = 48 utils, and it can be shown to be superior in utils to any other combination that also costs $240.

Now suppose that over time the unit price of beef rose from $10 to $40 per kilo while that of lamb remained unchanged at $30 per kilo. Using an indexation method that assumes the quantities in the previous basket to be unchanged – the Laspeyres method – the quantities would now cost ($40)(12) + ($30)(4) = $600. The increase recorded for the CPI, as a measure of inflation, would then be ($600/$240) = 250 per cent.

With a COLI, the consumers are expected to substitute beef for lamb in a way that keeps their *total satisfaction*, rather than their quantities, unchanged. For the given preferences and the new prices, the combination that yields the highest satisfaction at a level of 48 utils should become x = 6 kilos of beef and y = 8 kilos of lamb. This new basket would now cost ($40)(6) + ($30)(8) = $480. The increase recorded for the COLI would then be ($480/$240) = 200 per cent. Because the price substitution towards lamb is not considered, the Laspeyres-based CPI clearly overstates the real increase in the cost of living, by a factor of 50 per cent. Too much weight is given to the commodity for which prices have risen. The substitution may be more severe if the similarities between commodities are at an aggregation level that is 'high' rather than 'low', for example, if different cuts of one type of meat were considered rather than different types of meat.

3 Minimising and estimating price-substitution bias

Price-substitution bias can be minimised if the base-quantities of a Laspeyres index are regularly updated to the most current period. Hausman (2003) recommended this by replacing price surveys with instantaneous scanner data of current-period prices and quantities. Current-period quantities are required in the construction of a Paasche-based index. When combined with a Laspeyres index, the geometric mean of the two indices is a Fisher index, which more closely approximates a COLI. The Fisher index is also a superlative index; that is, it has the advantage of exhibiting price and quantity predictions that can be strongly associated with well-known utility functions (it treats prices and quantities equally across periods: Diewert, 1976).

Superlative indices were applied by Manser and McDonald (1988) to US data concerning personal consumption expenditures for 1959–1985. The authors found an annual substitution bias of between 0.14 and 0.22 per cent a year. For similar US data between 1982 and 1991, Aizcorbe and Jackman (1993) estimated an annual substitution bias of about 0.2 per cent. Another superlative price index based on a weighted geometric mean of basket price-changes – the Törnqvist index – was applied to price and consumer expenditure data for Taiwan between 1991 and 2006 (Lieu et al., 2009). When compared against the results of a Laspeyres-based CPI index, the CPI was found to be biased by around 0.1 percentage points annually.

In New Zealand, the Törnqvist method was applied to Australian supermarket scanner data obtained weekly between May 2007 and July 2010 (Krsinich, 2011). When compared against a base-invariant indexation method – the RGEX method proposed by Ivancic, Diewert and Fox (2009) – the results showed a significant divergence between the two indices, and between either of them and a third index that involved controlling for changes in commodity characteristics. While the measurement of bias was not the goal of the study, it revealed how indices could diverge significantly depending upon which one is regarded as being closer to a COLI.

Substitution bias is also uncovered by directly estimating the interrelated demand equations implied by an underlying utility function. An early approach proposed a class of utility functions that allowed for the quantities demanded to depend upon the prices of other commodities without excessive restrictions (Braithwait, 1980). Fifty-three commodities were considered, and these comprised nearly 90 per cent of all types of US consumption expenditures for the 15-year period between 1958 and 1973.

The regression results for the quantities demanded showed significant substitutions within commodity groups. The substitution elasticities were found to be especially high for clothing, shelter and recreation, implying high CPI biases for these commodity groups: in the order of 0.8, 1.0 and 7.0 percentage points respectively over a period of 15 years. For all commodity groups, the overall CPI bias was 1.5 percentage points over 15 years, or about one-tenth of one point per year. However, this was less than the one-fourth of one point per year proposed by the Boskin Commission (Boskin et al., 1997).

4 Price substitution across commodities

Substitutions *across* commodity groups are also known to be a source of CPI bias. A special case is the substitution over time that occurs between food and other components of consumption – a food substitution bias. One cause is the declining importance that consumers place upon food as their incomes rise, a relationship between food expenditures and income that is known as an Engel curve. But even so, the substitution might occur because of lower relative food prices, a widening of income distribution, decreases in family size, or a number of other factors. The combined effect of these additional factors is ideally referred to as Engel drift (bias), because they refer to shifts in an Engel curve rather than movements along it.

Hamilton (2001) estimated the size of the food substitution bias by conducting regressions of a demand function for 'food at home' based upon 1974–1991 data provided by the US Panel Study of Income Dynamics. Food at home was modelled as being dependent upon household income, its price relative to the prices of other components, and other determining factors. After considering all of these potential effects, the food substitution bias was estimated to be around 1.5 percentage points a year.

Gibson and Scobie (2010) improved upon this procedure by considering the reverse-causality errors that may arise from household income being dependent upon food at home. Using information concerning the CPI and household consumption expenditures, they estimated a food substitution bias for New Zealand of around 1.4 percentage points a year. Many studies of other countries have supposedly found something similar (see also Gibson and Scobie, this volume).

5 Outlet-substitution bias from discounted prices: A welfare approach

Bias across *outlets*, rather than across commodities, can occur because of the benefits to consumers of being able to substitute toward discounted prices. This became particularly important in the 1980s when so-called budget US warehouses like Walmart and the Price Club offered lower prices for virtually identical products. In New Zealand, the trend has been mirrored by the market entry of discount outlets like The Warehouse and Pak'nSave. Acknowledging this trend, the Boskin Commission estimates that the US CPI bias from outlet substitution is around 0.1 per cent a year.

To illustrate a hypothetical example, consider using the previous example of a utility function $U = x\,y$. But instead of the usual commodities, let x be the quantity of lamb available for sale in one outlet, A, and y the quantity of the same lamb available in another outlet, B. If the unit price of lamb was $40 per kilo in both outlets and the consumers' total budget was $640, total satisfaction would be maximised by the consumers choosing $x = 8$ kilos in each of the outlets, for a maximum utility of 64 utils. The price authorities can infer these quantity combinations by dividing the observed expenditure in each outlet ($320) by each outlet's unit price ($40).

Now, for simplicity, suppose that outlet A dropped its price from $40 to $10 per kilo while outlet B held its own unchanged at $40. With the Laspeyres indexation method, the original quantities in the previous basket are assumed to be unchanged. The originals would now cost ($10)(8) + ($40)(8) = $400. The CPI would then have recorded an index of ($400/$640) = 62.5 per cent, which is equivalent to a 37.5 per cent decrease in prices.

This recorded decrease fails to consider the substitution that consumers would have undertaken *for an unchanged maximum utility*. For the previous maximum of 64 utils, consumers would have chosen to purchase more lamb from outlet A, of $x = 16$ kilos, while purchasing less from outlet B, of $y = 4$

kilos. These choices can be shown as the ones preferred given the lower price and an unchanged utility function. A COLI would consider these quantities according to a cost of ($10)(16) + ($40)(4) = $320 necessary to maintain 64 utils. The resulting index, of $320/$640 = 50 per cent, is equivalent to a 50 per cent decrease in prices. By comparison, the CPI's 37.5 per cent price decrease understates the improvement in the cost of living.

6 Empirical estimates of outlet bias

The measurement of outlet bias is tricky because the lower prices might be accompanied by a reduction in service, variety or quality. Reinsdorf (1993) mitigated some of these difficulties by comparing the gasoline and food components of the CPI against the same components of the average price series (AP) of the US Bureau of Labor Statistics (BLS). The AP was deemed closer to a COLI than the CPI because of its procedure for monitoring a single variety for a group of commodities rather than the group itself, for example, 'unleaded 91 octane' for a gasoline group, and 'T-bone' for a group of steaks. The tracking of a variety rather than of the group it belonged to made it possible to eliminate changes in variety or quality as the leading cause of a price change.

For US data between January 1980 and January 1989, the CPI's gasoline components decreased by an annual average rate of 1.4 per cent while the same AP components fell by 2.3 per cent. In this context, the CPI would thus have potentially understated the outlet-related welfare improvements by 0.9 per cent a year. For the food components, the CPI *increased* at an annual average rate of 4.2 per cent, while the AP grew by only 2.1 per cent, suggesting an understatement of around 2 per cent a year.

7 Outlet bias from Laspeyres weights

The findings by Reinsdorf (1993) also suggest that a CPI bias can arise because even if new outlets offered lower prices, a Laspeyres-based approach may not accord them proper weights. This is referred to by Moulton (1996) as a type of formula bias resulting from sample rotation.

As an illustration, consider a succession of three periods for which there are no changes in *average* prices, basket components, quantities and preferences, and therefore no possible change in overall consumer satisfaction (see also Moulton, 1996, for an extended example). In the first period, outlets A and B are the ones sampled. The recorded expenditure is $120 for each of these outlets, for a total expenditure of $240. With the price of lamb being $30 in each outlet, the sampling authorities infer that 4 kilos are purchased at each one. These weights are then used for a Laspeyres index in the second period.

In the second period, new outlets C and D emerge to become the new sample. The recorded expenditure is unchanged at $120 for each of the outlets. However, one of them, outlet C, charges a higher unit price of $40 per kilo, while the other one, outlet D, charges a lower price of $20. Using a Laspeyres-based approach, the previous period-quantities are used as weights so that the Laspeyres numerator for the second period is $40(4) + $20(4) = $240. The ratio of this to previous total expenditure, $240/$240, is a Laspeyres index of 100 per cent, thereby implying, rightfully so, that there has been no change in the cost of living. However, because the prices have diverged, the sampling authorities update their inferred base quantities. For outlet C, the new base is $120/$40 = 3 kilos. For outlet D, it is $120/$20 = 6 kilos. In the third period, if the new outlets were to maintain their prices, the revised numerator would become $40(3) + $20(6) = $240. The Laspeyres index would continue to be $240/$240 = 100 per cent and there would be no bias in the CPI.

However, suppose that in the third period, the new outlets reverse their prices. Outlet C charges a lower price of $20, while outlet D charges a higher one of $40. (The recorded expenditure is still $120 for each of the outlets and this is used for a future updating of quantities.) With the most recent quantities being 3 kilos for outlet C and 4 kilos for outlet D, the Laspeyres numerator becomes $20(3) + $40(6) = $300. The Laspeyres index becomes $300/$240 = 1.25, despite neither inflation nor a change in the cost of living, implying a bias of 25 per cent. This occurs because a reversal of prices has inadvertently placed too little weight upon the outlet that reduced its price, and too much weight upon the one that increased its price.

A bias would also occur if average prices actually fall. For example, suppose outlet C charges a lower price of $20 per kilo while outlet D merely charges the previous average of $30, instead of reverting to $40. The Laspeyres numerator becomes $20(3) + $30(6) = $240. The Laspeyres index becomes $240/$240, or 100 per cent, indicating no change in the cost of living, despite the fact that consumers have benefited from lower *average* prices.

8 Bias from new commodities

With newly introduced commodities, the potential bias is difficult to measure because there is no previous quantity that can be inferred. A way around this problem is to first imagine what consumers would have been willing to pay if the new commodity had been provided at a quantity that is close to zero. This estimate for willingness to pay is known as a virtual price (see Hausman, 2003). Because of the downward-sloping nature of demand curves, a virtual price is typically higher than any price recorded for an index, which would be for some quantity currently demanded that is obviously not zero. That the price actually paid by consumers is lower than the virtual one suggests that consumers benefit from the new commodity being introduced. These benefits are known as consumer surplus.

A problem is that the demand curve usually implies an infinitely large virtual price even for very simple utility functions. To find a practicable price, Hausman (2003) proposes to find either a linear or a log-linear version of the demand curve. The price intercept of this version is an estimate of the virtual price.

As a hypothetical example, consider the introduction of electronic mail (e-mail) in the 1980s, the quantities (y) of which have been anecdotally known to have increased, while those of postal mail (x) have decreased. Setting aside any quality differences between the two services, let the current price of postal mail be 10 cents per letter, and the cost of e-mail 1 cent per message in a utility function of the same previous form, $U = x\,y$. Suppose that consumers have a budget of 20 cents to be expended on both. At this budget and at the unit prices, consumers are able to maximise their utility by choosing $x = 1$ message sent by postal mail and $y = 10$ messages sent by e-mail, and the maximised utility is $U = 10$ utils. Suppose that these prices and quantities are the ones recorded for the current period, so that the numerator of a cost-of-living index corresponds to the expression $(10)1 + 1(10) = 20$ cents.

For the base period preceding the current one, assume a unit price of 10 cents for postal mail, but let that of electronic mail be unknown, as it has just been introduced. Based upon the form of the utility function, a demand curve for electronic mail can be derived for an unchanged utility of 10 utils. This demand curve has an infinitely large virtual price at a quantity demanded of zero. Following Hausman (2003), a linear version of this demand can be derived based upon the gradient of the curve at the choice of $x = 1$ and $y = 10$ messages. From applying calculus, this gradient is –0.2 cents per message. From finding an intercept for a straight line, the virtual price is found to be equal to six cents. That is, consumers would have been willing to pay up to six cents per message at the pre-introduction quantity of zero, less two-tenths of a cent for every additional message made available for their demand.

It is unclear what quantity is to be used for this virtual price in a COLI. One possibility is the current one recorded. If this were the one used, the denominator for the base index of a COLI would be equal to $10(1) + 6(10) = 70$ cents, the number '6' being the virtual price for '10' email messages demanded. For the numerator previously derived, the result is a COLI of $20/70 = 28.57$ per cent. Relative to a base of 100 per cent, the cost of living has thus gone down by over 70 per cent, a bias potentially unrecorded by the CPI.

9 Empirical findings for new-commodity bias

By way of real examples, Hausman (1999) constructed a price index for a new commodity, mobile phone usage in the United States, for the years between 1985 and 1998 preceding the inclusion of such an index into the CPI. Using 1985 as a base, he estimated a 27 per cent decrease in the price index that was completely neglected by the broader telecommunications index, which showed instead a 10.1 per cent increase in prices for the same period – an increase of 1.07 per cent a year.

A log-linear demand curve for monthly usage and prices was estimated for data between 1989 and 1993. The virtual price for mobile phone usage was found to be US$97 per month and the price elasticity was −0.51 per cent of usage for every 1 per cent increase in price. When these estimates were included, the COLI for telecommunications was estimated to have dropped by 0.8 per cent a year, implying an annual bias in the telecommunications index of around 1.9 per cent.

Hausman (2010) used a similar approach to estimate the welfare gains from the introduction of mobile phones in India. The virtual price in the year 2009 for a log-linear version of the demand for mobile phones was found to be as high as 15 cents per minute, based upon an average price of about one US cent per minute and an average monthly mobile expenditure of $5.68. After considering that total expenditures on all consumer items were around $118.30 per month, he estimated that mobile phones reduced the cost of living by a range of between 1.1 per cent and 4.14 per cent per month, a reduction not necessarily mirrored by the corresponding CPI.

10 Biases due to changes in quality

Biases can also arise because the characteristics of the CPI commodities may change over time, resulting in a change in quality. If combined with the introduction of new commodities, the corresponding bias in the US CPI is thought to be around 0.6 percentage points a year (Boskin et al., 1997).

If the quality of a commodity has increased but is not considered, the CPI overstates the change in the cost of living, i.e. the bias is upward. If the quality has decreased, the CPI understates the change, i.e. the bias is downward. The reason for this is that consumers acquire utility from the *characteristics* of commodities they desire, as well as from the quantities of those commodities. This assumption is known as the hedonic approach to utility maximisation (see e.g. Rosen, 1974). If consumers' utilities are to be held unchanged at some COLI base period, changes in prices that are the result of quality changes must therefore be purged from the CPI.

An empirical solution is to infer that the quality changes are simply the differences between the prices of new items and the inflation or deflation of their corresponding group. This was a method used by the US and many Western democracies until the late 1990s. Thereafter, it became more common to conduct a regression of observed commodity prices against their known characteristics. The coefficient estimates for such a regression are then used to identify what portions of the observed prices are to be purged. This is theoretically justified because the 'demand equations' that emerge from a hedonic approach can be unit prices, rather than quantities, that depend upon the indicated characteristics of the commodities desired.

As an illustration, consider that the screen characteristics of television sets have changed from cathode ray tubes (CRTs) to liquid crystal displays (LCDs). If other characteristics remain unchanged, LCDs provide a superior viewing experience to CRTs. Thus, if the utility function for television sets had been $U = x\,y$, the variable x might be for an unchanged characteristic such as the sound, while the variable y might be for the viewing experience, which has changed. Being a discrete variable rather than a continuous one, variable y could be assigned either a '0' if the item surveyed was a CRT, or a '1' if it was an LCD. For a sufficient number of items observed, the regression estimate associated with the viewing experience will then represent some dollar estimate for the benefit of viewing through an LCD. In practice, there would be many such dollar estimates associated with many evolving characteristics.

11 Estimates of quality biases

Indeed, television sets were among the first items for which hedonic methods were applied. For 1993 US data, Moulton and colleagues (1999) obtained regression estimates for the price valuations of such characteristics as LCDs, larger screens and picture-in-picture features. LCDs were found to be valued by 17.4 per cent more than CRTs; larger screens by 6.5 per cent more per additional inch, and picture-in-picture by up to 25.4 per cent more if a second tuner were included.

The increasing market penetration of such improvements over four succeeding years after 1993 would have increased the overall quality of sets in a way that might have biased the published CPI. The bias was estimated to be upward, and it ranged between 4.7 and 7.8 percentage points, an average of between 1.175 and 1.95 points annually. The published CPI had declined to 86.8 per cent by August 1997, from a 100 per cent base in August 1993, because of falling television prices. By comparison, the 'hedonic' index was estimated to have been lower, at between 79.0 and 82.1 per cent (Moulton et al., 1999, Table 5).

The use of hedonic methods has since expanded to consider biases from a wider range of commodities. For clothes dryers in the US consumer market, the published CPI fell by 0.43 percentage points, from 98.119 per cent in September 1999 to 97.695 per cent by June 2000. But after adjusting for quality improvements such as capacity, electronic controls and moisture sensors, the hedonic-adjusted CPI was estimated have been 97.741 in June 2000, implying a small downward bias of 0.04 percentage points (Liegey, 2001). Downward biases were also found for US personal computers and camcorders. Upward biases were estimated for VCRs and audio equipment (Shepler, 2000).

For personal computers in Korea, the published CPI fell from 56.7 per cent in January 1999 to 45.6 per cent by December 2000. But after adjusting for brand, processing power, memory and the presence of a DVD, the hedonic index was supposed to have been 40.7 per cent by December 2000, suggesting an upward CPI bias of 4.9 percentage points over two years (Lee, 2001).

More recently, hedonic methods have also been applied to New Zealand scanner data concerning consumer electronic products (Krsinich, 2011). While estimating quality bias was not the purpose, the indices of a hedonic regression approach were found to differ from those of two superlative index approaches, though by less than 10 percentage points over two years (2009–2010).

12 Concluding remarks

Acknowledging biases from many angles, some governments have undertaken improvements in the way that the CPI is obtained. Of particular interest has been the initiatives undertaken by the United States Bureau of Labor Statistics (BLS).

In 1996, the BLS mitigated outlet bias by changing how outlets were sampled (Greenlees and Mason, 1996). That same year, the BLS revised its indices for medical care to allow for a greater substitution by consumers towards cheaper ways of obtaining health services. The trend had been for consumers to shift away from fee-for-services arrangements towards better-value health plans provided by health maintenance providers (see e.g. Ford and Ginsburg, 2001). This trend was not previously captured because of a fixed-quantity approach which made it appear that medical care prices were rising far more than they actually were.

Later on, the medical-care indices were further refined to focus on the combined costs reflected in patients' bills, rather than on pricing individual inputs to treatment. A greater substitution by consumers towards generic drugs was allowed for by a change of sampling procedure. The previous procedure included generic drugs into the market basket only if a sampled pharmacy discontinued selling the expensive variety. This had an unintended effect of placing too little weight upon expenditures on generics (Ford and Ginsburg, 2001). The new procedure included generic drugs whether or not the sale of expensive varieties was discontinued.

Greater substitution was also allowed for by replacing a fixed-quantity approach with a geometric-mean approach to calculating quantities from expenditure shares (Cashell, 2000). From 1999 this was applied to over 61 per cent of the index. It was not applied to commodities that were not expected to have a great deal of substitution, such as housing and medical care. Later on, in 2002, the BLS began publishing a supplementary index that allowed for even greater substitution between very similar commodities, i.e. substitution at a 'high' level of aggregation.

Hedonic methods continued to be regarded as useful for measuring biases from quality change. However, for computers, the BLS adopted a monthly attribution method based upon internet prices in order to cope with rapidly changing configurations (see e.g. Johnson et al., 2006). This method proved nearly as accurate as using hedonic regressions. Furthermore, from 1998, sample rotation was increased for all goods from 20 per cent a year to 25 per cent a year, implying a full sample rotation every four years rather than every five years. For rapidly changing commodities in electronics, sample rotation was increased to 50 per cent a year, equivalent to a full sample rotation every two years.

There is little doubt that other types of bias will eventually be uncovered. Invariably, some new method will then be proposed to reduce the bias. Unfortunately, the concept of a COLI is also bound to evolve. Its current emphasis upon market goods and services does not yet consider the impacts upon living standards of changes in the consumers' external environment, or of changes in their sources of satisfaction, such as from the provision of non-market services or from altruistic intentions (see e.g. Victorio, 2002; 2009). About all that can be hoped is that some evolving version of a COLI will continue to be the main framework by which the merits of a CPI are judged.

References

Aizcorbe, Ana M., and Patrick C. Jackman, 'The Commodity Substitution Effect in CPI Data, 1982–91', *Monthly Labor Review*, December 1993, 116:12, 25–33.

Boskin, Michael J., Ellen R. Dulberger, Robert Gordon, Zvi Griliches and Dale W. Jorgenson, 'The CPI Commission: Findings and Recommendations', *The American Economic Review*, May 1997, 87:2, 78–83.

Braithwait, Steven D., 'Substitution Bias of the Laspeyres Price Index: An Analysis Using Cost-of-Living Indices', *American Economic Review*, March 1980, 70:1, 64–77.

Cashell, Brian W., 'The Consumer Price Index: Recent Improvements and Prospective Changes', January 2000, Congressional Research Service, The Library of Congress. Available at http://congressional research.com/RL30019/document.php

Diewert, W. E., 'Exact and Superlative Index Numbers', *Journal of Econometrics*, May 1976, 4:2, 115–145.

Ford, Ina Kay, and Daniel H. Ginsburg, 'Medical Care in the Consumer Price Index', in D. M. Cutler, M. E. Manser and E. R. Berndt (eds.) *Medical Care Output and Productivity*, Chicago: University of Chicago Press, January 2001, pp. 203–220.

Gibson, John, and Grant Scobie, 'Using Engel Curves to Estimate CPI Bias in a Small, Open, Inflation-Targeting Economy', *Applied Financial Economics*, 2010, 20:7, 1327–1335.

Greenlees, John S., and Charles C. Mason, 'Overview of the 1998 Revision of the Consumer Price Index', *Monthly Labor Review*, December 1996, 119:12, 3–9.

Hamilton, Bruce W., 'Using Engel's Law to Estimate CPI Bias', *American Economic Review*, June 2001, 91:3, 619–630.

Hausman, Jerry, 'Cellular Telephone, New Products and the CPI', *Journal of Business and Economic Statistics*, April 1999, 17:2, 188–194.

———, 'Sources of Bias and Solutions to Bias in the Consumer Price Index', *Journal of Economic Perspectives*, Winter 2003, 17:1, 23–44.

———, 'Mobile Phones in Developing Countries', unpublished manuscript, May 2010. Available at http://www.crei.cat/conferences/cornucopia/confpapers/Jerry Hausman_Barcelona%20paper.pdf

Ivancic, L., W. E. Diewert and K. J. Fox, 'Scanner Data, Time Aggregation and the Construction of Price Indexes', Discussion Paper 09-09, 2009, Department of Economics, The University of British Columbia, Vancouver, Canada.

Johnson, David S., Stephen B. Reed and Kenneth J. Stewart, 'Price Measurement in the United States: A Decade After the Boskin Report', *Monthly Labor Review*, May 2006, 129:5, 10–19.

Krsinich, Frances, 'Price Indices from Scanner Data: A Comparison of Different Methods', Paper Presented at the Ottawa Group, May 2011. Available at http://www.stats.govt.nz/ottawa-group-2011/agenda.aspx

Lee, Eunjeong, 'How to Reflect Quality Change in the CPI: The Case of Korea', Paper Presented at the Sixth Meeting of the International Working Group on Price Indices, April 2001, Canberra, Australia.

Liegey, P. R., Jr, 'Hedonic Quality Adjustment Methods for Clothes Dryers in the U.S. CPI', 2001, U.S. Bureau of Labor Statistics. Available at http//www.bls.gov/cpi/cpidryer.htm

Lieu, PangTien, Jui-Hui Chen and Chih-Jung Chang, 'Study on Taiwan Consumers; Cost of Living: An Application of the Törnqvist Price Index Formula', *International Journal of Business*, January 2009, 1:1, 1–18.

Manser, Marilyn E., and Richard J. McDonald, 'An Analysis of Substitution Bias in Measuring Inflation: 1959–85', *Econometrica*, July 1988, 56:4, 909–930.

Moulton, Brent R., 'Bias in the Consumer Price Index: What is the Evidence?' *The Journal of Economic Perspectives*, Fall 1996, 10:4, 159–177.

————, Timothy La Fleur and Karin Moses, 'Research on Improved Quality Adjustment in the CPI: The Case of Televisions', *Proceedings of the Fourth Meeting of the International Working Group on Price Indices,* January 1999, Bureau of Labor Statistics, Washington DC.

Reinsdorf, Marshall, 'The Effect of Outlet Price Differentials on the U.S. Consumer Price Index', in M. F. Foss, M. E. Manser and A. H. Young (eds) *Price Measurements and Their Uses,* Chicago: University of Chicago Press, 1993, pp. 227–54.

Rosen, Sherwin, 'Hedonic Prices and Implicit Markets: Product Differentiation in Pure Competition', *Journal of Political Economy*, January 1974, 82:1, 34–55.

Shepler, Nicole, 'Developing a Hedonic Regression Model for Camcorders in the U.S. CPI', U.S. Bureau of Labor Statistics, 2000, Available at http://www.bls.gov/cpi/cpicomco.htm

Victorio, Andres, 'Non-Market Insurance and Intrafamily Transfers', *Applied Economics Letters,* February 2002, 9:2, 99–102.

————, 'Altruism and Externalities', *Applied Economics Letters*, October 2009, 16:15, 1529–1531.

Acknowledgements

Gratitude is extended to Sharleen Forbes, Gary Hawke and Chris Pike. Funding and administrative support were provided by StatScience (NZ) Limited and the School of Government at Victoria University of Wellington.

Using Engel Curves to Estimate CPI Bias in a Small, Open, Inflation-Targeting Economy*

John Gibson & Grant Scobie

Abstract

A cost-of-living bias concerning the New Zealand Consumer Price Index (CPI) is calculated by estimating Engel curves for the food budgets of demographically similar households at different points in time. For the 17 years between 1984 and 2001 the bias is estimated to have averaged over 1 per cent annually. The estimates are similar to those found in the United States.

1 Introduction

The Consumer Price Index (CPI), a widely used measure of inflation, is known to overstate the true increase in the cost of living (Hausman, 2003). One reason has to do with households spending a smaller proportion of their budget on necessities, such as food-at-home, as they become richer. These decreases in the proportion of the budget spent on necessities may not match even the best statistical predictions. If the actual decreases exceeded the predictions in a period of rising prices, there is an excess importance placed upon necessities. This produces an exaggerated measure of the increased cost required to maintain the same standard of living. This exaggeration is a source of bias in the measurement of the cost of living. There are other sources of bias, but it is this cost-of-living bias that is considered here.

There is considerable debate concerning the size of this bias. The 1996 Boskin Commission (Boskin, 1996) estimated this bias in the USA CPI to be in the order of 1.1 annual percentage points. Some government agencies questioned this estimate because of alleged weaknesses in the methods by which they were derived.[1]

---

*   This chapter is a revised version of Gibson and Scobie (2010).

1   Examples include Australia (Edwards, 1997), France (Lequiller, 1997) and the United Kingdom (Fenwick, 1997). The New Zealand Government Statistician claimed that "The CPI in the United States is not updated as frequently as in New Zealand. . . . I do not believe that the level of bias estimated in the Boskin report for the USA CPI is relevant to New Zealand" (Morris, 1997, p.50). Similarly, the Reserve Bank of New Zealand note "Statistics New Zealand appears to be more thorough than many foreign statistical bureaus in trying to account for these biases" (Ebert, 1994, p.25).

In this article, a cost-of-living bias for the New Zealand CPI is estimated from household data using the method of Hamilton (2001). The method is based on a presupposed relationship, known as an Engel curve, between budgeted expenditures and levels of household income. Empirically, the bias is estimated based upon regressions of the budget share of food against important independent variables across time.

The method has previously been applied to the USA (Costa, 2001), Canada (Beatty and Larsen, 2005), Norway (Larsen, 2007), Russia (Gibson et al., 2008), Australia (Barrett and Brzozowski, 2010) and Indonesia (Olivia and Gibson, 2013).

Beatty and Crossley (2012) note that this method does not necessarily equate to constructing a cost-of-living index. A cost-of-living index is based on a basket of goods, and that basket will vary across a distribution of expenditures. For example, poorer households will typically spend more on food than others. As a consequence, a 'true' cost of living index can be obtained only for a point in the expenditure distribution (approximately at the median), which in turn, may not be representative of the underlying population.

New Zealand is an interesting case for measuring any cost-of-living bias in the CPI because the Reserve Bank of New Zealand was the first central bank to set monetary policy around an inflation target.[2] If the goal of monetary policy were to preserve the value of money, an inflation target should aim for increases in the CPI that are equal to the bias in the cost of living (Crawford et al., 1998). Presumptions of a 1 per cent point bias in the New Zealand CPI had an important influence on chosen inflation targets (Sherwin, 2000, p. 22). The inflation target was raised to 0–3 per cent in 1996 and to 1–3 per cent in 2002 on the hunch that the CPI bias was increasing, even though such a finding had never been obtained for New Zealand.

Being a small, open economy, New Zealand is also vulnerable to other sources of bias in the cost of living. Changes in its terms of trade may fail to consider that consumers substitute away from higher-priced goods to cheaper ones, thereby unintentionally giving more weight to the higher-priced goods. This type of bias is considered to be no more than one-fifth of the total CPI bias in the USA, a large economy, although it may be greater in economies with larger relative price shocks.[3] Despite the research, we do not presume that the bias in the CPI always overstates the true cost of living. Some findings suggest

---

2   A chronology of New Zealand's financial market reforms is given by Boyle and Eckhold (1997).

3   The Boskin Commission estimated commodity substitution bias of 0.15 percentage points out of a total annual bias of 1.1 points. This was comparable to the outlet bias of 0.1 points, and smaller than the formula bias of 0.25 points and the bias due to quality change and new products of 0.6 points.

that a bias may actually understate, rather than overstate, changes in the cost of living in a small country (Larsen, 2007).[4]

2 The Engel curve method for measuring CPI bias

Budget expenditures for necessities like food usually decline as household incomes increase, giving rise to an Engel curve that is downward-sloping. If the curve does not shift, its shape can be used to predict expenditures in relation to changes in household incomes, and it is on this basis that changes in the cost of living can be measured. Empirically, finding an Engel curve requires conducting a regression of budgeted expenditures that controls for movements in relative prices and household characteristics. If the predicted expenditures stray away from actual ones measured later on, the differences may be the result of the curve having drifted over time. The differences can then be used to estimate the extent by which changes in the cost of living have not been accurately reflected in the CPI. They are especially important for food expenditures because food's income elasticity is very low, implying that its budget share is extremely sensitive to any inaccuracies in the measurement of income.

The Engel-curve method can best be illustrated by considering three cross-sections of New Zealand household budgets, those of 1984, 1991 and 1998 (Figure 1).

In this figure, a 1984 household with a Current Consumption Expenditure (CCEX) of $40,000 has a predicted food share of 9.7 per cent, controlling for other variables that might affect that share. This is a point on the 1984 Engel curve. The same household in 1991 had a real expenditure of $20,800 (in 1984 prices), with only the prices changing. If the CPI measures the true cost of living, this household should slide up the Engel curve to have a food budget share of 15.0 per cent. But in reality, households in 1991 with CPI-deflated expenditures of $20,800 had food budget shares of only 14.4 per cent, not 15.0 per cent.

Similarly, a 1984 household with a CCEX of $40,000 would have had CPI-deflated total expenditures of $18,300 in 1998, all else unchanged except for price changes. According to the original (1984) Engel curve, that real income level would predict a food share of 16.1 per cent. In actuality, households in 1998 with a CCEX of $18,300 had food shares of only 13.6 per cent. Thus, when viewed from the standard of their food budget shares, New Zealand households in both 1991 and 1998 acted as if they were better off than their CPI-deflated income would have indicated.

4   Here the CPI failed to capture rising costs of housing services in a credit-financed house price boom.

Figure 1. Food Engel curves for 1984, 1991 and 1998

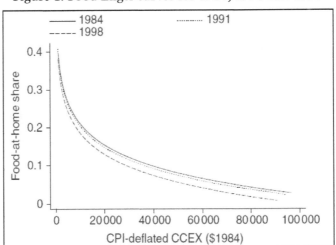

The extent by which the CPI may over-estimate the true cost of living in this particular case, is herein defined as an Engel-drift bias. To formalise its mathematical derivation, consider a form of the equation for the Engel curve, in which the budget share is a linear function of the logarithm of real household income and a relative price term:[5]

$$w_{i,j,t} = \phi + \gamma(\ln P_{F,j,t} - \ln P_{N,j,t}) + \beta(\ln Y_{i,j,t} - \ln P_{j,t})$$
$$+ X'\theta + u_{i,j,t} \tag{1}$$

In this equation, $w_{i,j,t}$ is the budget share of food for household i in region j and time period t, $P_{F,j,t}$, $P_{N,j,t}$ and $P_{j,t}$ represent the true but unobserved prices of food, non-food, and all goods, Y is the household's total income, X is a vector of individual household characteristics and u is the disturbance. The true cost of living is treated as a geometric weighted average of food and non-food prices:

$$\ln P_{j,t} = \alpha \ln P_{F,j,t} + (1 - \alpha) \ln P_{N,j,t} \tag{2}$$

Also, it is assumed that the prices of a good G (either food, non-food or all goods) are measured with error:

$$\ln P_{G,j,t} = \ln P_{G,j,0} + \ln(1 + \Pi_{G,j,t}) + \ln(1 + E_{G,t}) \tag{3}$$

---

5   This provides the basis of the Almost Ideal Demand System (AIDS) of Deaton and Muellbauer (1980). Results when a quadratic in log income is used are also described later in this chapter.

In Equation (3), $\Pi_{G,j,t}$ represents the cumulative percentage increase in the CPI-measured price of good G from period 0 to period t and $E_{G,t}$ is the period-t per cent cumulative measurement error in the cost-of-living index since the base period. By inserting Equation (3) into (2), it is apparent that:

$$\ln(1 + E_t) = \alpha \ln(1 + E_{F,t}) + (1 - \alpha) \ln(1 + E_{N,t})$$

Following Hamilton (2001), an estimable model of the budget share is given by Equation (4), assuming no cross-sectional variation in relative food prices:[6]

$$w_{i,t} = \hat{\phi} + \beta[\ln Y_{i,t} - \ln(1 - \Pi_t)] + X'\theta + \sum_{t=1}^{T} \delta_t D_t + u_{i,t}$$

$$(4)$$

In this equation, the time dummy variable, D_t is equal to 1 in period t. The cumulative cost-of-living bias in the CPI at time t, in percentage terms, is calculated as:

$$1 - \exp\left\{\frac{\delta_t - \bar{\gamma}[\ln(1 + \pi_{F,t}) - \ln(1 + \pi_{N,t})]}{-\beta}\right\} \qquad (5)$$

Equation (5) is an expression for the Engel-drift bias, in cumulative terms. For this bias to be completely estimated, a value for the mean exponential parameter $\bar{\gamma}$ must be obtained from outside of the estimated parameters for Equation (4). These must then be combined with estimates of food inflation $\pi_{F,t}$ and non-food inflation $\pi_{N,t}$.

3 Data and estimation results

For estimating Equation (5), the expenditures and characteristics of 53,455 households were obtained from New Zealand's Household Economic Survey (HES) and combined with CPI data for 16 survey years between 1983/1984 and 2000/2001 (the survey was not carried out in 1998/1999 and 1999/2000).[7] The HES requires households to keep an expenditure diary for two weeks, a requirement similar to that of the UK's Family Expenditure Survey (FES) and many other household budget surveys.

6   New Zealand does not have a spatial price index, so a model which relies on cross-sectional variation in relative food prices could not be utilised.

7   These years are henceforth referred to by the latter year, i.e. 1983/1984 becomes 1984. The 2001 survey was on a June year basis while all previous surveys were on a March year basis. The survey has only been carried out twice since 2001 and micro data from these years are not yet available.

Households whose share of expenditure devoted to food was either less than 2 per cent or greater than 80 per cent were treated as extreme-valued respondents and therefore excluded. This selection rule, also used by Hamilton (2001), removed 1 per cent (n=569) of the households. Household expenditures that provided consumption benefits exceeding one year (e.g. consumer durables) were also removed to get an estimate of current consumption expenditure, henceforth referred to as 'consumption' or CCEX.

Despite these data refinements, there was the possibility of regression-analysis inaccuracies resulting from reverse causality. On the one hand, the chosen dependent variable, food share, would clearly have depended upon consumption, a supposedly independent variable. But on the other hand, consumption would also clearly have depended upon food share. Thus, a decision was made to ameliorate the interdependency by including an instrumental variable (IV), household income, as an explanatory variable in some of the regressions (see e.g. Gibson et al., 2008). The independence of household income was partly ensured by the fact that its method of collection – from a separate survey form and from a different reporting period – was largely uninfluenced by the method for food share and for consumption.

A description of the dependent and explanatory variables is given in Table 1.

To show how food shares and household characteristics have changed over time, the beginning- and end-period averages of the variables are reported in addition to the full sample average.

The dependent variable, which is the share of consumption devoted to food-at-home, averages 19 per cent and falls by two percentage points over the sample period. This fall, which indicates improved living standards, occurs despite some stagnation in CPI-deflated total consumption, the values for which were slightly lower in 1998–2001 than they were in 1984–1987.

The explanatory variables included a number of demographic changes that could have accounted for the fall in food shares, for example, a reduction in household size and in number of children per household. Also included were the budget share for restaurant and takeaway meals, not measured in the dependent variable and important because restaurant meals are imperfect substitutes for food-at-home (see e.g. Hamilton, 2001). Had better data been available, the substitution would have been quantified and the relative price of restaurant meals (rather than spending on them) would instead have been the explanatory variable.

Table 1. Descriptive statistics for the sample

	Full sample		1984–1987	1998–2001
	Mean	SD	Mean	Mean
Budget share for food-at-home	0.187	0.095	0.196	0.177
ln CPI-deflated total consumption	9.316	0.637	9.355	9.340
Share of food eaten out	0.038	0.042	0.037	0.040
Demographic variables				
ln household size	0.861	0.560	0.910	0.836
Share of household ≤2 years old	0.035	0.102	0.036	0.032
Share of household 3–14-year-old boys	0.063	0.138	0.074	0.062
Share of household 15–17-year-old boys	0.017	0.070	0.018	0.016
Share of household 3–14-year-old girls	0.060	0.134	0.070	0.055
Share of household 15–17-year-old girls	0.017	0.070	0.018	0.015
Maori or Pacific Islander household head	0.114	0.317	0.080	0.115
Female household head	0.412	0.492	0.257	0.505
Age of household head	47.393	17.107	46.655	48.336
Household type				
Couple with no children	0.250	0.433	0.247	0.257
Sole-parent household	0.079	0.270	0.070	0.081
Couple with children	0.342	0.474	0.388	0.314
Mixed family	0.078	0.268	0.064	0.106
Nonfamily household	0.042	0.200	0.048	0.018
Dwelling tenure variables				
Rent-free (unowned)	0.036	0.186	0.048	0.038
Owned with mortgage	0.337	0.473	0.367	0.310
Owned without mortgage	0.381	0.486	0.350	0.381

Notes: Estimates weighted by population sampling weights. The excluded household type is sole occupant and the excluded tenure status is renting. The full sample covers 1984–2001 and has $N = 52\,886$.

Table 2 presents Ordinary Least Squares (OLS) estimates of the Engel functions, with food-at-home as the dependent variable. The negative coefficient for the CPI-deflated total consumption indicates that food budget shares fall as households become richer. Its expenditure elasticity is estimated at around 0.567, evaluated at the mean of the food budget share.

The other key feature is that the year dummy variables are all negative and statistically significant. Moreover, with the exception of 1990, 1991 and 2001, each dummy variable is larger (i.e. more negative) than in the preceding survey year. Thus, there is an almost continual downwards drift in the food Engel curve, as previously shown in Figure 1 for three selected years.

The last column of Table 2 reports the results for a functional form where the food share depends on a quadratic form of the total consumption variable. While the squared consumption term is statistically significant, its presence adds almost nothing to the explanatory power of the model. More importantly, the δ_t coefficients on the year dummy variables are unchanged from their values in the linear specification, so it is very unlikely that the drift in the Engel curve was due to some misspecification in the choice of functional form. On this basis, log-linear form was the one used for eventually calculating the CPI bias expressed in Equations (4) and (5).

Table 2. Food-at-home Engel curve regression results

	β	$|t|$	β	$|t|$
ln CPI-deflated current consumption	−0.081	80.19	0.030	1.73
[ln CPI-deflated current consumption]^2			−0.006	6.54
Share of food eaten out	−0.176	18.00	−0.177	18.22
Demographic variables				
ln household size	0.080	30.84	0.082	31.54
Share of household ≤ 2 years old	−0.006	1.11	−0.007	1.42
Share of household 3–14-year-old boys	0.015	3.51	0.013	3.20
Share of household 15–17-year-old boys	0.040	6.43	0.040	6.36
Share of household 3–14-year-old girls	0.010	2.50	0.009	2.16
Share of household 15–17-year-old girls	0.011	1.55	0.011	1.47
Maori or Pacific Islander household head	0.005	2.99	0.005	2.91
Female household head	0.003	3.24	0.003	3.42
Age of household head	0.001	19.21	0.001	19.65
Household type				
Couple with no children	0.005	2.54	0.002	0.96
Sole-parent household	−0.010	3.81	−0.013	4.90
Couple with children	0.002	0.67	−0.001	0.31
Mixed family	−0.004	1.25	−0.007	2.11
Nonfamily household	−0.010	3.45	−0.012	4.16
Dwelling tenure variables				
Rent-free (unowned)	0.035	10.95	0.036	11.31
Owned with mortgage	0.005	4.40	0.005	4.66
Owned without mortgage	0.019	13.96	0.019	14.07
Year dummies				
1985	−0.003	1.71	−0.003	1.65
1986	−0.008	4.16	−0.008	4.14
1987	−0.008	4.49	−0.009	4.57
1988	−0.014	7.28	−0.014	7.25
1989	−0.015	7.47	−0.015	7.46
1990	−0.008	3.81	−0.008	3.75
1991	−0.006	2.97	−0.006	2.91
1992	−0.013	6.16	−0.013	6.13
1993	−0.015	8.14	−0.015	8.12
1994	−0.015	7.14	−0.015	7.15
1995	−0.021	10.25	−0.021	10.29
1996	−0.023	11.16	−0.023	11.18
1997	−0.027	13.15	−0.027	13.16
1998	−0.025	12.18	−0.025	12.17
2001	−0.017	7.46	−0.017	7.48
Intercept	0.842	85.45	0.326	3.87
R^2	0.336		0.338	
F-test (slopes = 0)	$F_{(34, 52851)} = 534.8 \ (p < 0.00)$		$F_{(35, 52850)} = 625.3 \ (p < 0.00)$	
F-test H_0: Year dummies = 0	$F_{(15, 52851)} = 26.7 \ (p < 0.00)$		$F_{(15, 52850)} = 26.9 \ (p < 0.00)$	

Notes: Estimates weighted by population sampling weights and *t*-statistics based on heteroscedastically consistent SEs. $N = 52\,886$. The excluded household type is sole occupant and the excluded tenure status is renting. Expenditures and food share based on current consumption expenditures, which are defined in text.

Table 3 presents findings in relation to two sensitivity analyses. The first analysis ignores the sampling weights, since there is debate about the use of these in regressions (Deaton, 1997). The results for this are almost exactly the same as those in Table 2, so the drift in the Food Engel curves does not appear to be due to the use of incorrectly weighted estimates. The second analysis uses an instrumental variable (IV) procedure previously explained and justified. The standard errors in Table 3 show that for both estimation methods the cumulative bias is statistically significant over all periods except 1984–1985.

Table 3. Sensitivity analysis results for food Engel curve regressions

	Ignoring weights		IV estimates[a]	
	β	$|t|$	B	$|t|$
ln CPI-deflated current consumption	−0.082	111.64	−0.093	44.72
Share of food eaten out	−0.172	19.74	−0.155	14.90
Demographic variables				
ln household size	0.083	39.48	0.089	30.73
Share of household ≤ 2 years old	−0.007	1.57	−0.022	3.95
Share of household 3–14-year-old boys	0.012	3.47	0.001	0.30
Share of household 15–17-year-old boys	0.038	6.85	0.035	5.60
Share of household 3–14-year-old girls	0.010	2.68	−0.002	0.44
Share of household 15–17-year-old girls	0.008	1.41	0.005	0.71
Maori or Pacific Islander household head	0.007	5.96	0.002	1.35
Female household head	0.002	2.77	0.002	2.58
Age of household head	0.001	26.67	0.001	14.45
Household type				
Couple with no children	0.004	2.48	0.007	3.06
Sole-parent household	−0.007	3.50	−0.008	3.17
Couple with children	0.000	0.03	0.004	1.34
Mixed family	−0.004	1.43	−0.003	0.92
Nonfamily household	−0.011	4.18	−0.009	2.98
Dwelling tenure variables				
Rent-free (unowned)	0.032	16.05	0.032	9.61
Owned with mortgage	0.004	3.83	0.007	6.28
Owned without mortgage	0.017	16.05	0.019	14.16
Year dummies				
1985	−0.003	1.68	−0.003	1.43
1986	−0.008	4.16	−0.008	4.34
1987	−0.008	4.53	−0.009	4.76
1988	−0.014	8.09	−0.014	7.21
1989	−0.013	7.18	−0.014	7.26
1990	−0.008	4.41	−0.008	4.06
1991	−0.006	3.25	−0.006	2.86
1992	−0.011	5.85	−0.013	6.21
1993	−0.014	8.34	−0.015	8.35
1994	−0.015	7.79	−0.016	7.58
1995	−0.021	10.71	−0.021	10.40
1996	−0.023	11.57	−0.023	11.20
1997	−0.027	13.94	−0.027	13.28
1998	−0.024	12.21	−0.024	11.88
2001	−0.017	8.54	−0.016	7.11
Intercept	0.855	119.04	0.956	48.68
R^2	0.340		0.334	
F-test (slopes = 0)	$F_{(34,52469)} = 799.5\ (p < 0.00)$		$F_{(34,52603)} = 417.1\ (p < 0.00)$	
F-test H_0: Year dummies = 0	$F_{(15,52469)} = 29.7\ (p < 0.00)$		$F_{(15,52603)} = 27.0\ (p < 0.00)$	
F-test (instrument = 0 in first stage regression)			$F_{(1,52469)} = 11594\ (p < 0.00)$	
F-test (Hausman test for consistency of OLS)			$F_{(1,52468)} = 41.9\ (p < 0.00)$	

Notes: See Table 2.

[a] ln CPI-deflated total consumption is treated as the endogenous variable, with ln CPI-deflated disposable income as the instrument.

A Hausman test of differences between the two analyses in Table 3 indicated no statistically significant differences between the first one (an OLS procedure) and the second one (an IV). Also, there is only a small practical effect from using IV: the coefficient on the consumption variable increases in absolute value terms from −0.081 to −0.093. Moreover, the pattern for the coefficients on the dummy variables for each survey year is very similar to when OLS is used, again corroborating the view that the drift in the food Engel curve was neither spurious nor dependent upon the choice of regression procedure.

4 Estimating the bias

The apparent drift in the food Engel curves might have been caused by some growth in real expenditures that was unmeasured. Barring any understatement in the reporting of nominal expenditures, which is unlikely, one can conjecture that the growth was the Engel-drift bias.

To verify this conjecture, the cost-of-living bias proposed in Equation (5) had to be estimated, bearing in mind that an estimate of the exponential parameter $\bar{\gamma}$ was needed to remove any effect upon the bias arising from differences in inflation rates between food and non-food items. One way of deriving a value of $\bar{\gamma}$ was to work backwards from estimates of the own-price elasticity of food demand, e_{ii}. This is because e_{ii} can be expressed as:

$$e_{ii} = -1 + \frac{\gamma - \alpha\beta}{w} \qquad (6)$$

In this equation, α is the share of food in the overall price index. The other parameters are defined according to Equations (1) and (2). Also in this equation, it is possible to obtain an estimate of $\bar{\gamma}$ by obtaining estimates for e_{ii}, for β, for the mean food budget share, expressed as $\bar{\omega}$, and for the share of food in the CPI, α.

For obtaining an estimate of e_{ii}, we used the Frisch (1959) method for additive demand systems. This method enables e_{ii} to be derived from the food budget share, from the expenditure elasticity of food demand (η), and from a parameter, ω, known as the 'flexibility of money':

$$e_{ii} = \frac{1}{\omega}\eta_i(1 - w_i\eta_i) - w_i\eta_i \qquad (7)$$

For the flexibility of money ω, we used an estimate of –2.2 percentage points, one that arises from the flexibility being a function of per capita Gross National Product, x, according to an estimated equation of the form, $\omega=36X^{-0.36}$ (Lluch et al., 1977).[8] For the other parameters, we used a mean food budget share of 0.187 (based upon Table 1), an estimate of $\beta = -0.081$ (based upon Table 2), and a food share in the CPI of 0.179.

From using these values, we obtained an estimate for $\bar{\gamma}$ of 0.109. By comparison, Hamilton (2001) found a value of $\bar{\gamma}=0.07$ for the USA. Others

8   The Gross Domestic Product (GDP) estimates are used rather than GNP, with real per capita GDP averaging $23,500 between 1984 and 2001 (in 1995 prices) and the GDP deflator being 422.6 in 1995 and 40.5 in 1970. Combining this information with an exchange rate in 1970 of US$1.12 per NZ$ gives an estimate of X=2,500.

found $\bar{\gamma}$ to be in the range of 0.09–0.16 for other countries (see e.g. Beatty and Larson, 2005).

The Engel-drift bias in the New Zealand CPI implied by these estimates is reported in Table 4. There are two sets of estimates, one using the OLS results from Table 2 and one using the IV results from Table 3. The cumulative bias peaked in 1997, at either 0.174 (OLS) or 0.154 (IV). This was slightly lower in 1998 and considerably lower in 2001. It is difficult to know how much weight can be placed on the results for 2001 since there may have had been changes in the operation of the HES when it moved from an annual to a triennial frequency.

When the cumulative bias is converted into an annual average it exhibits a declining trend (columns 6 and 7 of Table 4). Across the whole period the average of the annual bias estimates is 0.016 using the OLS results and 0.014 using the IV results. In all the years except for four (the first two years plus 1991 and 2001) the average annual bias is between one and two percentage points.

Table 4. Cumulative CPI bias, SEs and annual average bias estimates

Years	OLS estimates (Column 1, Table 2)		IV Estimates (Column 2, Table 3)		Annual average bias estimates	
	Cumulative bias	SE	Cumulative bias	SE	OLS	IV
1984–1985	0.034	(0.022)	0.024	(0.019)	0.034	0.024
1984–1988	0.071	(0.021)	0.065	(0.019)	0.035	0.032
1984–1987	0.053	(0.022)	0.051	(0.019)	0.018	0.017
1984–1988	0.081	(0.021)	0.069	(0.019)	0.020	0.017
1984–1989	0.099	(0.022)	0.082	(0.019)	0.020	0.016
1984–1990	0.074	(0.024)	0.066	(0.020)	0.012	0.011
1984–1991	0.056	(0.025)	0.046	(0.022)	0.008	0.007
1984–1992	0.098	(0.023)	0.087	(0.020)	0.012	0.011
1984–1993	0.123	(0.020)	0.112	(0.017)	0.014	0.012
1984–1994	0.110	(0.023)	0.105	(0.020)	0.011	0.010
1984–1995	0.140	(0.022)	0.126	(0.019)	0.013	0.011
1984–1996	0.131	(0.022)	0.115	(0.020)	0.011	0.010
1984–1997	0.174	(0.021)	0.154	(0.019)	0.013	0.012
1984–1998	0.161	(0.021)	0.137	(0.019)	0.012	0.010
1984–2001	0.102	(0.025)	0.082	(0.022)	0.006	0.005
			Average of averages		0.016	0.014

Notes: Cumulative bias is estimated using Equation 5 in the text, with parameters from either Table 2 (OLS) or Table 3 (IV) and a value of $\bar{\gamma}$ of 0.109. SEs are calculated from the delta method, using a heteroscedastically robust variance–covariance matrix.

To see if the results are sensitive to the value of this parameter, two alternative values for $\bar{\gamma}$ were tried: 0.07 and 0.13. The lower value was used by Hamilton 2001) when applying Equation (5) to his USA sample. The higher value is the weighted mean of the $\hat{\gamma}$ estimates reported by Beatty and Larsen for four subsets of their Canadian sample. If the lower value of $\hat{\gamma}=0.07$ is used, the Engel-drift estimates are slightly higher, averaging at 0.019 (OLS) and 0.016 (IV). If the higher one is used, the estimates are slightly lower, averaging 0.014 (OLS) and 0.012 (IV). These results suggest that an annual average bias of somewhat over one percentage point is reasonably robust.

5 Conclusions

In this article, a cost-of-living bias was estimated for the New Zealand CPI, beginning from food-budget Engel curves for demographically similar households at different points in time. The econometric estimates indicate a persistent and substantial downward drift in the Engel curves for the 17 years from 1984 to 2001. This drift suggests unmeasured growth in real expenditures. The annual average of the Engel-drift bias was typically between one to two percentage points, with a preferred point estimate of 1.4 percentage points.

The estimated bias is considerably higher than the level of bias assumed by New Zealand statistical authorities. It is also quite similar to estimates made with the same method for the USA and Canada. For the period between 1981 and 1999, Hamilton (2001) found for the USA CPI an annual bias of 1.5 percentage points. For 1978–2000, Beatty and Larson (2005) found for the Canadian CPI an annual bias of between 1.3 percentage points for single adult elderly households, and 1.9 percentage points for couples with children.

The cross-country similarities suggest that Engel-drift bias is not restricted to the USA CPI, contrary to claims made by some statistical agencies (Edwards, 1997; Fenwick, 1997; Lequiller, 1997). In the specific context of this article, the claim made by the New Zealand Government Statistician that 'I do not believe that the level of bias estimated in the Boskin report for the USA CPI is relevant to New Zealand' (Morris, 1997, p. 50) is clearly not supported.

An important implication is that the Reserve Bank of New Zealand may have to reconsider its inflation target. If the goal of a target is to preserve the value of money, targeted inflation must not deviate substantially around some estimate of the cost-of-living bias. The findings in this article are not far from the presumption of there being a one percentage point bias in the New Zealand CPI (Sherwin, 2000). They are consistent with an old inflation target of 0–2 per cent. The revised inflation target since 2002, of 1–3 per cent, is too high relative to our findings. Furthermore, the trend shown in Table 4 is that of a bias that will progressively decline in succeeding years.

References

Barrett, G. and Brzozowski, M. (2010). Using Engel curves to estimate the bias in the Australian CPI. *Economic Record*, 86(272), 1–14.

Beatty, T. and Larsen, E. (2005). Using Engel curves to estimate bias in the Canadian CPI as a cost of living index. *Canadian Journal of Economics*, 38, 482–499.

Beatty, Timothy K. M. and Crossley, Thomas F. (2012). Lost in translation: What do Engel curves tell us about the cost of living? University of Minnesota, unpublished paper.

Boskin, M. (1996). *Final Report of the Advisory Commission to Study the Consumer Price Index.* S.Prt 104–172, US Government Printing Office, Washington, DC.

Boyle, G. and Eckhold, K. (1997). Capital structure choice and financial market liberalization: evidence from New Zealand. *Applied Financial Economics*, 7, 427–437.

Costa, D. (2001). Estimating real income in the United States from 1888 to 1994: correcting CPI bias using Engel curves. *Journal of Political Economy*, 109, 1288–1310.

Crawford, A., Fillion, J.-F. and Laflèche, T. (1998). Is the CPI a suitable measure for defining price stability? In *Price Stability, Inflation Targets and Monetary Policy*, Proceedings of a Conference held by the Bank of Canada, May 1997, Bank of Canada, Ottawa, 39–73.

Deaton, A. (1997). *The Analysis of Household Surveys: A Microeconometric Approach to Development Policy.* Baltimore: Johns Hopkins University Press.

Deaton, A. and Muellbauer, J. (1980). An almost ideal demand system. *American Economic Review*, 70, 312–326.

Ebert, C. (1994). Defining price stability: what should we aim for? *Reserve Bank Bulletin*, 57, 23–34.

Edwards, R. (1997). Measuring inflation in Australia. In L. M. Ducharme (ed.), *Bias in the CPI: Experiences from Five OECD Countries.* Ottawa: Statistics Canada, 5–12.

Fenwick, D. (1997). The Boskin report from a United Kingdom perspective. In L. M. Ducharme (ed.), *Bias in the CPI: Experiences from Five OECD Countries.* Ottawa: Statistics Canada, 45–52.

Frisch, R. (1959). A complete system for computing all direct and cross demand elasticities in a model with many sectors. *Econometrica*, 27, 177–196.

Gibson, J., Stillman, S. and Le, T. (2008). CPI bias and real living standards in Russia during the transition. *Journal of Development Economics*, 87, 140–160.

Gibson, John and Scobie, Grant (2010). Using Engel curves to estimate CPI bias in a small, open, inflation-targeting economy. *Applied Financial Economics*, 20(17), 1327–1335.

Hamilton, B. (2001). Using Engel's law to estimate CPI bias. *American Economic Review*, 91, 619–630.

Hausman, J. (2003). Sources of bias and solutions to bias in the consumer price index. *Journal of Economic Perspectives*, 17, 23–44.

Larsen, E. (2007). Does the CPI mirror the cost of living? Engel's law suggests not in Norway. *Scandinavian Journal of Economics*, 109, 177–195.

Lequiller, F. (1997). Does the French CPI overstate inflation? In L. M. Ducharme (ed.), *Bias in the CPI: Experiences from Five OECD Countries.* Ottawa: Statistics Canada, 25–43.

Lluch, C., Powell, A. and Williams, R. (1977). *Patterns in Household Demand and Saving.* Oxford: Oxford University Press for the World Bank.

Morris, J. (1997). Managing Measurement Limitations in the Consumers Price Index. Consumers Price Index Revision Advisory Committee, New Zealand.

Olivia, Susan and Gibson, John (2013). Using Engel curves to measure CPI bias for Indonesia. *Bulletin of Indonesian Economic Studies*, 49(1),85-101.

Sherwin, M. (2000). Strategic choices in inflation targeting: the New Zealand evidence. In M. Blejer, A. Ize, A. Leone and S. Werland (eds) *Inflation Targeting in Practice: Strategic and Operational Issues and Application to Emerging Market Economies*. Washington: International Monetary Fund, 15–27.

Special Consumer Price Indices for Particular Groups of Households

Alan Bentley

Abstract

Dissemination of consumer price indices for particular groups of households in New Zealand has been limited to the Beneficiaries Price Index in 1975 and the Superannuitants Price Index 1993–99, supplemented with research studies by Jackson (1978) and Statistics New Zealand (2013a). How and why these indices have been calculated is unearthed along with discussion on why official production has not been more widespread.

1 Introduction

This chapter reviews consideration and availability of price indices for specific groups of households in New Zealand over the past century. The impact of changes in the coverage and purpose of the Consumers Price Index (CPI) is outlined to provide the context of discussions on whose inflation is of interest and why. The necessity of a comprehensive household budget survey, to provide expenditure weights for particular groups of households, is highlighted. The evolution of such surveys serves as a backdrop to the possibilities available to construct group-specific consumer price indices. Availability of group-specific indices in New Zealand is compared with international practice. Finally, the discussion is brought up-to-date by considering a feasibility study undertaken for the 2013 CPI Advisory Committee.

2 Changing focus of the CPI

Consideration of special group indices is closely related to questions regarding the purpose and construction of the headline measure of consumer price change. Indeed, group-specific indices can be considered mini-CPIs for a particular group with a specific purpose in mind. In contrast, if only one CPI is published then this leads to compromises in the design to meet multiple uses, or an index that only fully meets one particular purpose.

Today's CPI measures the change in price of goods and services acquired by New Zealand-resident private households. It is an aggregate measure which represents the price change experienced on average by households. Production of a single CPI to meet multiple purposes is reflected in the current design which is not purely aligned with any one purpose. The 2013 CPI Advisory Committee recommended that the principal use of the CPI is to inform monetary policy setting, and acknowledged that the design of the CPI is a compromise between the principal use and other uses such as adjusting a range of public and private payments.[1]

Figure 1. Evolution of special indices for particular groups of households

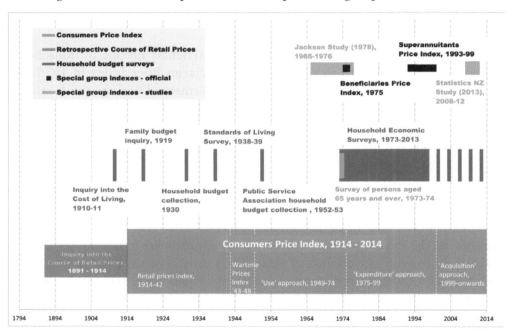

The design of the CPI has evolved over time as methods, data availability and the primary focus of the index have changed. Material modifications to design features of the CPI, worth noting in the context of considering price change for particular groups in society, are noted in this section. For a more comprehensive account of the history of consumer price indices in New Zealand see Forbes and colleagues (2012).

2.1 Retail Prices Index, 1914–42

The focus of the early CPI, then known as the Retail Prices Index, calculated between 1914 and 1942, was on understanding price change as it affects the 'cost of living'. *The Report on the Cost of Living in New Zealand, 1891–1914*, which

1   Statistics New Zealand (2013c).

retrospectively calculated price indices back to 1891 from retailers' historical records of prices, and outlined the founding principles of the ongoing production of the Retail Prices Index from 1914, clearly states the emphasis:[2]

> It is said that the "pinching shoe" of rising prices has been at the root of much social discontent . . . To the average man no subject is of greater interest than that which directly touches his pocket and modifies his spending-power . . . The general level of prices, or the purchasing-power of money, is an abstraction which in itself is mainly of academic interest. What touches every one is the cost of living.

The scope of the initial index was limited to food and house-rent.[3] The food group included a small number of non-food groceries, namely: starch, blue, soap and tobacco. The limited coverage was justified firstly on the grounds that food and rent covered over 50 per cent of total household expenditure according to the collection of household budgets by the Labour Department in 1910–11. Moreover, coverage was considered to be even greater for households with expenditure below the average of all households:

> . . . these commodities become more and more important in cases where the expenditure is limited below the average. Food and shelter are the primary needs which must be satisfied before all others.

The Industrial Conciliation and Arbitration Act 1894 established the Court of Arbitration to adjudicate in industrial disputes.[4] Impartial evidence on the 'cost of living', notably provided by the Retail Prices Index, was a critical input into their wage determinations.

2.2 Wartime Prices Index 1943–48

In December 1942, the Government announced its intention to stabilise prices of essential commodities and services.[5] The plan was two-fold: a price-control policy aimed at limiting price increases; and use of the Wartime Prices Index to automatically adjust wage and salary rates. From a population group perspective it is interesting to note discussion on the variation between households:

> The index thus relates to the essential requirements entering into the cost of living of the average New Zealand household, and is not limited to what is commonly termed the "working-class" standard of living. In this connection it may be noted that in New Zealand social stratification does not show the wide cleavages common to older countries, industrialization is limited, and the

2   New Zealand Government (1915).
3   Prices for a fuel and light group were also collected, but not initially included in the main inquiry due to the variation in which these commodities (notably: wood, coal, gas, and electricity) were predominately used in different geographic regions.
4   Holt (1986).
5   New Zealand Government (1944).

dispersion of incomes relatively small, these factors making for a more uniform standard of living than is possible in countries with more complex social and economic structures.

2.3 Consumers Price Index 1949–74

The 1948 Index Committee made recommendations to widen the scope of the index so that it was no longer restricted to necessities:[6]

> While, in the past, considerable emphasis has been given to the criterion of "essentiality" in the selection of commodities and services for inclusion in retail price indices, the objective in modern index-number making is to include within the scope of a retail prices index all commodities and services used by the consumer group or groups to which the index relates . . . the Committee has not excluded any group of commodities and/or services because that particular class of living expenditure was regarded as non-essential or socially undesirable.

The widening of the coverage was not without bounds however. Notably, private motoring and alcoholic liquors were omitted.

The 1948 committee concluded that the variations in living habits in New Zealand were less pronounced than in most other countries, and therefore the index should not be limited to any "given economic group" or "specified type of community". However, discussion of the weighting methods used did note that the index was intended to be most representative for "family living-conditions", and that "the living-costs of persons not living as a family were not directly represented in the index":

> . . . the Committee did not select a "typical" family on which to base the pattern of the index, but relied on aggregate consumption statistics as the basis of the weighting. However, the index is intended to apply more particularly to family living-conditions . . . a general index can only apply to typical conditions, and special indices with probably very different weighting patterns would be necessary to represent correctly the expenditure patterns of "lodgers" and "roomers." . . . Newly established families or families just moved to a new locality would have abnormal expenditure patterns which would not necessarily be well represented by any general consumers' price index.

The 1955 revision further increased the scope of the index:[7]

> . . . there is a tendency to more liberal thinking on the part of the index number statisticians, so that commodities lately regarded as luxuries are now accepted as conventional necessaries . . . The inclusion of alcoholic liquor is a kindred example . . .

6   New Zealand Government (1948).
7   Department of Statistics (1956).

Coverage of the CPI again increased slightly in the 1965 revision, primarily due to a change in the conceptual treatment of consumer durables, and a scope change to explicitly include expenditure by newly established households.[8]

The variation of individual household expenditure from average household expenditure was discussed. It was concluded that the "likenesses in [households'] modes of living are generally greater than the differences", and again it was thought that "variations in living habits are less pronounced in New Zealand than in most other countries, so that there is not the strong need here to design special indices for groups of particular income range, occupational status category etc."

2.4 Consumers Price Index 1975–99

The 1971 CPI Advisory Committee recommendation to revise the CPI to be based on "actual expenditure rather than, as at present, on actual or notional consumption" was implemented in 1975.[9] In modern day terms,[10] this was a change from the 'use' approach to an 'expenditure' approach, which combined elements of the 'acquisition' and 'payment' approaches.

The difference between these approaches is due to timing differences and conceptual coverage between households' 'payment', 'acquisition' and 'use' of some commodities. The major impact of the different approaches is on the measurement of housing, interest and insurance.[11] The value of home grown fruit and vegetables was also excluded in the revised index, in line with the conceptual change, as there is no monetary expenditure attached to the consumption of these products.

The choice of the appropriate approach depends on the use of the price index. The International Labour Organization's (2003) *Resolution Concerning Consumer Price Indices* provides the following advice:

> The 'acquisition' approach is often used when the primary purpose of the index is to serve as a macroeconomic indicator. The 'payment' approach is often used when the primary purpose of the index is for the adjustment of compensation or income. Where the aim of the index is to measure changes in the cost of living, the 'use' approach may be most suitable.

The conceptual change can be viewed as the 1971 committee transitioning away from an index primarily focused on measuring changes in the 'cost of living' for wage adjustments to a more multi-purpose indicator of retail price change. An expenditure approach to index weights also facilitated development of the

8   Department of Statistics (1966).
9   New Zealand Government (1971).
10   See, for example, International Labour Organization (2003).
11   For further discussion of the practical differences between the approaches see Pike (2014).

proposed household budget survey (which began in 1973), since the expenditure concept is likely to be most easily reported by household respondents.

The potential to calculate special purpose indices looks to have been considered somewhat by the 1971 committee:

> It is not possible to have a single Consumers Price Index that will serve equally well all the purposes for which the index is used. It is proposed by the Committee that the concept of a single multi-purpose index be retained, but that, as far as possible, the items should be selected and the regimen so designed as to render the index adaptable for special purposes.

The 1978 CPI Advisory Committee continued to affirm the general-purpose nature of the CPI. The committee noted that historically the principal use of the CPI was adjustment of wages, but that the emphasis had widened to include the use of the index as a general measure of inflation and for "far-reaching economic policy decisions affecting the whole community".[12]

Both the 1978 and 1985 CPI Advisory Committees discussed suggestions for a special-purpose price index limited to "basics" or "necessities".[13] The committees rejected these suggestions, noting the practical difficulties of classifying items as "necessities" or "luxuries".

These two committees also discussed indices for special population, or socio-economic, groups. The 1978 committee noted the results of Jackson (1978), and both 1978 and 1985 committees referred to the Beneficiaries Price Index produced in 1975, to conclude that the movements in these group-specific indices were not significantly different from the CPI. It was thought this was in part due to these indices using the same underlying price data as the CPI. This led the 1978 committee to conclude:

> . . . the committee has no firm recommendation to make regarding the introduction of specific special-group consumer price indices . . . That if a retail price index for a special population group is introduced, it be based on relevant household expenditure statistics using price data directly applicable to the quality specifications of goods and services actually purchased by the special population.

The stance against special population indices was hardened in 1985 to a recommendation not to publish such indices on the grounds that these would be "resource-demanding and lead to public confusion".

The 1991 CPI Advisory Committee suggested ways to address the concerns raised in 1985, recommending that the Department of Statistics should consider the preparation of sub-indices for groups such as household types and income

---

12   New Zealand Government (1978).
13   New Zealand Government (1985).

levels.[14] They suggested resources could be obtained by producing additional indices on a "user-funded" basis, since they would meet a specific user need. This committee concluded that public confidence in the CPI could be maintained by sub-indices being produced on the same "methodological concepts" as the CPI so that there would be no alternative inconsistent all groups index.

The 1991 CPI Advisory Committee also discussed the use of expenditure weights from the total expenditure of all households, sometimes referred to as "plutocratic" weights. They noted that using aggregate expenditure means that households with above average expenditure have a greater influence in determination of the weights. This committee recommended that the Department of Statistics investigate the feasibility of using "democratic" weights, where each household is given equal importance.

2.5 Consumers Price Index 1999–2014

A further conceptual change took place in 1999 to remove interest payments from the headline CPI to better align with the 'acquisition' approach.[15] This represented a partial implementation of the 1997 CPI Advisory Committee recommendation that a set of three measures of consumer price change should be produced using each of the 'acquisition', 'payment' and 'use' approaches, and that the acquisition measure, excluding interest, should be known as the official CPI.[16] In 2001, Statistics New Zealand decided not to seek funding to produce the two additional measures, using payment and use approaches, reflecting an internal view (also expressed by the Advisory Committee on Economic Statistics) that improvements to existing price indices and other macro-economic statistics were a higher priority.[17]

The 1997 CPI Advisory Committee discussed the Superannuitants Price Index (SPI), a research index for superannuitant households published from 1995, and other population sub-group indices. The committee noted that there was "a case for measurement of well-being for population sub-groups", and that the SPI needed methodological and conceptual refinements but that such development work was not a high priority. Views expressed in the public submissions to the 1997 committee were both for and against the development of specific indices to meet the needs of sector groups.

The 2004 CPI Advisory Committee concluded that the headline measure of the CPI should remain an acquisition-based index and that a supplementary index (or indices) should be produced that would be more suited conceptually to measuring

14 New Zealand Government (1991).
15 Statistics New Zealand (2013b).
16 New Zealand Government (1997).
17 Statistics New Zealand (2004a).

changes in households' cost of living.[18] It was noted that the supplementary index (or indices) should take account of changes in the cost of living for different population subgroups. Example groups given were: superannuitants, wage and salary earners, low-income households and recipients of government transfer payments. In a media release about the 2004 committee's report, the Government Statistician said that he supported the potential value of these additional measures, but noted that current resources would not allow for the development of cost-of-living indices.[19] Funding was sought, but not obtained.

The call for additional indices was endorsed by the 2013 CPI Advisory Committee, which recommended that "Statistics NZ provides additional indices that reflect changes in the purchasing power of the incomes of particular subgroups of the population".[20] The 2013 committee recommended that Statistics New Zealand reduces the number of regional pricing centres in order to fund other CPI-related initiatives, including production of indices for population subgroups. They gave the following population subgroups as examples: ethnic groups (particularly Māori), government transfer recipients, income groups, and wage and salary earners.

3 Evolution of household budget surveys

The lack of special-group indices until 1975 is at least partly due to the absence of a comprehensive household budget survey prior to the Household Economic Survey, then called the New Zealand Household Survey, which commenced in 1973–74.[21] Calls were made for such a survey 60 years earlier, in 1915.[22] The required data and methods to produce price indices appropriate to specific groups were clearly known at that time:

> The usual method adopted to measure the cost of living for any group of persons is to obtain a typical budget of expenditure and then to measure the effects of changes in the price-level upon that budget . . . it is hoped that an expenditure inquiry may shortly be undertaken from which a typical actual budget for New Zealand may be evolved.

The call for a comprehensive family budget inquiry was repeated in 1948, which noted the potential application to group specific price indices:[23]

18   Statistics New Zealand (2004b).
19   Statistics New Zealand (2013b).
20   Statistics New Zealand (2013c).
21   The Household Economic Survey was known as the New Zealand Household Survey from 1973 to 1983, the New Zealand Household Expenditure and Income Survey from 1983 to 1993, the New Zealand Household Economic Survey from 1993 to 1995, and the Household Economic Survey from 1995 onwards.
22   New Zealand Government (1915).
23   New Zealand Government (1948).

In designing the basis of compilation of a consumers' price index, statistical experts favour the taking of a family budget inquiry. Indeed, if the application of the index is to be limited to any "given economic group" or to a "specified type of community", a family budget inquiry is necessary in order to ascertain the spending habits of the particular group or groups covered by the index.

The 1948 committee labelled early attempts at budget surveys as "uniformly disappointing". These early surveys all suffered from low response rates and consequently small sample sizes. The report gave a frank account of the problems encountered:

> . . . while the national virtues in spending habits were generously represented in the family budgets received, the national vices were curiously absent.

The committee outlined the key features of what they considered constituted a "properly designed" family budget inquiry conducted by "modern methods", to include interviews conducted by skilled enumerators of a random selection of sampled families. Table 1 shows the achieved sample size of each of the early family budget inquiries.

Table 1. Family budget inquiries, 1910–1939

Year of survey	Carried out by	Achieved sample size (families/households)
1910–11	Department of Labour	69
1919	Census and Statistics Department	109
1930	Census and Statistics Department	318
1938–39	Department of Scientific and Industrial Research	250*

* Survey population covered only tramwaymen and boot operatives

Information on household budgets was collected by the Public Service Association in 1952–53. These data were used, along with retail trade data from the Census of Distribution 1953, to weight the CPI in the 1955 revision.[24]

3.1 Household Economic Survey 1973–2013

By the mid-1960s it was becoming increasingly apparent that New Zealand's absence of a comprehensive household budget survey to weight the CPI was out of line with general international practice.[25] From 1966 some investigatory work was undertaken on the feasibility of such a survey.[26] In October 1969, the

24 Statistics New Zealand (1993).
25 New Zealand Government (1971).
26 Thorne (19––).

Technical Committee on Statistics recommended that a comprehensive household expenditure survey of over 10,000 budget-weeks, extending over 12 months, should be conducted by the Department of Statistics as soon as practicable.

A comprehensive household budget survey became a reality in 1973 with the Government accepting the 1971 CPI Advisory Committee recommendation that household expenditure surveys be instituted to provide the basis of the expenditure weighting for the CPI. Survey results were first published in May 1975, and were used to reweight the CPI for the March 1975 quarter. The achieved sample, for the first survey, comprised 3,812 households, representing 62.9 per cent of eligible households contacted.[27]

A major design feature that sets this survey apart from its predecessors was the use of an interviewer-administered recall questionnaire in addition to a self-completed two-week expenditure diary. The survey design was based on the United Kingdom's Family Expenditure Survey. The survey was conducted annually from 1973 to 1998. Comprehensive surveys have been run on a three-yearly timetable since, most recently in the year to June 2013.[28] Of interest from a population group perspective is the decision in the initial survey design to include collection of income data, in class intervals, to allow income-group analysis of expenditure.[29]

3.2 Survey of persons 65 years and over 1973–74

Another budget survey, the Survey of persons 65 years and over, 1973–74, was run alongside the Household Survey starting in the latter part of 1973. It was a joint initiative between the Department of Social Welfare and the Department of Statistics, and was used to weight the group-specific Beneficiaries Price Index in 1975. Field collection and survey operations were conducted by the Department of Statistics between November 1973 and June 1974.[30]

The sample for the survey was drawn from Social Security beneficiaries aged 65 years and over.[31] Participants numbered 2,303 people, out of 3,120 eligible people sampled. Expenditure data was collected in much the same way as the Household Survey, using an interviewer questionnaire of recall expenditure and a one-week diary. The survey also covered several other topics including food, health, work and leisure, and mobility and transport.

---

27 For the collection period July 1973–June 1974 (Department of Statistics, 1975b).
28 Since 2008, a shortened version of the Household Economic Survey that focuses on income data has been conducted in the years between comprehensive expenditure surveys.
29 Department of Statistics (1972).
30 Department of Statistics (1977).
31 The sample was drawn from people aged 65 years and over receiving a Superannuation Benefit, Age Benefit or War Veteran's Allowance in the period November 1973–January 1974 (Department of Statistics, 1975d).

4 Availability of group-specific indices

4.1 Beneficiaries Price Index 1975

The first formal attempt to construct a consumer price index for a particular group of the New Zealand population was the Beneficiaries Price Index, which was produced in 1975 at the request of Government.[32] The group-level weighting pattern was based on expenditure reported in the Survey of persons 65 years and over. Weights below this level were based on the expenditure pattern of households in the Household Survey where the head of the household was aged 65 and over. The index used the same underlying price data as the CPI; no additional price collection was undertaken.

The first Beneficiaries Price Index *News Release* stated that the "index will be compiled quarterly, and for all New Zealand only". Production of the Beneficiaries Price Index was stopped after a year. The 1978 CPI Advisory Committee did not explicitly state the reasons for ceasing production, but alluded to the circumstances at the time:

> At the request of the Government of the time the Department of Statistics did prepare an Age Beneficiaries Price Index [sic] in 1975 . . . the index was discontinued early in 1976. The index did not display movements significantly at variance from those of the Consumers Price Index . . .

Public pension policy was a hot topic in the 1970s.[33] A compulsory contributory superannuation scheme was set up in 1975. It was short-lived, however, as the general election of 29 November 1975 saw a change of government, and the scheme was repealed in 1976.

The 1985 CPI Advisory Committee was also elusive on the reasons for discontinuing the Beneficiaries Price Index, but again noted that the index did not show significantly different results from the CPI:[34]

> Movements recorded in the index, which was subsequently discontinued, were not significantly different from those measured by the CPI . . .

Both the 1978 and 1985 committees commented on the Beneficiaries Price Index using the same underlying price data as the CPI, noting that additional price collection would be desirable but resource demanding. They also thought that dissemination of more than one CPI could lead to "public confusion" or "undermine the special authoritative status" of the CPI.

The 1978 committee considered that a "properly constructed special-group

---

32   Department of Statistics (1975a).
33   Preston (2008).
34   New Zealand Government (1985).

index should use price data applicable to the quality specifications . . . purchased by the index subpopulation". The 1985 committee thought that using the same price data as the CPI may have been inappropriate "as the CPI is less sensitive to variations in its weighting pattern than to variations in current price data used in the index calculations".

Table 2. Beneficiaries Price Index 1975

	Beneficiaries Price Index			Consumers Price Index		
		Per cent change			Per cent change	
	Index	Quarterly	Annual	Index	Quarterly	Annual
1974 Q4	1000	–	–	1000	–	–
1975 Q1	1025	2.5	–	1031	3.1	–
1975 Q2	1063	3.7	–	1072	4.0	–
1975 Q3	1103	3.8	–	1111	3.6	–
1975 Q4	1155	4.7	15.5	1157	4.1	15.7

Source: Department of Statistics

Figure 2. Beneficiaries Price Index and CPI Expenditure Weights,
December quarter 1974

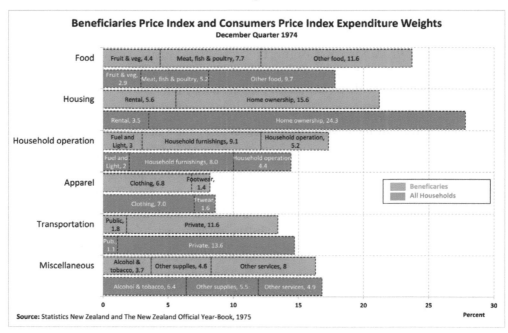

4.2 Jackson study

Jackson (1978) used the Household Survey (now called the Household Economic Survey) to calculate a 'consumers price index' for groups within the following categories of households:

- Total weekly income (10 groups)
- Income of head of household (11 groups)
- Age of head of household (8 groups)
- Occupation of head of household (10 groups)
- Family type (9 groups)

Figure 3. Jackson's 'Consumers Price Index' by weekly income groups

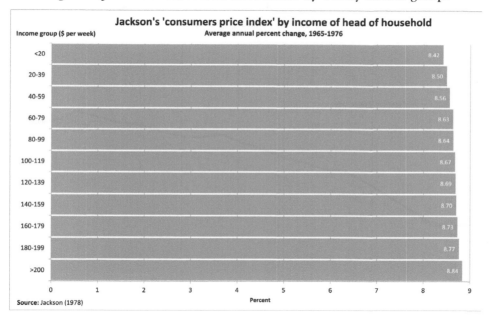

Indices were produced using the Household Survey 1974–75 to reweight the CPI at an eight expenditure-group level (and at a 15 expenditure-group level for income groups) for the period between the December 1974 quarter and the June 1977 quarter, and using annual price data 1965–76. Jackson found "very limited variability arising from household characteristics observed", but noted that this may have been a "statistical artefact" of the aggregate, expenditure-group-level reweight for each household group (i.e. due to the lack of household group-specific price data).

Jackson found the clearest pattern of any group was households grouped by income of head of household, shown in Figure 3 above. He noted that the differences "were not large but should be viewed as significant".

4.3 *Superannuitants Price Index*

Statistics New Zealand published a research series called the Superannuitants Price Index (SPI) in the mid-to-late 1990s.[35] The SPI measured change in consumer prices as it affected superannuitant households (a household with one or more people aged 60 or over who received New Zealand Superannuation and where a superannuitant had the highest income within the household). The SPI was published as two sub-indices, split by tenure of the household ('renters' and 'owner-occupiers'). The index time series are shown in Figure 4.

Figure 4. Superannuitants Price Index and Consumers Price Index

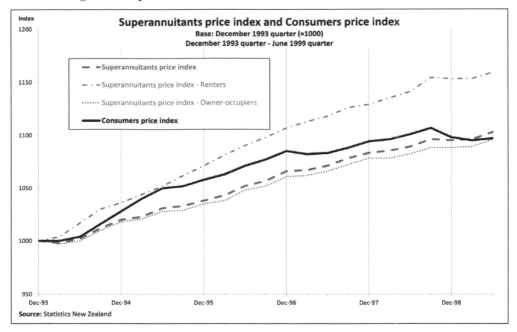

The index was discontinued after the June 1999 quarter. The main reasons given at the time were:[36]

- The 1997 CPI Advisory Committee recommended that further development of the SPI was a low priority.
- There were known limitations to the SPI when it was first constructed in 1995 (e.g. it assumed superannuitants purchased similar goods and services at similar outlets and prices to the average New Zealander). Several

---

35   First published in 1995, the time series is available for the period from the December 1993 quarter to the June 1999 quarter.
36   Ewing (1999).

organisations had expressed reservations about the usefulness of a measure with these sorts of limitations.

- A major conceptual change was made to the CPI in 1999 to exclude interest payments and section prices, which made the headline measure less suited as a living-cost index. The SPI was originally based on a living-cost definition. Continuing to calculate the SPI based on the new CPI definition would mean covering a reduced range of goods and services.
- It was stated that Statistics New Zealand would not be able to update superannuitant spending patterns as frequently as the CPI weights, with available resources. Consequently, the difference between the CPI and the SPI was viewed as likely to become less meaningful.

5 International practice of constructing special-purpose indices

The scope and coverage of CPIs varies internationally. Likewise, calculating and publishing CPIs for subpopulations also varies across countries. Some national statistical agencies produce official CPI estimates for subpopulations. Research on this topic has been done in many countries that do not have official estimates. The research and publication practices in selected countries are outlined in this section (summarised in Table 3).

The International Labour Organization's (2003) *Resolution Concerning Consumer Price Indices* provides the following advice:

> Significant differences in the expenditure patterns and/or price movements between specific population groups or regions may exist, and care should be taken to ensure that they are represented in the index. Separate indices for these population groups or regions may be computed if there is sufficient demand to justify the additional cost.

The Report by the Commission on the Measurement of Economic Performance and Social Progress, which has been helping to shape the future development of economic statistics internationally, highlighted the importance of understanding the distributional aspects of inflation from a welfare perspective.[37]

A point of particular relevance from a welfare perspective is the question about whose price index is evaluated. Often, conceptual discussions about price indices are conducted as if there were a single representative consumer. Statistical agencies calculate the increase in prices by looking at the costs of an average bundle of goods. However, different people buy different bundles of goods (e.g. poor people spend more on food and less on entertainment) and they may buy their goods and services in different types of stores (which sell 'similar' products at very different prices). When all prices move together, having different indices

37   Stiglitz et al. (2009).

for different people may not make much of a difference. But recently, with soaring oil and food prices, these differences may have become more marked and people at the bottom of the income distribution may have seen real incomes fall by much more than those at the top of the income distribution.

Table 3. Comparison of international practice

Country	CPI reference population	Population group consumer price indexes*	Household budget surveys		
			Title	Frequency	Achieved sample size (households)
New Zealand	Private resident households expenditure whilst in NZ	None	Household economic survey	3 yearly	3,000
Australia	Metropolitan private households (households in six state capital cities, Darwin and Canberra)	Five analytical living cost indexes (ALCIs): 1. employee 2. self-funded retiree 3. age pensioner 4. other government transfer recipient 5. pensioner and beneficiary (groups 3 and 4 combined)	Household expenditure survey	6 yearly	10,000
Canada	Private resident households expenditure	None	Survey of household spending	Yearly	18,000
Japan	All households	☐ income quintiles ☐ retired elderly households For head of household: ☐ age group ☐ occupation ☐ tenure	Family income and expenditure survey	Monthly	9,000
			National survey of family income and expenditure	5 yearly	57,000
United Kingdom	CPI – household expenditure in UK (including expenditure by foreign visitors) RPI – resident households (including expenditure abroad), excluding high-income and pensioner households	☐ four consumer price indexes (with different methods and/or coverage) ☐ retail price index pensioner indexes	Living cost and food survey	Yearly	6,000
United States of America	Urban households	Three consumer price indexes: 1. CPI – U (urban consumers) 2. CPI – W (wage earners and clerical workers) 3. CPI – E (aged 62 years and older)	Consumer expenditure survey	Yearly	36,000 (interview); 7,100 (diary)

*Current known official publication. Regional indexes excluded.

5.1 Australia

Australia's headline CPI is based on the 'acquisition' approach. The reference population is metropolitan private households (households in six state capital cities, Darwin and Canberra). This coverage represents about 64 per cent of all

Australian private households.[38]

The Australian Bureau of Statistics also publishes analytical living cost indices (ALCIs) for four household groupings, based on a 'payment' approach:[39]

- employee
- age pensioner (households whose principal source of income is the age pension or veterans affairs pension)
- other government transfer recipient (households whose principal source of income is a government pension or benefit other than the age pension or veterans affairs pension)
- self-funded retiree

In addition, a pensioner and beneficiary living cost index (PBLCI) is published which combines the age pensioner household and other government transfer recipient indices.

Analytical living cost indices have been published by the Australian Bureau of Statistics since June 2000. Initially quarterly indices were published once a year. They have been published quarterly since the September 2009 quarter.[40] From September 2009, most Australian social security pensions have been indexed by the greater of the CPI and the PBLCI. Pension rates are also adjusted for improvements in wages, as measured by male total average weekly earnings.[41]

The Australian Household Expenditure Survey is used to weight the Australian CPI and living cost indices. The 2009/10 sample was increased by about 3,000 households (compared with the 2003/04 survey) to include additional sampling of metropolitan households whose main source of income was a government pension, benefit and/or allowance.[42] The main purpose of the inclusion of this additional sample was to improve the commodity weighting of the PBLCI, to better reflect the different expenditure patterns of pensioner households compared with the general population. The achieved sample size for the 2009/10 survey was nearly 10,000 households, compared with an achieved sample size of about 3,000 households for New Zealand's Household Economic Surveys in 2009/10 and 2012/13.

---

38   Australian Bureau of Statistics (2011a).
39   Australian Bureau of Statistics (2012b). The 'payment' approach measures the change in the price of goods and services 'paid for' (regardless of the timing of 'acquisition' or 'use'). The major differences between the payment and acquisition approaches are: the inclusion of interest payments, the exclusion of net purchase of housing, and the use of total payments for insurance premiums under the payment approach. The acquisition approach uses net insurance payments (premiums paid less claims paid out).
40   Australian Bureau of Statistics (2011b).
41   Department of Families, Housing, Community Services and Indigenous Affairs (2012).
42   Australian Bureau of Statistics (2012a).

5.2 Canada

The reference population for Canada's CPI is private resident households.[43] It is available with a regional breakdown, but no further subpopulation CPIs are currently published. An analytical study of CPIs for different subgroups of the reference population found little difference in price change, for the period 1993–97, for the following three groups:[44]

• Low-income households
• Low-income senior citizens
• Senior citizens

CPI expenditure weights are based on the Survey of Household Spending, an annual survey which had a sample size of nearly 18,000 households in 2011.[45]

5.3 Japan

The reference population for Japan's CPI is households nationwide. Japan's CPI is also published for the following groups:[46]

• Income quintiles
• Retired elderly households
• Age group of household head
• Occupation of household head
• Tenure of dwelling of household head

Expenditure weights for Japan's CPI are updated from two household surveys. The Family Income and Expenditure Survey is a monthly survey of 9,000 households (one-person households are surveyed for three months, larger households for six months). The National Survey of Family Income and Expenditure runs every five years and has a sample size of 57,000 households.[47]

5.4 United Kingdom

Four consumer price indices are currently published in the UK:[48]

• Consumer Prices Index (CPI)
• Consumer Prices Index including owner occupiers' housing costs (CPIH)
• Retail Prices Index (RPI)
• Retail Prices Index calculated using the Jevons formula (RPIJ)

43   Statistics Canada (2013a).
44   Taktek (1998).
45   Statistics Canada (2013b).
46   Statistics Bureau of Japan (2010).
47   Statistics Bureau of Japan (2009).
48   Evans and Restieaux (2013).

The CPI is an acquisition-based index compiled using the methodology of the European Harmonised Index of Consumer Prices (HICP). HICPs exclude most elements of owner-occupied housing costs, due to lack of consensus on appropriate methods.[49] CPIH includes owner-occupied housing costs, using a 'rental equivalence' approach. The CPI reference population covers all UK households, including institutional households, and foreign visitors to the UK. Expenditure by UK households abroad is excluded.

The RPI includes mortgage interest payments, house depreciation, insurance, council tax, and house purchase costs (e.g. estate agents' and conveyancing fees).[50] The RPI uses the 'Carli' elementary aggregate formula (which does not meet international standards). The RPIJ uses the 'Jevons' elementary aggregate formula (which meets international standards). The RPI reference population excludes institutional households, pensioner households (households with at least 75 per cent of their income from state pensions and benefits), and high-income households (the top 4 per cent of the income distribution). RPI pensioner indices are published for one- and two-person pensioner households (pensioner households are not within the scope of the main RPI). Housing costs are excluded from these subpopulation indices.[51]

In 2011, the Institute for Fiscal Studies produced estimates of the Retail Prices Index for 2000–10 by income deciles, benefit dependency, age of head of household, family composition, and housing tenure.[52]

The sample size of the Living Cost and Food Survey, equivalent to New Zealand's Household Economic Survey, is around 6,000 responding households per year.[53]

5.5 United States of America

The Bureau of Labor Statistics publishes several CPIs with different reference populations. The CPI for all urban consumers (CPI-U) excludes households living in rural non-metropolitan areas, and institutional households. The CPI for urban wage earners and clerical workers (CPI-W) is based on the expenditure of households included in the CPI-U definition that also meet two requirements: more than half the household's income comes from clerical or wage occupations, and at least one of the household's earners has been employed for 37 weeks or more during the previous 12 months.

Since 1987, the Bureau of Labor Statistics has produced an experimental CPI

49   Eurostat (2004).
50   Office for National Statistics (2010).
51   Office for National Statistics (2013).
52   Levell and Oldfield (2011).
53   Office for National Statistics (2012).

for Americans aged 62 years and older (CPI-E).[54] The index is calculated using the same basket items, retail outlets, and price quotes as the headline CPI. The upper-level weighting is calculated from the expenditure patterns of older Americans.

Social security benefits are adjusted using the CPI for urban wage earners and clerical workers (CPI-W). Some policymakers have advocated using the CPI-E to adjust benefits instead. In 2009, the achieved sample size of the US Consumer Expenditure Survey, used to weight the CPIs, was about 36,000 in the interview survey and 7,100 in the diary survey.[55]

6 CPI Advisory Committee 2013 feasibility study

Statistics New Zealand undertook a feasibility study on producing indices for population subgroups, as part of the work undertaken for the 2013 CPI Advisory Committee.[56] The empirical investigation used data from existing collections to reweight the CPI for the specific spending patterns of particular groups of households. The following three population subgroupings were considered:

- ethnic groups (including Māori households)
- recipients of government transfer payments (superannuitants and beneficiaries)
- income groups

A 'payment' approach, which would be suitable for index(es) primarily used for compensation purposes, was explored in the feasibility study. The major difference between the 'payment' and 'acquisition' approaches is the inclusion of interest payments under the payment approach.

The study found that many population subgroups have expenditure weights that differ from the all-households expenditure weights (using information from the 2006/07 and 2009/10 Household Economic Surveys; see Figure 5a). Over the study period (2008–12), differences in expenditure patterns resulted in statistically significant differences in consumer price change for some population subgroups compared with all households.

Figure 5b shows the average annual per cent change over the study period for each group, and the associated expenditure-group-level contributions to change. The error bars are 95 per cent confidence intervals. They show the uncertainty in the estimates of price change, due to the sampling of households in the Household Economic Survey (which was used to calculate population subgroup expenditure weights for the feasibility study).

The 2013 committee welcomed the analysis in the feasibility study and recognised that there was a need for measures of consumer price change that

54   Stewart (2008).
55   Mathiowetz et al. (2011).
56   Statistics New Zealand (2013a).

Figure 5a. Feasibility study 2013 results – expenditure weights

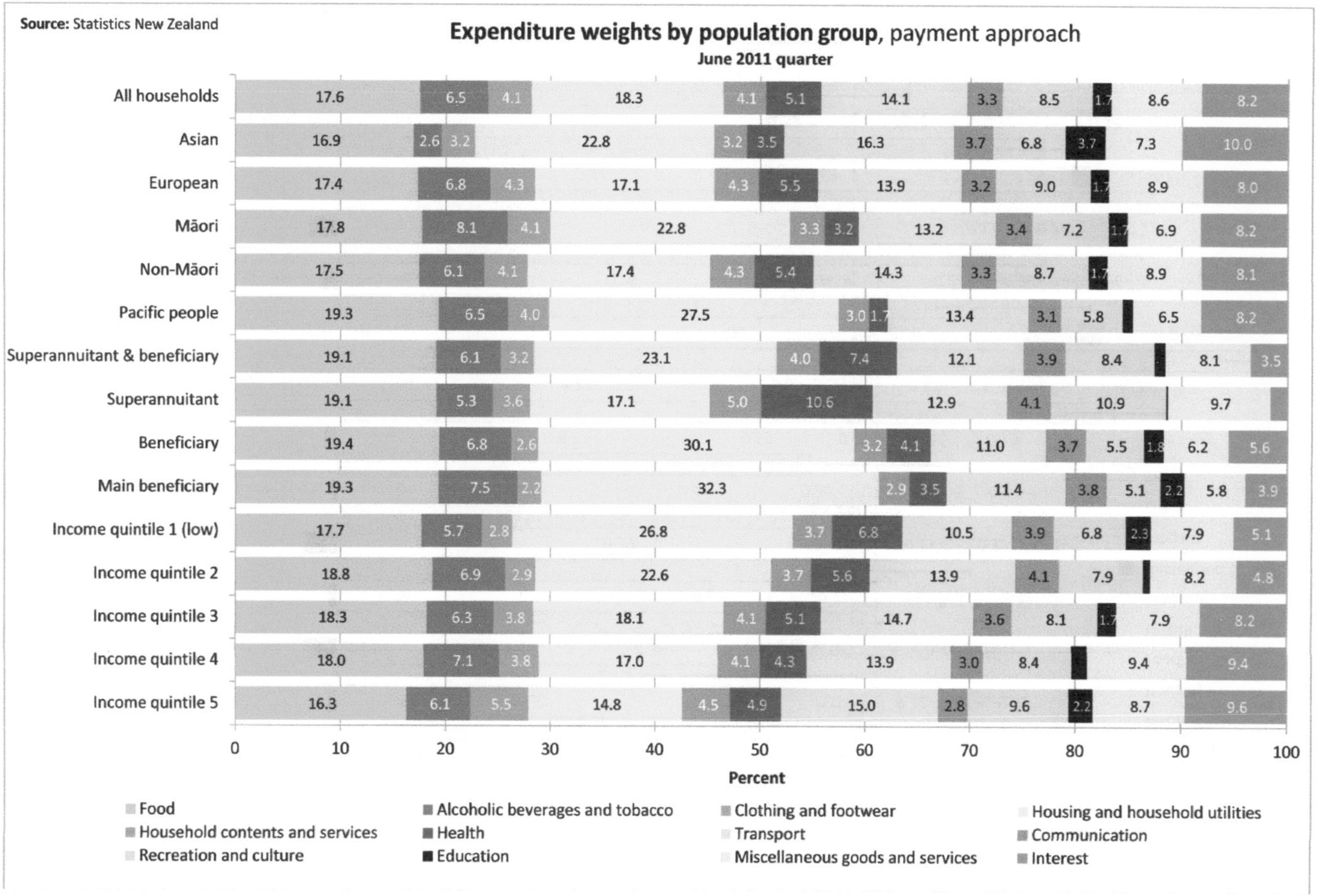

Source: Statistics New Zealand

Expenditure weights by population group, payment approach
June 2011 quarter

Population group	Food	Alcoholic beverages and tobacco	Clothing and footwear	Housing and household utilities	Household contents and services	Health	Transport	Communication	Recreation and culture	Education	Miscellaneous goods and services	Interest
All households	17.6	6.5	4.1	18.3	4.1	5.1	14.1	3.3	8.5	1.7	8.6	8.2
Asian	16.9	2.6	3.2	22.8	3.2	3.5	16.3	3.7	6.8	3.7	7.3	10.0
European	17.4	6.8	4.3	17.1	4.3	5.5	13.9	3.2	9.0	1.7	8.9	8.0
Māori	17.8	8.1	4.1	22.8	3.3	3.2	13.2	3.4	7.2	1.7	6.9	8.2
Non-Māori	17.5	6.1	4.1	17.4	4.3	5.4	14.3	3.3	8.7	1.7	8.9	8.1
Pacific people	19.3	6.5	4.0	27.5	3.0	1.7	13.4	3.1	5.8	1.7	6.5	8.2
Superannuitant & beneficiary	19.1	6.1	3.2	23.1	4.0	7.4	12.1	3.9	8.4		8.1	3.5
Superannuitant	19.1	5.3	3.6	17.1	5.0	10.6	12.9	4.1	10.9		9.7	
Beneficiary	19.4	6.8	2.6	30.1	3.2	4.1	11.0	3.7	5.5	1.8	6.2	5.6
Main beneficiary	19.3	7.5	2.2	32.3	2.9	3.5	11.4	3.8	5.1	2.2	5.8	3.9
Income quintile 1 (low)	17.7	5.7	2.8	26.8	3.7	6.8	10.5	3.9	6.8	2.3	7.9	5.1
Income quintile 2	18.8	6.9	2.9	22.6	3.7	5.6	13.9	4.1	7.9	1.7	8.2	4.8
Income quintile 3	18.3	6.3	3.8	18.1	4.1	5.1	14.7	3.6	8.1	1.7	7.9	8.2
Income quintile 4	18.0	7.1	3.8	17.0	4.1	4.3	13.9	3.0	8.4	1.7	9.4	8.2
Income quintile 5	16.3	6.1	5.5	14.8	4.5	4.9	15.0	2.8	9.6	2.2	8.7	9.6

Percent

Legend: Food; Alcoholic beverages and tobacco; Clothing and footwear; Housing and household utilities; Household contents and services; Health; Transport; Communication; Recreation and culture; Education; Miscellaneous goods and services; Interest

Figure 5b. Feasibility study 2013 results – price change

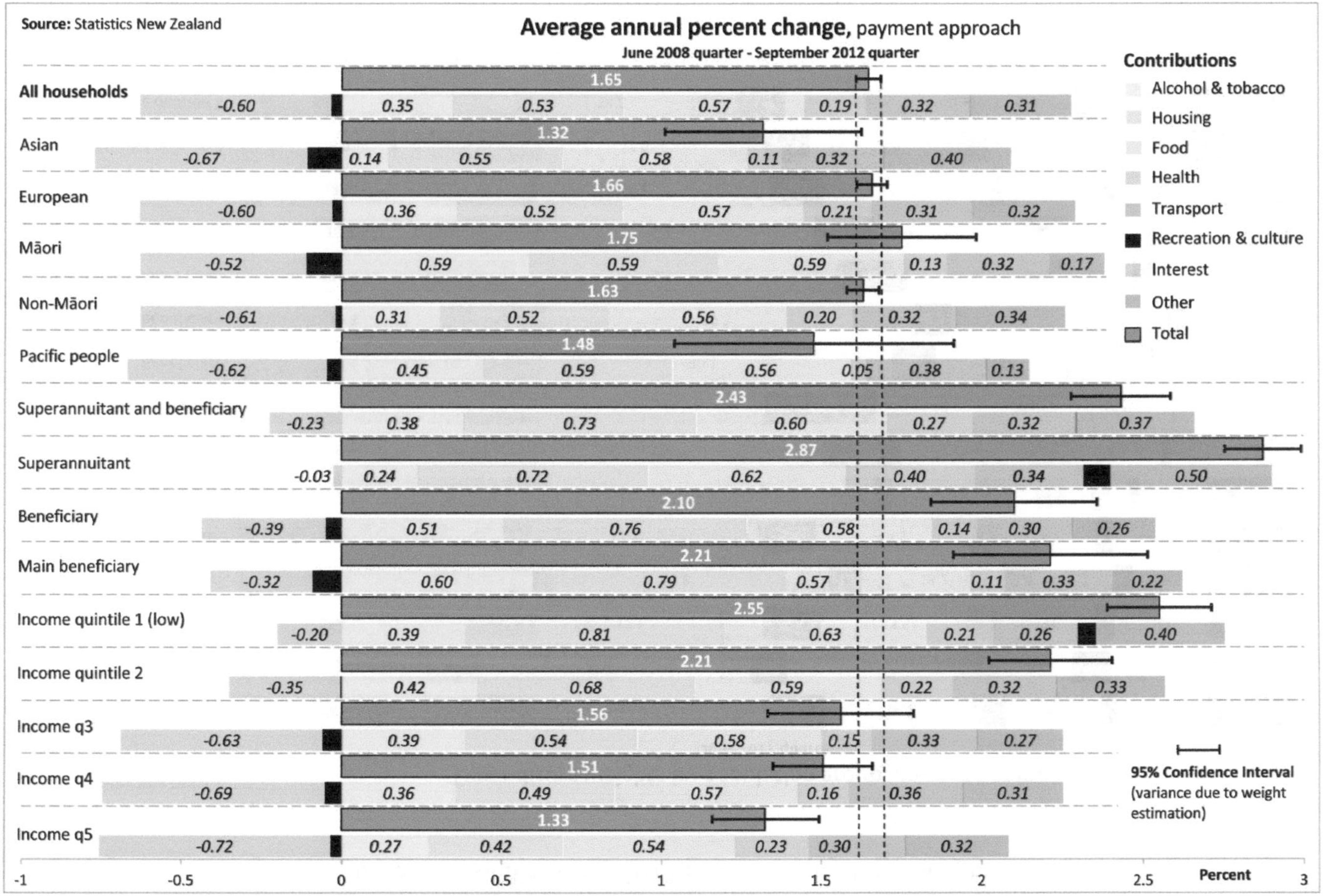

took into account the unique spending patterns of population subgroups, so recommended the publication of indices for population subgroups. A resource trade-off was suggested by the committee: to reduce the amount of regional price collection to fund, amongst other things, production of indices for population subgroups.[57]

7 Concluding remarks

The focus of the New Zealand CPI has changed over the past century from attention being devoted to measuring changes in the 'cost of living', primarily for wage adjustments, to increasing emphasis being placed on the use of the index for general inflation measurement, and most recently to the stated principal use: to inform monetary policy setting. Consequently, the coverage of household expenditure by the index has increased over time. This has seen a move from an index focused on the necessities of food and housing, to the present near universal coverage of consumption expenditure by resident households in New Zealand.

For much of the early part of the twentieth century, successive reviews of the CPI stated a view that the variation in expenditure patterns between New Zealand households was likely to be less than in some other countries. This view, combined with the lack of a comprehensive household budget survey, resulted in no formal attempts to construct group-specific indices until 1975.

Since the first modern Household Economic Survey in 1973–74, the construction of special indices for particular groups of households has been technically feasible. Views about the merits of producing such measures have varied over time (and no doubt from individual to individual). Concerns expressed about producing and disseminating such indices include:

- costs of production (or priority versus other areas of focus)
- validity of a reweight of the CPI, with no modification to underlying price data, to account for variations in commodities purchased by specific population groups
- quality of group-specific weight estimates from the Household Economic Survey (including consideration of the achieved sample sizes, and the consequential sampling variation of estimates, for particular groups of households)
- user needs and potential user confusion of multiple CPIs.

New Zealand is far from alone internationally in the tensions between the multitude of different uses of the CPI. This is highlighted by the variation in dissemination practices between countries. Some national statistical agencies

---

57   Statistics New Zealand (2013c).

produce official CPI estimates for population groups, and research has been done in many countries that do not have official estimates.

The recent past has seen CPI Advisory Committees making recommendations in favour of special consumer price indices for particular groups of households. The 1991 committee recommended that the Department of Statistics should consider the preparation of sub-indices, such as for household types and income levels, but these should be on a user-funded basis. The 1997 committee stated that consideration should be given to the extent to which the CPI is representative of the expenditure patterns of different socio-economic groups. This committee thought that a range of consumer price indices (on each of the 'acquisition', 'payment', and 'use' approaches), combined with a suite of real disposable-income measures, would be required to provide users with an appropriate indicator of the changing purchasing power of households.

The 2004 and 2013 committees both made explicit recommendations to produce supplementary indices for different population groups. Example groups given were: government transfer recipients (including superannuitants), income groups, wage and salary earners, and, by the 2013 committee only, ethnic groups.

Statistics New Zealand's 2013 feasibility study, undertaken for the 2013 CPI Advisory Committee, demonstrated that production of special group indices would be technically feasible, using existing data. Enhancements that would be required to the methods and data sources used in the study have been identified. Time will tell if user demand for special consumer price indices for particular groups of households is sufficiently persuasive to lead to their regular production and dissemination.

References

Australian Bureau of Statistics (2011a). *A guide to the consumer price index: 16th series*, 2011. September 2011. Available from www.abs.gov.au

Australian Bureau of Statistics (2011b). *Analytical living cost indexes for selected Australian household types*. March 2011. Available from www.abs.gov.au

Australian Bureau of Statistics (2012a). *Household expenditure survey and survey of income and housing, User guide*, Australia 2009–10. Available from www.abs.gov.au

Australian Bureau of Statistics (2012b). *Selected living cost indexes, Australia*. September 2012. Available from www.abs.gov.au

Department of Families, Housing, Community Services and Indigenous Affairs (2012). *More pension increases – pension indexation*. Available from www.fahcsia.gov.au

Department of Statistics (1956). Consumers' price index 1955 revision, Special supplement to November 1956 issue of *Monthly Abstract of Statistics*. Wellington: Government Printer.

Department of Statistics (1966). Consumers' price index 1965 revision, Special supplement to September 1966 issue of *Monthly Abstract of Statistics*. Wellington: Government Printer.

Department of Statistics (1972). *Household expenditure survey feasibility study*, Report of the departmental advisory committee to the Government Statistician. Oct 1972. Unpublished paper, Department of Statistics.

Department of Statistics (1975a). Beneficiaries price index, News release. July 1975. Wellington: Author.

Department of Statistics (1975b). *Household sample survey 1 July 1973–30 June 1974*. Wellington: Author.

Department of Statistics (1975c). *The New Zealand official year-book, 1975*. Available from www.stats.govt.nz

Department of Statistics (1975d). *Survey of persons aged 65 years and over: A preliminary report*. Wellington: Author.

Department of Statistics (1977). *Survey of persons aged 65 years and over 1973–74*. Wellington: Author.

Evans, B. and Restieaux, A. (2013). *Users and uses of consumer price inflation statistics*. Office for National Statistics. October 2013. Available from www.ons.gov.uk

Ewing, I. (1999). Discontinuing the superannuitants price index. Unpublished letter from Deputy Government Statistician to CPI users, Statistics New Zealand.

Eurostat (2004). *Harmonized indices of consumer prices, A short guide for users*. March 2004. Available from www.europa.eu

Forbes, S., Higgs, C., Keating, J., and Roberts, E. (2012). Prescriptivism to positivism? The development of the CPI in New Zealand. *New Zealand Economic Papers*, 46:1, 57–77.

Holt, J. (1986). *Compulsory arbitration in New Zealand: The first forty years*. Auckland: Auckland University Press.

International Labour Organization (2003). *Resolution concerning consumer price indices*, adopted at the Seventeenth International Conference of Labour Statisticians. Available from www.ilo.org

Jackson, L. F. (1978). Household income and expenditure effects in inflation, *New Zealand Economic Papers*, Vol. 12, 1978.

Levell, P. and Oldfield, Z. (2011). *The spending patterns and inflation experience of low-income households over the past decade*. Institute for Fiscal Studies Commentary C119. Available from www.ifs.org.uk

Maruyama, A (2011). *The index for retired elderly households*. International Working Group on Price Indices. Available from www.ottawagroup.org

Mathiowetz, et al. (2011). Redesign options for the consumer expenditure survey, Bureau of Labour Statistics. Available from www.bls.gov

Mehrhoff, et al. (2009). *Is inflation heterogeneously distributed among income groups?* International Working Group On Price Indices. Available from www.ottawagroup.org

Moulton, B. R. and Stewart, K. J. (1997). *An overview of experimental U.S. consumer price indexes*. International Working Group on Price Indices. Available from www. ottawagroup.org

New Zealand Government (1915). *Report on the cost of living in New Zealand, 1891–1914*. November 1915. Wellington: Government Printer.

New Zealand Government (1920). *An inquiry into prices in New Zealand, 1891–1919*. September 1920. Wellington: Government Printer.

New Zealand Government (1944). Report on the New Zealand wartime prices index. *Appendices to the Journal of the House of Representatives* H-43.

New Zealand Government (1948). Report of index committee. *Appendices to the Journal of the House of Representatives* H-48.

New Zealand Government (1971). Report of the consumers price index revision advisory committee. Sep 1971. *Appendices to the Journal of the House of Representatives* H-40.

New Zealand Government (1978). Report of the consumers price index revision advisory committee. Oct 1978. *Appendices to the Journal of the House of Representatives* G-28A.

New Zealand Government (1985). Report of the consumers price index revision advisory committee. May 1985. *Appendices to the Journal of the House of Representatives* G-28A.

New Zealand Government (1991). Report of the consumers price index revision advisory committee. Nov 1991. *Appendices to the Journal of the House of Representatives* G-28A.

New Zealand Government (1997). Report of the consumers price index revision advisory committee. Nov 1997. *Appendices to the Journal of the House of Representatives* G-28A.

Office for National Statistics (2010). *Differences between the RPI and CPI measures of inflation*. Available from www.ons.gov.uk

Office for National Statistics (2012). Living cost and food survey quality and methodology information. Available from www.ons.gov.uk

Office for National Statistics (2013). CPI and RPI reference tables, January 2013, table 40. Available from www.ons.gov.uk

Pike, C. (2014). CPI Frameworks, 1949–2014. In S. Forbes and A. Victorio (eds) *The New Zealand CPI at 100: History and Interpretation*, Wellington: Victoria University Press.

Preston, D. (2008). *Retirement income in New Zealand: the historical context*. Retirement Commission. Available from www.cflri.org.nz

Statistics Canada (2013a). Consumer price index – detailed information for October 2013. Available from www.statcan.gc.ca

Statistics Canada (2013b). *User guide for the survey of household spending, 2011*. February 2013. Available from www.statcan.gc.ca

Statistics Bureau of Japan (2009). *2009 national survey of family income and expenditure overview*. Available from www.stat.go.jp

Statistics Bureau of Japan (2010). *Outline of the 2010-base consumer price index*. Available from www.stat.go.jp

Statistics New Zealand (1993). *Consumers price index revision report 1993.* Wellington: Author.

Statistics New Zealand (2004a). *Progress on the 1997 revision advisory committee recommendations.* Statistics New Zealand, Wellington. Available from www.stats. govt.nz

Statistics New Zealand (2004b). *Report of the consumers price index revision advisory committee 2004.* Statistics New Zealand, Wellington. Available from www.stats. govt.nz

Statistics New Zealand (2013a). Consumer price change for subpopulations. In *Consumers price index advisory committee 2013 discussion paper*, Statistics New Zealand, Wellington. Available from www.stats.govt.nz

Statistics New Zealand (2013b). *Consumers price index advisory committee 2013 background paper.* Statistics New Zealand, Wellington. Available from www.stats. govt.nz

Statistics New Zealand (2013c). *Report of the consumers price index advisory committee 2013.* Statistics New Zealand, Wellington. Available from www.stats. govt.nz

Stewart, K. J. (2008). *The experimental consumer price index for elderly Americans (CPI-E): 1982–2007.* Bureau of Labor Statistics. Available from www.bls.gov

Stiglitz, et al. (2009). *Report by the commission on the measurement of economic performance and social progress.* Available from www.stiglitz-sen-fitoussi.fr

Taktek, N. (1998). *Comparative study of analytical consumer price indexes for different subgroups of the reference population.* June 1998. Available from www. statcan.gc.ca

Thorne, B. M. (19--). A history of the household survey. Unpublished paper, Department of Statistics.

Acknowledgements

The author would like to thank Sharleen Forbes for the opportunity to write this chapter, and gratefully acknowledges the insightful comments and guidance to fruitful references from Chris Pike and Sarah Healey. I am also very appreciative of peer reviewer Gary Hawke, whose salient remarks have enhanced the social-economic context of this final version.

Quality Adjustment in the New Zealand CPI: Current Practice and Future Directions

Frances Krsinich

Abstract

We explain the range of different approaches currently used in the New Zealand Consumers Price Index for dealing with quality change. Since 2001 these have included a hedonic regression approach to estimating the price movements of used cars. A fixed effects index was used to benchmark the current matched-sample approach to quality-adjusting housing rental price movements. New data sources, in particular scanner data for consumer electronics and supermarket data, and web-scraped online retail data, present new challenges for quality adjustment. We summarise the recent methodological research contributed to by Statistics New Zealand in this area. Exploiting the longitudinal nature of the data in the hedonic framework appears to have significant potential for quality adjustment.

1 Introduction

A key issue when estimating price indices is ensuring that only 'like-for-like' price change is reflected in the index. Products are constantly evolving over time, with associated changes in quality. If this quality is not adjusted for appropriately, price indices will be correspondingly biased. For example, if a can of beans reduces in size but its price remains the same, this should contribute an increase to the price index.

The Boskin Commission report on the CPI in the United States (Boskin et al., 1996) highlighted the importance of appropriately adjusting for quality change to ensure a fit-for-purpose CPI.

Historically, quality adjustment in the New Zealand CPI has been dealt with by the maintenance of a fixed and representative basket of goods and services. Section 3 of this chapter summarises the different approaches to quality adjustment when goods and services initially in the fixed basket are no longer available for pricing.

Regular updating of the basket – in terms of the products priced, the outlets they are priced at, and their associated expenditure weights – keeps the basket representative of what New Zealand consumers are buying.

New data sources, such as scanner data and online data, give us significant opportunities to improve the quality and cost-effectiveness of estimating price change (Statistics New Zealand, 2013). But quality adjustment becomes more challenging when using this kind of data. Traditional price-index formulae do not work with such big datasets because of the high level of turnover in products sold, and the volatility in prices and quantities due to sales.

'Hedonic regression' is a common approach to deriving quality-adjusted price change, by statistically modelling prices against time and the price-determining characteristics of the products. The price index is then derived from the parameters estimated for time. Weighting these models according to quantities ensures that the measures of price change reflect the expenditure shares appropriately.

The hedonic approach is an obvious one for adjusting the quality of price indices from these new data sources. However, information on the product characteristics are not always available in the data. Our research has shown that there is potential for exploiting the longitudinal nature of price data to counter this lack of information on characteristics and produce appropriately quality-adjusted price indices.

2 Historical view on dealing with quality change

The following selected extracts from reports on revisions to the CPI give some insight into the evolving focus on quality adjustment in New Zealand price measurement historically.

The 1912 Royal Commission on the Cost of Living emphasised the importance of pricing products of a constant quality across time, and noted that quality is generally improving, but concluded that this could not be adjusted for 'in the price statistics themselves':

> In dealing with the material accumulated regarding prices, the Commission was alive to most of the leading principles to be observed in combining and interpreting them, viz:-
> ... That the things priced should be the same not only in kind but also in quality. This is a matter impossible to allow for in the price statistics themselves, as they cannot be manipulated to allow for improvement in quality. But it is important to note that most of the articles with which the inquiry has been concerned have improved in quality during the last twenty years – some of them very considerably; that is to say, not only has there been an improvement in quality in each grade of the commodity, but in many cases new and higher grades of the same article have appeared. If ordinary white bread, e.g., improves in quality and the money price remains the same there is a real fall in price, but there is no plain and convenient method of representing statistically such a fall. All that can be done is to call attention to the fact that the quality has changed. (New Zealand Government, 1912, p.12)

The 1948 report of the Index Committee discusses the requirement for clear specifications to ensure identical qualities of goods are being priced:

> A further point of considerable importance is the effect on family expenditure of changes in the quality of goods. It is, of course, essential that, where possible, the prices reported should relate to identical qualities of goods at each period of reporting. For this reason the Committee stresses the importance of careful specification of each item to be priced; and the Government Statistician has drawn up price-collection forms after close consultation with expert opinion as to specifications for each item.
>
> Even with such precautions, difficulties in ensuring quotations for comparable qualities at each price collection are not easily overcome; and supervision of this aspect of the price-collecting programme will form an important part of the work of the price-collectors.
>
> . . . While it is difficult to lay down any hard-and-fast rules regarding the reflection of changes in quality in a retail price index, the Committee considers that changes of importance should be taken into account, since a marked depreciation or appreciation in the quality of an article priced is equivalent to a price change and should be reflected in the index. In some countries samples of the goods to be priced are kept by the price-collectors; and; for the more difficult items, this practice is recommended. (New Zealand Government, 1948, p.9)

And recommendation 21 of the 1978 report of the Consumers Price Index Revision Advisory Committee stresses the importance of 'quality control of price data':

> That in order to maintain the statistical standards of the index the work of quality control of price data be pursued to the maximum degree possible and in line with accepted international practice. (New Zealand Government, 1978, p.28)

In 1985 the Committee supported the intention of the then Department of Statistics to introduce a price-relative method, noting that it was better at dealing with the quality adjustments required by substitutions for obsolete commodities.

> The price-relative method avoids the problem of incorrect implicit variable outlet price weighting, because absolute prices are not averaged. It also offers greater flexibility in handling on-going practical problems associated with actual compilation of the index such as quality adjustments resulting from the substitution of obsolete commodities in individual outlets. The committee supports on these technical grounds the department's intention to introduce the price-relative method of calculating the within-town price-change averages as soon as it is practicable to do so. (New Zealand Government, 1985, p.17)

And the report of the Committee also notes that quality control is a challenging issue in practice:

12.9 Only 'pure' price changes should be incorporated into the index calculation. Excluded are price movements, or contributions to price movements, which arise from variations in quantities or qualities of surveyed commodities. This is not a trivial task as change is endemic in the market place. The Department of Statistics has therefore had to develop techniques to not only detect change, but also to suitably quantify its effects on price. In general, this area of work is known as 'quality control'.

12.10 The quality of a commodity is determined by the quantity and standard of service or satisfaction it will provide to the customer. At a practical level it is, in most cases, very difficult to define the quality of a service with any objectivity, normally making it necessary to assume this remains unchanged over the life of the index.

12.11 In the case of goods, any differences in the physical characteristics (for example size, style, operating characteristics, etc.), and conditions of sale, such as associated customer services, may be considered quality differences in terms of index concepts. While the former can usually be objectively assessed the latter usually necessitate some subjective appraisal. Other criteria for assessing quality differences, such as functional efficiency and perceived value, are also dependent on individual interpretation. Quality control procedures are developed to minimise the element of subjectivity. (New Zealand Government, 1985, p.41)

The report of the 1991 Revision Advisory Committee defines more clearly what is meant by 'quality' in the CPI:

The fundamental conceptual principle of quality control in the CPI is that the quality of a commodity is determined by the quantity and standard of service or satisfaction it will provide to the consumer. This definition that quality is determined by perceived value to the consumer provides a different assessment of quality to one using functional efficiency or the manufacturer's specification as a criterion.

The 'quality assessor' must calculate, or else make judgements as to, the difference in perceived value to the consumer between the original and replacement commodities. Quality control procedures are developed to try and minimise the element of subjectivity involved.

In the case of goods, differences in quantity, componentry, size, style, packaging, functional or operating characteristics (e.g. durability, capacity and speed) and associated customer service at the point of sale are all examples of quality differences. For basic consumer goods these can be assessed with a reasonable degree of objectivity. However for more complex durable goods this is not so simple. A new motorcycle model may feature a bigger fuel tank and a more powerful engine, yet have poorer handling than the model it replaces. The challenge is to make a combined assessment of all the diverse quality changes. (New Zealand Government, 1991, pp.45–46)

And the 1991 Committee expressed its confidence in the quality-control practice of the time:

> The Committee noted with satisfaction that by international standards, the quality control techniques and procedures employed in the New Zealand CPI are particularly robust and expressed its confidence that the CPI is as good a measure of price level change of a basket of goods and services of constant quality as is technically and practicably possible. Furthermore the Committee considered that the Department of Statistics should do more to publicise its efforts with respect to quality control procedures in the interest of promoting confidence in the reliability of the CPI. (New Zealand Government, 1991, p.27)

3 Current quality adjustment practice in the NZ CPI

Currently, Statistics New Zealand uses quality-adjustment methods that are consistent with the international best practice outlined in the International Labour Organization's (ILO) resolution on CPIs (International Labour Organization, 2003). These practices ensure the CPI is fit for purpose by addressing both the representativeness of the CPI basket and the need to maintain a fixed quality. They include:

- updating the CPI basket and weights once every three years;
- reviewing product and retail outlet samples regularly;
- making quality adjustments when products tracked in the index have changed characteristics; and
- using hedonic modelling to quality-adjust the price movements of used cars.

The characteristics of the products being priced are monitored to ensure that any relevant differences can be excluded from the estimated price change. These changes can be in the size, performance or functionality of the product. Quality assessments put a monetary value on the change in characteristics between the old and new product, as perceived by the consumer. Several different techniques or methods are used, depending on the type of good or service being tracked.

3.1 Product or outlet unavailability

At times, products scheduled for pricing are not available – they may be temporarily out of stock or permanently removed from sale. If a product is temporarily out of stock, the price from the previous period is carried forward, and alternative products are identified for possible future use.

Usually, if the product is still unavailable at the next pricing period, it will be replaced with one of the products previously identified as a suitable replacement (or, if necessary, the outlet is replaced). If a class of item is removed from sale from an outlet, then it will be tracked in the future, where possible, in a similar outlet.

3.2 Cheapest available specifications

For many products in the CPI basket, a specific product of a specific brand is tracked consistently. For others, the cheapest available option is tracked, regardless of brand. This is done where products are judged to have little quality difference across different brands, and for which consumers are unlikely to show much brand loyalty. For these products, tracking the price of one particular brand would not represent consumers' buying patterns as well as tracking the 'cheapest available' specification would.

Examples of products where the cheapest available option is priced are frozen peas, white bread, white flour, standard homogenised milk, cheddar cheese, standard eggs, butter, and sugar.

All fresh fruit and vegetables are priced on the basis of cheapest available, as long as the variety chosen is of suitable quality for most uses. This approach also allows for a consistent pricing pattern in products where specific brands or varieties are not reliably available at all sampled retailers.

3.3 Changing pack sizes and quantity specials

A common example of explicit quality adjustment is related to a change in pack size. For example, tea bags usually sold in boxes of 100 bags may come with 10 per cent extra due to a promotion run by the distributor. In this case, consumers receive the benefit of an extra 10 bags, so the recorded price is adjusted to reflect the value of the extra tea bags to the consumer.

Similarly, 'quantity specials' are also taken into account. For example, if a loaf of white bread was $2.00 in March 2011, and three loaves of white bread were $4.80 in April 2011 (the single price remained $2.00), then the price per loaf has decreased from $2.00 to $1.60, so a 20 per cent fall in price would be shown. Such quantity specials are reflected only where they are considered to be representative of the quantities likely to be purchased by households.

3.4 Option costs

For some products, quality adjustments are based on the market value of optional features, or a proportion of the market value of optional features. This approach is currently taken for desktop computers.

In the case of new cars, when distributors report changes to the sample models, we ask for the 'perceived' dollar value of these changes to customers. To ensure the adjustments are consistent, these are checked against records of previous adjustments. When there are changes to the engine, the value of the quality change is estimated on the basis of maximum power and torque. The values of all changes between the two models are combined.

Most quality adjustments to new car prices are made to remove the effect of improved or additional features, which increase the quality of the vehicle. In these cases, the value of the changes is removed from the retail price of the updated model to generate the like-for-like price.

If, on the other hand, the quality adjustment is due to a removed or diminished feature, the value of the change is added to the retail price of the updated model. In the 10 years from 2001 to 2011, most adjustments for lower quality were due to reductions in engine power or torque.

Figure 1 shows that over the 10-year period from the June 2001 quarter to the June 2011 quarter, the index for new cars based on retail prices increased by 19.1 per cent. The quality-adjusted price series, which is used to calculate the CPI, decreased 1.5 per cent over the same time period. The large difference between these two price series – which implies an annual average increase in quality of 1.9 per cent – shows the importance of quality adjustments in the CPI. See Statistics New Zealand (2011a) for more detail.

Figure 1. Retail price and quality-adjusted price of new cars 2001–2011

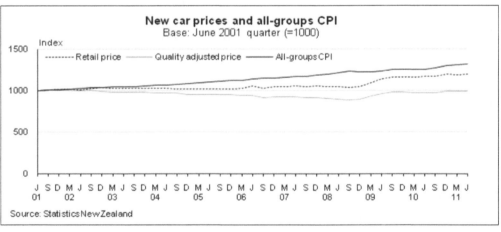

3.5 Hedonic regression

Statistics New Zealand runs a quarterly survey of used car dealers, which collects prices and characteristics of approximately 3,500 cars sold. A statistical technique called hedonic regression is used to estimate the price index for used cars from this data.

A used car can be seen as comprising a bundle of price-determining characteristics. Once these characteristics are identified and measured, the hedonic model can be interpreted as breaking down the car's price into the implicit prices and quantities of each characteristic. The price index can then be derived from the estimated price over time, after controlling for the changing quality composition of the cars being sold from quarter to quarter.

The hedonic method for used cars was implemented in the September 2001 quarter and updated in the June 2011 quarter (Statistics New Zealand, 2011b). Section 4 of this chapter describes hedonic regression and its application to used cars in more detail.

Hedonic regression was also briefly used to measure price change for whiteware in the early 2000s but this was discontinued as the approach was resource-intensive and resulted in index movements that were very close to those from the existing method.

3.6 Implicit quality adjustments

Section 3.1 above described what happens when products are unavailable. If a product is temporarily unavailable for two consecutive time periods, then a suitable replacement product, identified at the first instance of unavailability, will be used as a permanent replacement. In some instances it is assumed that any difference in price between the original product and its replacement reflects a difference in quality. This technique is called the 'overlap' method.

Statistics New Zealand uses the 'comparable replacement' method when the replacement product is judged to be very similar in quality to the old product, such as a newer model with only small, superficial changes. In this case, any change in retail price between the old and new models is shown in the price index.

When the replacement is judged to be of different quality to the old product, in some cases the price movement is inferred from products that are directly comparable from within the same geographic region as the product being replaced. This is called the 'class mean imputation' method.

For some products, quality is implicitly controlled by calculating price change based only on products that are available in consecutive time periods. This is a 'matched-model' or 'matched-sample' approach. Section 5 discusses the current use of a matched sample for the estimation of quality-adjusted dwelling-rental price change, and its evaluation against a hedonic benchmark.

4 Used cars hedonic index

4.1 The used cars survey

The measurement of price change for used cars is particularly challenging. The concept of a 'fixed basket' is difficult, if not impossible, to operationalise in this context. For example, even if we could measure the price of the same used car at a later date, it will have a different quality due to being older and having travelled further. So a different approach is needed to measure like-for-like price change for used cars.

Each quarter, data on the sales of approximately 3,500 cars are collected from a sample of used car dealers. Price, year of manufacture, make and model, engine size (cc rating), and odometer reading are collected for each car sold.

The sample was designed initially to support the calculation of average prices within estimation cells based on combinations of make and model, cc-rating ranges, and age of car. To ensure robust estimation of averages, cells with too few observations were excluded, which resulted in only around 25 per cent of the data being used. The average prices within each estimation cell were weighted together then the change in used-car price was derived from these.

4.2 Introduction of hedonic estimation for used cars in 2001

In order to make more efficient use of the used-cars survey data, a hedonic estimation was introduced in 2001. Price was modelled against quarter (i.e. time), region, make and model, age of car, cc rating, and odometer reading, as shown in equation (1):

$$P_c = \sum_k \beta_k C_{kc} + \sum_t \delta_t D_{ct} + \varepsilon_c \qquad (1)$$

Where:

P_c is the price of car c (note that there is no t term, as we can assume each individual car – at a given quality – is only sold once);
$D_{ct} = 1$ in the quarter t that car c is sold, and 0 otherwise;
C_{kc} is the kth characteristic of car c, where the k characteristics are:
  • town of purchase (15 categories)
  • make and model (47 categories)
  • age (in years)
  • size of engine (cc rating, e.g. 2300)
  • odometer reading (in kilometres);
ε_c is the error term, distributed normally; and
The quality-adjusted price index is derived from the parameter estimated on time (i.e. the δ_t).

In 2011 the hedonic model was improved, by:

• modelling the log of price, which fits the data better;
• incorporating a more detailed classification of make and model;
• adding squared terms for age of car and cc rating; and
• adding an identifier for used car dealer to the model.

The updated model is now:

$$\ln P_c = \sum_k \beta_k C_{kc} + \sum_t \delta_t D_{ct} + \varepsilon_c \qquad (2)$$

Where the k characteristics are:

- town of purchase (15 categories);
- dealer (approximately 300);
- make and model (96 categories);
- age (in years) and age squared;
- size of engine (cc rating, e.g. 2300) and cc rating squared; and
- odometer reading (in kilometres).

Hedonic indices are calculated separately for each of five broad regions of New Zealand (Auckland, Wellington, Rest of North Island, Canterbury, and Rest of South Island) and these regional-level indices are incorporated into the New Zealand CPI.

The New Zealand CPI is non-revisable so, to make the hedonic method operational, a rolling window of the latest eight quarters is used to estimate the hedonic model for each quarter and the index movement for the most recent quarter is linked to the previous quarter's index number. Statistics New Zealand (2011b) discusses the used-cars hedonic regression method in more detail.

5 Hedonic benchmarking of the matched-sample estimation of the rental index

5.1 The residential rents survey

The residential rents survey uses an area-based probability sample of approximately 2,800 rental dwellings. Landlords of the selected dwellings are asked each quarter for rental information. The sample is updated every quarter with dwellings that enter the rental market within the selected areas. These are identified from data on bond[1] payments by new tenants, by reconciling dwellings with newly lodged bonds against the existing sample, within sampled geographic areas.

Average rents are estimated from the sample within strata based on number of bedrooms and five broad regions. For example, average rent is estimated for three-bedroom rental dwellings in the Auckland region. Movements in these averages are weighted together using regional population-based expenditure shares to create a national index. The expenditure shares are updated at three-yearly CPI reviews.

A feature of the sample is that each quarter approximately 6.6 per cent of the rental dwellings in the sample are 'births' (i.e. dwellings new to the rental population), and around 3.2 per cent are 'deaths' (i.e. dwellings that are no longer

---

1   A bond is an initial payment made to the landlord, and lodged with the Ministry of Business, Innovation and Employment at the start of the tenancy, which is held until the end of the tenancy as a guarantee against damage to property, or non-payment of rent.

available for rent).[2] This reflects the increasing size of the rental population in New Zealand, as a result of population growth and a shift away from home ownership.

5.2 Introduction of a matched sample in 2000

The rental survey was initially designed in 1998, and in 2000 it was modified by restricting the price-movement estimation sample to those dwellings existing in both the previous and current quarters – that is, a 'matched sample'. This was done to ensure that differences in the composition of the sample due to newly rented dwellings and dwellings leaving the rental stock would not contaminate the estimation of price movements. This is a common approach to quality adjustment in price indices.

5.3 Hedonic benchmarking exercise

Smith (2008), of the Reserve Bank of New Zealand, speculated that the use of a matched sample might be biasing the index downwards by not reflecting like-for-like price changes associated with the dwellings new to the rental market (and, to a lesser extent, those leaving the rental market). As rents tend to follow a 'stepped' movement, with rent increases more likely when tenancies change and (implicitly) when dwellings are newly rented, this is a valid concern.

Krsinich (2009) measured the significance of this potential bias by constructing a benchmark hedonic index from the rental data. This showed that any bias due to the matched-sample estimation missing the implicit initial rent hikes associated with a newly rented dwelling was likely to be small.

Figure 2 shows the matched-sample index compared with both the hedonic benchmark and the index based directly on the full sample (i.e. based on the sample with no matching to ensure constant quality).

5.4 Fixed effects to control for unobserved characteristics

In the standard hedonic model,[3] price-determining characteristics are explicitly included in the model. In the case of the rental survey, however, the only available characteristics are fine-level region and number of bedrooms. These are not a sufficient measure of the quality of rental dwellings to provide a fully quality-adjusted index when included in the hedonic model. So instead, the hedonic formulation used to benchmark the rental index took advantage of the longitudinal nature of the rental data by fitting dwelling-specific intercepts. That is, a fixed-effects model (Allison, 2005) was used to control for all characteristics of the rental dwellings that are fixed across time.

2   On average over the years 2007 and 2008.
3   For example as described in Section 4 for the estimation of price movements for used cars.

Figure 2. Comparison of matched- and full-sample indices to the hedonic benchmark June 2006 to June 2008

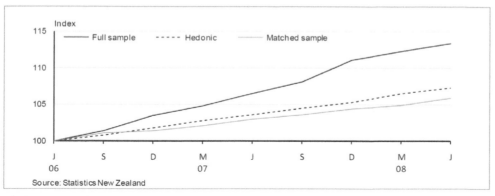

Source: Statistics New Zealand

Note: Base: June 2006 quarter (=100)

5.5 Validity of the fixed-effects approach

Questions were raised about the appropriateness of using fixed effects in the hedonic model. In particular, does the fixed-effects price index implicitly impute a price movement of zero for newly rented dwellings? If so, the benchmarking hedonic index might suffer from downwards bias in a similar way to the matched-sample index.

To give some context to these concerns, note that the continuously maintained probability sample of the rental survey is unusual in a price measurement context, where it is common for newly introduced products to be directly replacing old products in a fixed basket. If new rental dwellings in the sample were one-to-one replacements for rentals leaving the sample, then it does seem reasonable to hypothesise that a fixed-effects model – which models the difference from the mean rent across time of each dwelling – might be 'zeroing out' any price difference between old and new dwellings. In other words, it could be implicitly attributing any price difference between the old and new rentals to quality change.

To explicitly address the validity of the fixed effects formulation, Krsinich (2011b) extended a result from Aizcorbe, Corrado and Doms (2003) to show that the implicit price movement for a newly rented dwelling is appropriate: it is the movement from the average quality-adjusted[4] rents of continuing[5] dwellings in the previous quarter to the quality-adjusted rent of the new dwelling in the current quarter. In other words, the price movement that is implicitly contributed to the index by the new rental dwelling is fully quality-adjusted and, as such,

---

4   With respect to the characteristics of the dwellings that are fixed across time, as these are the characteristics controlled for by the fixed-effects formulation.

5   Continuing rental dwellings are those that are neither births nor deaths in a given quarter.

reflects only price change, with respect to the characteristics that are constant across time at the rental-dwelling level.

The properties of this fixed-effects price index have since been looked at more generally in the context of scanner and online data by Krsinich (2013, 2014) and de Haan (2013) and this is discussed further in Sections 6 and 7.

6 Quality-adjusted price indices from scanner data

Many products, such as those purchased at supermarkets, have their barcodes scanned at the time of purchase. This retail transaction data – or 'scanner data' – records prices, quantities sold, and associated information for all transactions across the full reference period. From the 2006 Consumers Price Index Review onwards, aggregated scanner data for supermarket products and for consumer electronics has been used to:

- determine the expenditure weights of some goods in the CPI basket;
- determine whether expenditure weight adjustments are required to reflect volume changes since the weight reference period (but before implementation of reviews) and, if so, by how much;
- select representative products to survey when price collectors visit retail outlets each month or quarter; and
- ensure that the mix of brands in the CPI price samples reflect market shares.

Since 2008, Statistics New Zealand has been actively researching the further potential of using more-detailed scanner data for directly estimating price change for products sold through supermarkets, and for consumer electronics products. The focus has been on determining appropriate methodologies to produce quality-adjusted price indices. A detailed research dataset of scanner data for consumer electronics products, from market research company GfK, was used for this purpose.

The potential benefits of using scanner data to measure price change include:

- improved accuracy, due to greater coverage of transactions and availability of real-time quantities;
- the ability to use existing administrative-type data sources;
- improved treatment of seasonal commodities; and
- the ability to account for commodity and product substitution between reweights.

However, the behaviour of prices and quantities at the detailed product-specification level, as reflected by scanner data, mean that traditional index methods do not work well. There are two reasons for this:

- high product churn – which makes fixed-base indices, such as the Laspeyres, quickly unrepresentative between rebases (see Section 6.1 below); and

- the volatile nature of prices and quantities due to discounting, seasonality, and the life-cycle of products – which may lead to chain-drift in chained indices (see Section 6.2 below).

6.1 Product churn

'Churn' refers to the turnover in products[6] being sold in the market. For some product groups, in particular consumer electronics, this turnover can be significant. Figure 3 shows the percentage of products sold in July 2008 that are still on sale each month over the subsequent three years, for the eight consumer electronics goods investigated. For laptop computers, only around 10 per cent of the July 2008 products were still being sold a year later.

Figure 3. Percentage of July 2008 product specifications still available from July 2008 to June 2011

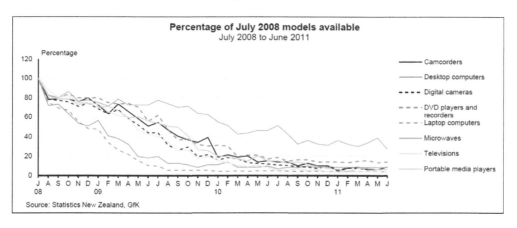

Note that current CPI practice for consumer electronics is to regularly update products being priced during the time between the three-yearly expenditure weight updates, with manual quality adjustment using a range of methods specific to the products (for example, option costs for computers).

Given this high degree of product churn, it might seem that one way of maintaining the representativeness of the basket being priced would be to use a chained superlative[7] index. That is, the index is calculated each period in reference to the products available in the current and previous period (rather than the current and base period) and that index number is linked to the previous index number. This would maximise the number of matched products

---

6   That is, products of a given specification, e.g. as reflected by barcodes.
7   A superlative index, such as a Törnqvist index, is one that utilises both current- and reference-period quantity shares symmetrically, which results in substitution between products being appropriately accounted for in the index.

included in the index calculation and reflect substitution across products by incorporating updated quantities each period. However, this is problematic, as explained in the next section.

6.2 Chain drift caused by price and quantity volatility

High-frequency chained superlative indices can result in substantial bias – known as 'chain drift' – when applied to scanner data. Ivancic, Diewert and Fox (2011) show this for Australian supermarket scanner data by a comparison with their rolling-year Gini-Éltető-Köves-Szulc (RYGEKS) method,[8] which is free of chain drift by construction.

Chain drift is the bias that occurs when a chained index diverges, or systematically 'drifts' away, from its direct (i.e. unchained) counterpart. A chained index in which the return of prices and quantities to previous levels does not correspond to the index also returning to its previous level, is exhibiting chain drift.

Supermarket products tend to be discounted frequently and, as might be expected, quantities bought increase sharply in response to these discounts as customers stockpile.

In 2010, Statistics New Zealand and Statistics Netherlands were given access to Australian supermarket-scanner research data as peer reviewers of the Australian Bureau of Statistics' research in this area. Krsinich (2011a) showed that, in general, the monthly chained Törnqvist was biased downwards relative to the RYGEKS for the products considered.

Figure 4. Effects of different indexing methods on Australian scanner data

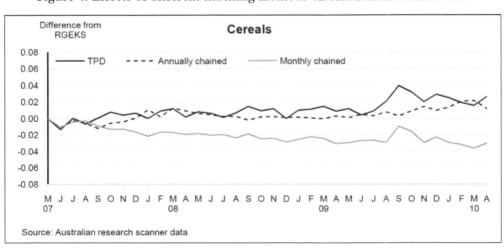

Source: Australian research scanner data

---

8   Discussed in more detail in Section 6.4.

For example, Figure 4 shows the results for cereals. Actual price indices cannot be shown for reasons of confidentiality, so instead the results are presented in terms of difference from the RYGEKS.[9] Note that the time-product dummy (TPD) index is the more usual name (in the Prices context) for the fixed-effects index.[10]

6.3 Methodologies for scanner data

Statistics New Zealand has collaborated with Statistics Netherlands by empirically testing, on New Zealand consumer electronics scanner data, a new benchmark index method called the Imputation Törnqvist Rolling Year GEKS (ITRYGEKS). This method extends the RYGEKS method, which had previously been regarded as the benchmark method for scanner data. De Haan and Krsinich (2014a) show that the RYGEKS, although free of chain drift, can be biased by not accounting for the implicit price movements associated with new and disappearing products. The ITRYGEKS method incorporates hedonic modelling into the RYGEKS approach in such a way that new and disappearing products are dealt with appropriately.

The ITRYGEKS method is a feasible method for the consumer electronics scanner data, which has extensive information on product characteristics available to incorporate into the hedonic models that the ITRYGEKS method utilises.

However, for supermarket scanner data, the ITRYGEKS method is not feasible because there is insufficient information on product characteristics available in the data. Research is ongoing, but the fixed-effects approach first used in the rental benchmarking exercise[11] looks promising (Krsinich, 2013), because the scanner data is longitudinal at the detailed product (i.e. barcode) level, with price-determining characteristics fixed across time by definition.[12]

6.4 The rolling year GEKS

Ivancic, Diewert and Fox (2011) proposed the RYGEKS method for producing price indices from scanner data. The RYGEKS uses all the prices and quantities in the data, and is free of chain drift. It is an extension to the time domain of the Gini-Élteto-Köves-Szulc (GEKS) method used for calculating multilateral

9   Referred to in the graph as 'RGEKS' for 'rolling GEKS'.
10   Called 'time-product dummy' because there are dummy variables included in the model for both time and products, as distinct from the more standard 'time-dummy' (TD) hedonic index which has dummies for time along with explicit inclusion of product characteristics in the model, e.g. as for used cars, discussed in Section 4.
11   See Section 5.
12   As any change in a product's characteristics will mean the barcode changes.

spatial price indices such as purchasing power parities.[13]

Within some window of time (generally one year plus a period, i.e. five quarters or 13 months)[14] the GEKS index between periods r and s is the geometric mean of all the superlative[15] bilateral indices between:

- time r and all the other periods in the window, and
- time s and all the other periods in the window.

Formulating the monthly RYGEKS with a 13-month rolling window is done as follows:

For the first window, i.e. $t=0$ to 12, the RYGEKS index is equal to the GEKS index:

$$P^{OT}_{RYGEKS} = P^{OT}_{GEKS} = \prod_{t=0}^{T}\left[P^{0t} \times P^{tT}\right]^{1/(T+1)} \tag{3}$$

Where P^{rs} is any superlative index (e.g. the Törnqvist) between periods r and s.

From $t=13$ onwards, the RYGEKS links on the most recent movement from the GEKS calculated on the next window (i.e. from $t=1$ to 13, then from $t=2$ to 14, and so on) as follows:

$$P^{0,13}_{RYGEKS} = P^{0,12}_{GEKS}\prod_{t=1}^{13}\left[P^{12,t} \times P^{t,13}\right]^{1/13} = \prod_{t=0}^{12}\left[P^{0,t} \times P^{t,12}\right]^{1/13}\prod_{t=1}^{13}\left[P^{12,t} \times P^{t,13}\right]^{1/13}$$

and then

$$P^{0,14}_{RYGEKS} = P^{0,13}_{RYGEKS}\prod_{t=2}^{14}\left[P^{13,t} \times P^{t,14}\right]^{1/13} \tag{4}$$

and so on.

A limitation of the RYGEKS method, however, is that it is based on the price movements between matched[16] products only. Any implicit price change associated with new or disappearing products is not reflected. So, for example, if the initial price of the latest model of a mobile phone is high relative to

13   Purchasing power parities compare prices in different countries at a given point in time.
14   The choice of a year plus a period means that the window will be long enough to counter periods of seasonal unavailability. This is the generally accepted default window length, but more research is required to formulate window-length optimality and the concepts defining it.
15   Any superlative index could be used (e.g. Fisher, Törnqvist, Walsh), but Ivancic, Diewert and Fox (2011) use the Fisher index.
16   That is, existing in both the two periods relating to the individual bilateral indices that feed into the RYGEKS.

its features when it is first introduced, then this implicit price increase is not reflected in the RYGEKS.

6.5 The imputation Törnqvist rolling year GEKS

An extension to the RYGEKS method was proposed by Jan de Haan, of Statistics Netherlands (de Haan and Krsinich, 2014a). The imputation Törnqvist rolling year GEKS (ITRYGEKS) uses hedonic models to impute for new and disappearing products. Unlike the RYGEKS, which is based on the geometric means of superlative bilateral indices, the ITRYGEKS is based on geometric means of hedonic bilateral indices.

The formulation is as above for RYGEKS, with the difference that the P^{ij} are bilateral time-dummy hedonic indices.

De Haan and Krsinich (2014a) show that, with appropriate weights,[17] the ITRYGEKS is algebraically equivalent to a Törnqvist index for the matched subset of products.[18] For new and disappearing products, the ITRYGEKS is algebraically equivalent to applying a Törnqvist formula to prices predicted from time-dummy hedonic models for the period in which there is no price available.

That is, the ITRYGEKS from period 0 to t can be expressed as follows:

$$P^{0t}_{ITRYGEKS} = \prod_{i \in M^{0t}} \left(\frac{p^t_i}{p^0_i}\right)^{\frac{s^0_i+s^t_i}{2}} \prod_{i \in D^{0t}} \left(\frac{\hat{p}^t_i}{p^0_i}\right)^{\frac{s^0_i}{2}} \prod_{i \in N^{0t}} \left(\frac{p^t_i}{\hat{p}^0_i}\right)^{\frac{s^t_i}{2}} \quad (5)$$

Where:

M^{0t} is the set of matched products with respect to periods 0 and t;

D^{0t} is the set of 'disappearing' products with respect to periods 0 and t – that is, the subset of products that exist in period 0 but not in period t;

N^{0t} is the set of 'new' products with respect to periods 0 and t – that is, the subset of products that exist in period t but not in period 0;

p^t_i is the actual price for product i in period t;

$\hat{p}^t_i$ is the predicted price for product i in period t from the time-dummy hedonic model based on the pooled bilateral data of periods 0 and t;

s^t_i is the expenditure share for item i in period t;

and this expression can be generalised to the ITRYGEKS between any two periods r and s.

---

17 The mean expenditure shares are the weights used for the matched items, and half of the expenditure shares are the weights used for the unmatched products.

18 By 'products' here, we mean products with a particular specification, that is, at the level of the barcode.

The ITRYGEKS method was empirically tested using scanner data for eight New Zealand consumer electronics products (camcorders, desktop computers, digital cameras, DVD players and recorders, laptop computers, microwaves,[19] televisions and portable media players) resulting in the following conclusions:

- The monthly chained Törnqvist is not a viable method for consumer electronics products, as it exhibits downwards chain drift for most products examined.
- RYGEKS shows evidence of bias due to not accounting for the price movements of new and disappearing products, particularly for computers.
- The easier-to-implement[20] rolling-year time-dummy (RYTD) hedonic index, based on multilateral pooled data,[21] gives very similar results to the ITRYGEKS.
- In some cases, such as supermarket data, few or no characteristics are likely to be available for explicitly incorporating into time-dummy hedonic models. Therefore neither the ITRYGEKS or RYTD methods are feasible. The fixed-effects method (called the rolling-year time-product dummy, or RYTPD, method in the paper) sits closer to the benchmark ITRYGEKS than does the RYGEKS, and therefore should be further investigated.

6.6 Fixed effects

As noted above, ITRYGEKS is a feasible method for production only when there are sufficient characteristics in the data to estimate the underlying bilateral time-dummy hedonic indices. The research data obtained for consumer electronics has extensive characteristics data so can support the estimation of ITRYGEKS indices.

However, for supermarket data, the only explicit characteristics likely to be consistently available in the data across all products are weight, volume or size. This means ITRYGEKS will not be feasible for supermarket products.

Methods which do not require explicit information on characteristics are chained superlative indices, such as the Törnqvist (which has been shown to suffer from chain drift, as discussed above), the RYGEKS and the fixed-effects index (also known as the time-product dummy, or TPD, method).

De Haan and Krsinich (2014a) showed empirically that the fixed-effects index tends to sit closer to the ITRYGEKS benchmark than the RYGEKS approach does. However they noted that, by construction, price movements

---

19 Microwaves are not strictly a consumer electronics product but, as a product with relatively little technological change, they offer a useful comparison.
20 But less able to be expressed in terms of traditional price index formulae.
21 That is, the hedonic models are based on the data for the full estimation window of, for example, 13 months.

of new items are systematically omitted due to the splicing, or 'linking on', of only the most recent period's movement. Fixed-effects regression requires two price observations before a product is non-trivially included in the estimation. Krsinich (2013) proposed and empirically tested a modified version of the splicing procedure – where the movement of the entire estimation window is incorporated rather than just the most recent period's movement. This approach ensures that the price movements of new products will be reflected in the index, in the period of entry, with one period's lag. This was shown to be consistently closer to the ITRYGEKS than either the RYGEKS or the fixed-effects index which splices on just the most recent period's movement – i.e. the RYTPD empirically tested by de Haan and Krsinich (2014a).

Figure 4 shows this fixed-effects window-splice (FEWS) index compared to the RYGEKS and the ITRYGEKS, for laptop computers and televisions.

Figure 4. Methods requiring no information on characteristics, compared with the benchmark ITRYGEKS

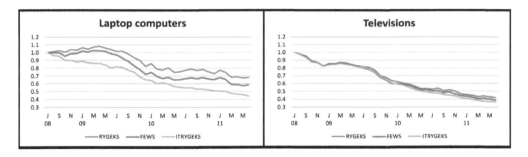

The work on the rentals fixed-effects benchmark, described above in Section 5, showed that the implicit price movement being estimated for new rental dwellings is appropriate, and the results on the consumer electronics scanner data show that the method performs better than the RYGEKS with respect to the ITRYGEKS benchmark.

Intuitively, though, it is difficult to see why this should be the case. How can the fixed-effects index work more effectively than the RYGEKS, if there is no extra information being incorporated? As with the RYGEKS, only prices, quantities and detailed product identifiers are utilised.

In fact there *is* extra information being utilised by the fixed-effects method – the longitudinal aspect of the data. Unlike the RYGEKS, the full longitudinal record for each product (once there are at least two price observations) is modelled in the fixed-effects index. In the RYGEKS, only two-period, or bilateral, movements of matched products are incorporated into the estimation.

Krsinich (2014) extends a result from de Haan (2013) to show that the fixed-effects index is equivalent to a fully interacted time-dummy hedonic index,[22] where all the characteristics are incorporated into the model as categorical variables.

In other words, the fixed-effects index may be a *better* quality-adjusted index than the time-dummy hedonic index (including only main effects), which explicitly incorporates information on characteristics. This is partly because all time-invariant characteristics[23] are (implicitly) controlled for, not only the observed characteristics, and partly because all the interactions between these characteristics are (implicitly) incorporated into the model.

This is a new idea which is still being debated, but it holds significant potential for very simple and effective quality-adjustment of price indices from 'big data' such as scanner or online data, where information on characteristics is limited or non-existent, but where product specifications are at a level of detail that ensures constant characteristics over time in the longitudinal data.

Very recent research by de Haan and Krsinich (2014b) utilises the New Zealand consumer electronics scanner data to show that the time-dummy hedonic index (i.e. where characteristics are explicitly included in the model) corresponds very closely to a 'quality-adjusted unit value' (QAUV) index, defined according to established econometric principles (de Haan, 2004). If the fixed-effects index is equivalent to a fully interacted time-dummy hedonic index, then it will follow that it can similarly be related to the concept of a quality adjusted unit value index.

7 Quality-adjusted price indices from online data

Statistics New Zealand has recently started to consider the potential of web-scraped online retail data for constructing price indices. We have done some initial exploratory analysis on 15 months of daily online prices for a major New Zealand consumer electronics retailer. This data was shared with us by the Billion Prices Project of the Massachusetts Institute of Technology (MIT), an academic initiative that uses prices collected from hundreds of online retailers around the world on a daily basis to conduct economic research. See Cavallo (2012b) for a description of how inflation measures based on the online data were first used to find evidence of bias in the official Argentine CPI measure.

Online data has product identifiers at the model level – similar to scanner data – but will tend to have little, if any, data on the characteristics of products. It also lacks any information on the quantities sold.

---

22 That is, a time-dummy hedonic index where the hedonic model includes all the interactions between characteristics, as well as the main effects.

23 Note that all characteristics at the barcode level are time-invariant by definition, because a change in any of them will result in a changed barcode.

The question then is how to produce quality-adjusted indices from this data. Daily inflation measures marketed by PriceStats[24] for over 20 countries use a daily chained Jevons index. This is a matched-model approach to quality adjustment, where the price movement is calculated based on the products that are available in the previous and current day. The absence of quantities in the data means that there is likely to be less potential for chain drift[25] but, as with any matched-model approach, the implicit price movements associated with new products appearing and old products disappearing will not be reflected in the index. Cavallo (2012a) examined this issue by using overlapping prices to adjust for quality change. Lacking data on quantities is also a problem because the indices will not fully reflect different expenditure shares across products, and the changes in these.[26]

Statistics New Zealand is investigating the potential of the fixed-effects approach in the context of this online data, and initial results are promising.

Figure 5 shows indices with no quality adjustment (the 'average price' graphs) compared to RYGEKS,[27] weekly chained Jevons and fixed-effects indices. Note that the data collection was interrupted during February and March 2013, so the prices were carried forward over this period (hence the indices are flat for these two months). Because of the difficulty of estimating RYGEKS for very high frequency data due to the very large number of bilateral index calculations required, we took day-per-week samples of the daily data, and computed the indices for each of these. This is interesting in itself, as it shows the effect of sampling in the time dimension which, in this case, can have an impact on estimates of short-term movements, though not on estimates of the longer-term trend.

While for televisions the three quality-adjusted index methods are very similar, for mobile computers they can differ quite significantly, reflecting the potential for chain drift in the chained Jevons, and bias (due to not accounting for the price change of new goods appearing and old goods disappearing) in both the RYGEKS and the chained Jevons. At the aggregate consumer electronics level, the methods give very similar results, suggesting a certain amount of 'cancelling out' of biases across products.

---

24   PriceStats is a US company which is related to, but distinct from, the Billion Prices Project academic initiative of MIT. It is a US-based company that seeks to bring to market innovation in the inflation measurement field. See http://www.pricestats.com/

25   Because it appears to be the slightly assymmetrical behaviour of the price and quantity spikes that causes chain drift, though the author is unsure whether this has been formally established in the literature.

26   Note that at the higher levels of aggregation in the CPI structure, the PriceStats inflation measures utilise expenditure weightings from the relevant countries' CPIs.

27   This RYGEKS is a modification of the usual approach that would be used in production, where a year-long GEKS index would be recalculated each period (e.g. day or week, depending on the frequency of the index). Instead, two 53-week GEKS are linked together in the middle of the three-year period.

Figure 5. Comparison of four different indexing methods on online data

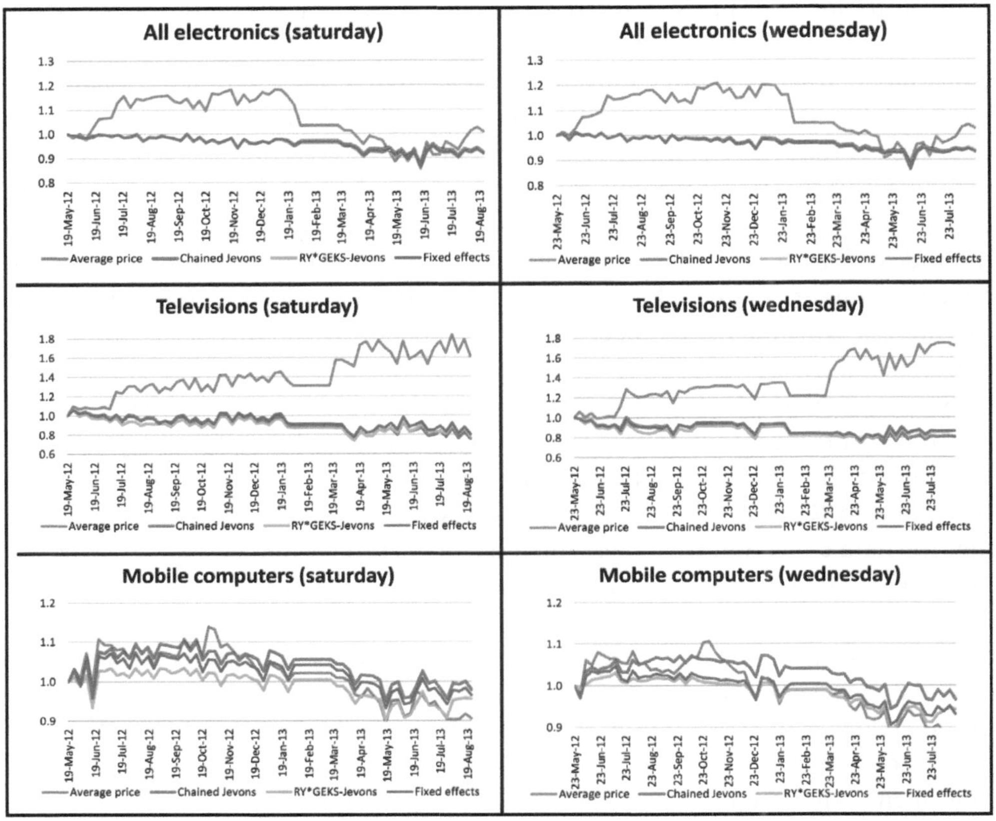

This initial analysis indicates that the fixed-effects method may be an appropriate one for producing quality-adjusted indices from online data.[28] Statistics New Zealand is in the beginning stages of a collaborative research agreement with PriceStats to share their daily online data for a range of New Zealand retailers who sell their products online.

8 Conclusion

Ensuring that the New Zealand CPI reflects 'like-for-like' price change is important. Products such as consumer electronics are rapidly evolving and have correspondingly shorter life-cycles in the market than other consumable goods. This makes the traditional approach of pricing a representative fixed basket challenging.

---

28 The issue remains that online data lacks information on quantities sold, though existing CPI weighting information could be used to aggregate the product-level indices at higher levels of the index hierarchy.

Hedonic regression has been used in production of the New Zealand CPI for over 10 years, to measure quality-adjusted price movements of used cars. The hedonic approach was also recently used to benchmark the performance of the current matched-sample approach to measuring housing rentals. This was the first example of Statistics New Zealand exploiting the longitudinal nature of the data to control for unobserved price-determining characteristics using fixed effects.

New data sources, in particular scanner data and web-scraped online data, have significant potential benefits, but they require new methodologies to ensure that the price indices derived from them are appropriately quality-adjusted. This has been an active area of research for Statistics New Zealand over the last five years. Collaborative research with Statistics Netherlands on a method extending the RYGEKS method to incorporate hedonic indices has been well-received in the Prices research community, and the imputation Törnqvist RYGEKS (ITRYGEKS) may now be considered a benchmark method for quality-adjusting price indices from scanner data. Statistics New Zealand intends to incorporate scanner data into production for the New Zealand CPI in the September quarter of 2014, for consumer electronics products, using the ITRYGEKS method.

Supermarket scanner data and web-scraped online data, however, do not contain sufficient information on characteristics to use the ITRYGEKS method. This has led to a revisiting of the fixed-effects index, along with a modification of the standard splicing procedure to ensure that the index is non-revisable and reflects the price movements of new products appropriately. At the time of writing, this looks very promising as an approach to producing non-revisable fully quality-adjusted price indices where there is longitudinal price and quantity information at a detailed product-specification level. Research in this area is ongoing.

References

Allison, P. D. (2005). *Fixed effects regression methods for longitudinal data using SAS*. Cary, NC: SAS Institute Inc.

Aizcorbe, A., Corrado, C., and Doms, M. (2003). *When do matched-model and hedonic techniques yield similar price measures?* Working Paper no. 2003–14, Federal Reserve Bank of San Francisco.

Boskin, M., Dulberger, E., Gordon, R., Griliches. Z., and Jorgenson, D. (1996). *Toward a more accurate measurement of the cost of living: Final report to the Senate Finance Committee*. Washington: Advisory commission to study the consumer price index, December 1996.

Cavallo, A. (2012a). *Overlapping quality adjustment using online data*. Paper presented at the 2012 Economic Measurement Group, Sydney, Australia.

Cavallo, A. (2012b). Online versus official price indexes: Measuring Argentina's inflation. *Journal of Monetary Economics*, December 2012.

de Haan, J. (2004). *Estimating quality-adjusted unit value indexes: Evidence from scanner data*. Paper presented at the SSHRC International Conference on Index Number Theory and the Measurement of Prices and Productivity, Vancouver, Canada, 30 June–3 July 2004.

de Haan, J. (2013). *Online data, fixed effects and the construction of high-frequency indexes*. Paper presented at the 2013 Economic Measurement Group, Sydney, Australia, November 2013.

de Haan, J. and F. Krsinich (2014a) Scanner data and the treatment of quality change in non-revisable price indexes, *Journal of Business & Economic Statistics* (forthcoming).

de Haan, J. and F. Krsinich (2014b) *Time dummy hedonic and quality-adjusted unit value indexes: do they really differ?* To be presented at the inaugural conference of the Society of Economic Measurement, Chicago, August 2014.

International Labour Organization (2003). *Resolution concerning consumer price indices*. Available from www.ilo.org.

Ivancic, L., Diewert, W. E., and Fox, K. J. (2011). Scanner data, time aggregation and the construction of price indexes. *Journal of Econometrics*, 161(1), 24–35.

Krsinich, F. (2009) *Use of hedonics at Statistics New Zealand*. Paper presented at the 2009 Economic Measurement Group, Sydney, Australia, December 2009.

Krsinich, F. (2011a). *Price indexes from scanner data: A comparison of different methods*. Paper presented at the 12th meeting of the Ottawa Group, Wellington, New Zealand, May 2011.

Krsinich, F. (2011b). *Measuring the price movements of used cars and residential rents in the New Zealand consumers price index*. Paper presented at the 12th meeting of the Ottawa Group, Wellington, New Zealand, May 2011.

Krsinich, F. (2013) *Using the rolling year time-product dummy method for quality adjustment in the case of unobserved characteristics*. Paper presented at the 2013 Ottawa Group, Copenhagen, Denmark, May 2013.

Krsinich, F. (2014) *Fixed effects with a window splice: quality-adjusted price indexes with no characteristic information*. Paper presented at the 2014 UNECE/ILO meeting of price index experts, Geneva, Switzerland, May 2014.

New Zealand Government (1912). Cost of Living in New Zealand (report and evidence of the Royal Commission on). Department of Labour. *Appendices to the Journal of the House of Representatives* H-18.

New Zealand Government (1948). Report of index committee. *Appendices to the Journal of the House of Representatives* H-48.

New Zealand Government (1978). Report of the consumers price index revision advisory committee. October 1978. *Appendices to the Journal of the House of Representatives* G-28A.

New Zealand Government (1985). Report of the consumers price index revision advisory committee. May 1985. *Appendices to the Journal of the House of Representatives* G-28A.

New Zealand Government (1991). Report of the consumers price index revision advisory committee. November 1991. *Appendices to the Journal of the House of Representatives* G-28A.

Smith, M. (2008). Measuring rents in the CPI. Unpublished document, Reserve Bank of New Zealand.

Statistics New Zealand (2011a). *Bigger, safer, better: tracking retail and quality adjusted new car prices in the CPI.* http://www.stats.govt.nz/browse_for_stats/economic_indicators/prices_indexes/new-car-prices.aspx

Statistics New Zealand (2011b). *Updating the CPI used cars index hedonic model.* http://www.stats.govt.nz/browse_for_stats/economic_indicators/prices_indexes/used-cars-hedonic-model.aspx

Statistics New Zealand (2012). Accounting for quality change in the CPI. *Price Index News*, July 2012, http://www.stats.govt.nz/tools_and_services/newsletters/price-index-news/jul-12-article-cpi-quality-change.aspx

Statistics New Zealand (2013). Retail transaction data. Chapter 5, *Consumers Price Index Advisory Committee 2013 Discussion Paper.* http://www.stats.govt.nz/browse_for_stats/economic_indicators/CPI_inflation/2013-cpi-review-advisory-committee.aspx#discussion

Acknowledgements

The author gratefully acknowledges the assistance and encouragement of Chris Pike, Jan de Haan, Alistair Gray, Soon Song, Sharleen Forbes and Richard Arnold. Alan Bentley was the lead author of an earlier article (Statistics New Zealand, 2012) which formed the basis of Section 3. Also we are very grateful to Alberto Cavallo of MIT for sharing Billion Prices Project online data with us for exploratory research.

An Analysis of Provincial Prices in New Zealand: 1885–1913

Ekaterina Sadetskaya & Les Oxley

Abstract

This chapter discusses the construction of a new Consumer Price Index (CPI) for New Zealand, 1885–1913, based upon aggregation of data from the four largest provincial districts: Auckland, Canterbury, Otago and Wellington. Using these new provincial data we explore the degree of market integration within the New Zealand dairy and meat sectors, and consider whether anecdotal evidence on South–North price convergence is supported statistically.

1 Overview

Measuring prices, both in terms of levels and rates of change, plays a fundamentally important role in a wide range of economic applications. Whether we consider individual goods and services or baskets of commodity aggregates, price data allow us to explore changes in 'real' values, as well as measure, estimate and test a wide range of economic hypotheses and relationships including, for example, changes in the cost and standard of living, real wages, purchasing power parity, and relative price changes. In most developed economies, the recent post-war history has been one of universal price inflation, where the differences that we see are only in terms of the rates of inflation and global spatial variation. However, long-term price series, where they exist (e.g. Australia – Bambrick, 1973; McLean, 1999; Britain – Mitchell, 1988), remind us that these post-World War II experiences are far from typical. Long periods of price stagnation and significant periods of decline were punctuated with relatively short periods of inflation, often caused by the need for the State to finance wars. Furthermore, the recent economic downturns associated with the global financial crisis led some to consider the possibility that the world might return to the spiralling deflations of the 1930s, thereby renewing an interest in historical analyses of prices for items such as housing and land.

    Summary measures such as the Consumers Price Index (CPI) are based upon our ability to appropriately aggregate weighted combinations of goods and services to provide a summary cost-of-living measure. In New Zealand, the first cost-of-living index was created in 1915 by the Government Statistician, Malcolm Fraser. His estimates were based on the records of people who were engaged in retail trade over the period 1891–1913. In 1982, Margaret Arnold constructed an alternate aggregate CPI by revising the weighting scheme used by Fraser and including additional provincial data, which she extracted from Statistics New Zealand Annual Reports.

For many, the Arnold series remains the most reliable for that period, and in our new work, reported here, we use Arnold's series as a benchmark to reconstruct a New Zealand CPI for the period 1885–1913 from a spatial perspective, i.e. disaggregated at the level of the four most populous provincial districts: Auckland, Canterbury, Otago, and Wellington.[1] The starting point coincides with the availability of district level nominal price series reported in Statistics New Zealand Annual Reports. The construction of provincial CPIs is achieved by using nominal prices for a chosen basket of goods based on the Labour Department Household Survey of 1893 and other sources, including New Zealand censuses and official yearbooks, and the Appendices to the Journals of the House of Representatives (New Zealand Department of Statistics, 1873–1935, 1893, 1894, 1911; New Zealand Parliament, 1884, 1887, 1965; Tremblay et al., 2005).

Using these new data, we then identify and analyse regional price movements and trends of the leading New Zealand sectors between 1885 and 1913 and test for evidence of spatial convergence in prices, using both simple coefficients of variation and more specific time-series methods,[2] allowing us to establish the extent of regional market integration. From an economic perspective, we use these techniques to consider the integration of traded commodity markets across provinces to consider whether the findings support the story of a South–North convergence generated initially via the refrigeration boom and subsequent shift in population from south to north.

2 New Zealand's historical prices series

2.1 McIlraith series (1861–1910)

The earliest price index for New Zealand (based on wholesale prices) was developed by McIlraith in 1911, most likely in response to heightened inflation prior to World War I (Nesbitt-Savage, 1993). The objective of that series was to measure changes in the general level of prices from 1860. In particular,

1 *Statistics of New Zealand* in its yearly publications reported average prices of produce, provisions etc. for each provincial district of New Zealand from approximately 1847 onwards.

2 Bernard and Durlauf (1995) and Johansen (1988)-type tests are used to test for common trends, which we refer to in more detail in Section 5.1.

McIlraith was interested in examining changes in the purchasing power of money and ascertaining the causes of the changes in the local price level. McIlraith (1911) did not attempt to weight the commodities used in the series, but rather derived the unweighted wholesale prices from import and export schedules, including the prices of non-consumer items (e.g. zinc, lead, bar iron). He further assumed that prices would deviate little among the largest centres, mainly upon the assumption that transport and communication between the different commercial centres of New Zealand was frequent and cheap. He therefore adopted Wellington prices for the most frequently imported goods, and Christchurch retail prices for agricultural produce items such as cereals and meats. McIlraith also used the Sauerbeck (1895) and 'Economist' series3 to compare New Zealand and English price levels. He found "a marked coincidence during 1880–89 between the two series" where the average prices were falling between 1880 and 1887 in both countries. McIlraith (1911, p.75) also compared his series to the United States Falkner series and found that "America, like New Zealand, did not experience the wave of inflated prices till 1872".

McIlraith was not always clear on the sources and references to the price series he used. As noted by Nesbitt-Savage (1993), the McIlraith wholesale price index is not an adequate consumer price series and provides only approximate measures of the annual rate of change in retail prices.

2.2 Fraser series (1891–1914)

Sudden price inflations in the 1890s reinvigorated the interest of the Department of Statistics in surveying relative price movements. In 1915, Government Statistician Malcolm Fraser produced a report on the long-term cost-of-living index, based on the records of people who were engaged in retail trade over the period 1891–1913 (Nesbitt-Savage, 1993). From that point on, regular monthly and quarterly surveys were undertaken to monitor consumer prices.

Fraser's cost-of-living index is the first weighted retail price series index, and represents a more appropriate CPI estimate than that of McIlraith. Despite that, Fraser's price series has its limitations. The retail prices for the Grocery group in Christchurch were not collected prior to 1899 although series for other centres were collected from 1891. The expenditure weights used by Fraser only approximate the results obtained by the Department of Labour as he did not include certain items of fruit and vegetables (Fraser, 1915). He also omitted the Other Items/Miscellaneous group, which by the 1910 expenditure survey constituted about 40.34 per cent of the household expenditure basket (Collins, 1912). Most importantly, Fraser "neglected" (Arnold, 1982) the *Statistics of New Zealand* annual return of retail prices published for each year since 1847,

3   McIlraith (1911) claimed to derive the series from the *Economist* magazine.

with the number of items expanding from 1885.[4] Fraser's series is therefore restrictive in scope (as it covered only food and rent) and was "further limited because the compliers relied on less than optimum sources" (Arnold, 1982; Nesbitt-Savage, 1993). Although both the McIlraith and Fraser price series are probably reliable in relation to the general trend, they appear to be less reliable in terms of annual fluctuations (Arnold, 1982).

2.3 Arnold series (1870–1919)

In order to address problems with the Fraser series (e.g. incomplete or limited expenditure basket and data source reliability), and to extend the series (the Fraser series commences in 1891), Margaret Arnold developed an aggregate CPI by revising the weighting scheme used by Fraser. To construct the new CPI she extracted annual average returns of prices reported in *Statistics of New Zealand* from 1870 to 1919 (Arnold, 1982) as collected by the Police Force (New Zealand Official Year-book, 1910).

Arnold's long-term series consisted of the five major subgroups of expenditure: Food, Housing, Clothing, Fuel and Light, and Miscellaneous items. She collated the prices for individual items for the years 1870–1901 and then linked them to the Fraser series "as to provide an adequate overlap with the Fraser series". She constructed the individual series by first taking the midpoint of the range of values given for each province, and then weighting these midpoints by the proportion of the population in each province. To develop her final CPI, she linked the five subseries together. Although for her final series she used various weights (Karamea,[5] Department of Labour, and Fraser), Arnold (1982) reports that using different weights "made relatively little impact on the series." Arnold concluded that the five subseries all move together, showing the same U-shape as the general trend. Arnold's CPI series is probably the most commonly used index of changing consumer prices in New Zealand for the 1870–1919 period.

2.4 Nesbitt-Savage series (1847–1990)

Nesbitt-Savage (1993) used Arnold's series from 1870 to 1919 as the basic starting point to construct his long-run CPI series (1847–1990). He developed two models to construct (rather than directly measure) a long-run CPI from 1847 to 1992. The first model used an overlap between McIlraith and Arnold to construct the series for 1861–1869. The second model used the correlation

---

4   In 1885 the Department of Statistics expanded the range of goods for which it published prices, to include, for example, farm yard produce (eggs, ham, bacon etc.), garden produce (potatoes, onions, carrots, cabbages etc.), and miscellaneous items (coal, firewood etc.).

5   Karamea Store Book, 1875–1876, NP Series 23, Box 5, item 6, Archives New Zealand (ANZ).

between Sauerbeck's British Wholesale Price Index and Arnold's series to derive an approximation for the period between 1847 and 1860. The first two models were then linked to Arnold's (1870–1919) and the Department of Statistics' (1920–1992) CPI series. Nesbitt-Savage assumed the same consumption patterns (i.e. an unchanged basket of goods) throughout that whole period (1847–1919). The models then used simple linear regression techniques to predict the series. The methods used to generate the long-term CPI series can probably be refined using more sophisticated time series methods not available then.

3 Methods and Data

3.1 Basket choice

The construction of any CPI generally begins with a compilation of the average prices of a wide range of commodities and their relative expenditure weights (shares). For example, Table 1 reports consumer basket weights for three different time periods for New Zealand and two other countries with comparable labour markets (Australia and Britain). In New Zealand, the proportion of overall expenditure spent on food declined from 63.05 per cent to 34.13 per cent during the period 1875–1911. The relatively high proportion of expenditure on food in Australia can be noted from the earliest expenditure survey (1861); this expenditure subsequently declined to around 30 per cent by 1911.

For both New Zealand and Australia, there is a shift from the dominant expenditure on food in the early years before 1900 to correspondingly larger shares being spent on miscellaneous items after 1900. Similarly to Australia, expenditure on housing/rent more than doubled in New Zealand between 1875 and 1911. For Australia, there is some divergence in the basket weights between the McLean (1999) and Knibbs (1911) series. Markedly, Knibbs's basket shows a very small share of income spent on food and a correspondingly large share spent on 'Miscellaneous' items. McLean (1999), however, was sceptical about the results of Knibbs's 1911 expenditure survey, which he indicated were "deemed unsatisfactory".

Interestingly, in Britain the expenditure on food has a reverse pattern: expenditure on food increased by 24 per cent from 1900 to 1914. In part this may have been due to some miscellaneous items being erroneously included in the food portion of the expenditure, thereby inflating the amount spent on food.

The basket of goods chosen for construction of the New Zealand Provincial CPIs corresponds to that reported in Arnold (1982), but with minor changes (i.e. we include eggs, dried fruits, potatoes and vegetables, and omit fish from the grocery basket). Arnold used three different weighting schemes for different periods: 1875 Karamea weights (for 1870–1893); 1893 basic expenditure weights (1885–1919); and 1910 Fraser budget study weights (1895–1919). However, she

Table 1. Country-specific expenditure weights for consumer price indices (% of total expenditure)

Items of expenditure / Country	New Zealand			Australia				Britain	
Survey year	1893	1910-11	1875	1861	1900	1913	1911	1900	1914
Source	Household survey	Labour Depart.	Karamea weights	McLean (1999)			Knibbs (1911)*	Prest (1954)	Shergold (1982)
Food	52.7	34.13	63.05	45.12	39.40	38.52	32.23	34.9	54.45
Rent (housing)	10.38	20.31	6.14	12.09	15.54	19.43	13.7	11.6	17.65
Clothing	17.52	13.89	14.6	12.09	23.31	21.39	12.72	10	11.95
Fuel and Light	8.08	5.22	2.08				3.46	5.1	5.95
Tobacco							0.63	1.8	
Alcohol	1.16		3.22	14.27	13.46	12.12	0.74	12.8	2.6
Miscellaneous	10.16	26.45	10.91	16.43	11.82	8.54	36.52	23.8	7.4

Notes and Sources: * Extracted from R. Allen (1994): Australia, Knibbs (1911: 14, 19), food includes non-food groceries and non-alcoholic beverages.

noted that the final aggregate series were robust when subjected to different weighting schemes. We chose the 1893 basic expenditure weights for the entire 1885–1913 period because the Karamea weights were based on one store book rather than a representative sample, and the Fraser weights covered only a portion of the total expenditure.

It is not known if consumption patterns differed across the provinces. For example, when estimating differences in the cost of living between Christchurch and Auckland for food and rent, Collins (1912) notes:

> the figures show an increase of 20 % in the cost of living (food and rent) in Christchurch as against an increase of about 34 % for Auckland. Auckland's budget shows an increase in food by 25 %, while Christchurch indicated an increase of about 21 % by 1910–11.

However, Collins included only a small selection of items and failed to consider the weights for the whole basket. Furthermore, the expenditure weights were also limited to the two selected provinces. He commented on the limitations of the cost-of-living figures provided by the Royal Commission: "the report of the Royal Commission represents a rudimentary summary of the statistics on prices in the Dominion at that time" (Collins, 1912, p. xii).

More recently, Greasley and Oxley (2004) reported that the prices of foodstuffs in 1896 were cheaper in New Zealand than in Manchester, while the overall cost of living in New Zealand was higher than in Manchester. Workers' living costs were, respectively, 23 per cent and 28 per cent higher in Auckland and Wellington than in Manchester. They suggested that such results may overstate the extent of living costs in New Zealand since there could be differences in expenditure patterns between the North and the South: "much of the North Island is frost free for most of the year, which lessened the need for domestic fuel." Such an interpretation would be difficult to incorporate in the construction of a CPI since it is not clear how much more would be spent on fuel by people who reside in the South Island.

3.2 CPI calculation

From approximately 1885, Statistics New Zealand published a wider range of product prices, extending the vegetable and home produce section, as well as prices for fuel and light. Factories and manufacturing production series were also reported from 1885.[6] Grocery prices for items such as jam and dried fruits were taken from the import schedule (1885–1890 except for Canterbury, 1885–1899) and then linked with corresponding items reported in Fraser (from 1890 for most series). The price series for Dairy, Meat, Fuel and Light, and

6   The clothing series had to be extracted from that data.

Clothing are identical to those reported in Arnold (1982), with Housing and Miscellaneous deviating only slightly.

For the housing price index, consideration was made of most people living in four- or five-bedroom homes, with many owning their own homes. Also considered was the practice of most tenants leasing their homes at a fixed rent rather than bargaining for their rents weekly (Fraser, 1916). Two series for the index were eventually constructed: *Statistics New Zealand* pre-1902 (calculated from the number of boroughs and the rental value of rateable property), and the housing prices reported in Fraser (1915) from 1902 to 1913.

The assigned individual weights for some items (the ones that imply variety, e.g. dried fruits) were derived from consumption expenditure figures reported for individual items in Fraser (1915). The base used for the indices was the average between 1909 and 1913 (1909 – 1913 = 100).

The subseries for Food (combined Grocery, Dairy and Meat) and Housing were found to be positively correlated with the Fraser series (see Table 2). A negative correlation was found for the Fuel and Light series, probably because of the limited time spans considered by Fraser (no data was available prior to 1893 for Wellington, 1903 for Christchurch, and 1907 for Auckland and Dunedin). Estimating the cost of housing prior to 1901 was also problematic. The borough statistics (used to derive the new Housing series) did not necessarily reflect the cost of paying rent (the cost of rateable properties was divided by the number of people living in each of the main boroughs), but rather reflected the cost of upkeep and mortgage payments. The mean values of the Food and Housing sub-index series were not significantly different between the new estimates and those of Fraser.

Table 2. Pearson's correlation between the new subseries and Fraser's

Index	Correlation Coefficient
Dairy	0.854
Grocery	0.28
Meat	0.31
Housing	0.42
Fuel and Light	-0.36

3.3 Index choice and construction

The choice of an appropriate index for the analysis of our new provincial CPIs was constrained by data availability (prior to 1913 only annual data is reported) and the limited information on expenditure patterns across provinces. Modern literature on index numbers offers several axiomatic approaches to the choice of a price index. Under the first axiomatic approach, the quantities and prices are independent variables (the cross-elasticity of demand is zero). There are approximately 20 tests under which indices are now evaluated (International Labour Organization et al., 2004). The Fisher index satisfies all 20 axioms, while the Young, Laspeyres and Paasche indices fail three time-reversal tests. The Walsh index fails four tests, and the Törnqvist index fails nine tests. In the case where data follows relatively smooth trends, the Törnqvist and Fisher indices are expected to approximate each other numerically (ILO et al., 2004).

In the second axiomatic approach, in which a price index is defined as a function of the two sets of prices, or their ratios, and two sets of values, the Törnqvist is the only price index that satisfies all 17 axioms. This is one of the many reasons why this index is currently favored by many researchers. Following the general consensus, we chose the Törnqvist index formula for the calculation of our new provincial CPIs. Alternative index formulas were also considered, although, due to the limited information available on the historical prices and consumer basket, we were not able to calculate the exact Törnqvist, Fisher, Laspeyres or Paasche indices.

Figure 1. Provincial CPI constructed via alternative index formulas

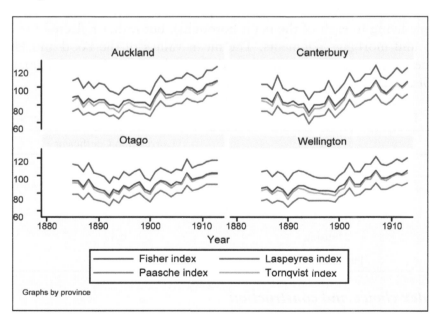

Figure 1 shows that the CPI series constructed using alternative index formulas all follow a similar pattern; however, as predicted by the theory, some of them are at the higher bound, while others are at the lower bound. Estimates derived via the Törnqvist and Fisher index formulas are closely approximated, and are in between the lower and the upper bounds.

A correlation matrix showed the Törnqvist and Fisher indices to be statistically identical. The Törnqvist price index was also highly correlated with both the Laspeyres and Paasche index estimates, with a correlation coefficient of between 0.96 and 0.99.

4 Provincial analysis

The period 1885–1913 was one of the most controversial and interesting in New Zealand's history: a period of depression and price deflation, rapid increases in production in the export industries (frozen meat and dairy), and intensive technological change in both agriculture and manufacturing. We endeavored to study price trends nationally and regionally, while also examining any inequalities in commodity prices at the provincial level.

4.1 Sub-index series provincial analysis

Studies for Australia and Britain identify the lack of convergence in commodity or labour markets between the mid-nineteenth and early twentieth centuries. McLean (1999), for example, concluded that for the four capital cities in Australia 1870–1914, there was no clear trend towards greater integration of commodity markets, with the exception of selected food items (bacon and potatoes). In New Zealand, Fraser (1915) also found divergence in the general grocery group series (the lowest prices were found in Canterbury and the highest in Dunedin). Significant disparities were also recognised in the meat series, where Auckland was consistently above the other centres and Dunedin consistently below. The patterns also varied for the other subseries, but overall Dunedin was identified as the least expensive city and Wellington as the most expensive. Aggregate expenditure series derived by Fraser (1915) did not show any signs of convergence by 1914.

We derive new provincial CPI series which are different in composition and in expenditure weights to those of Fraser, and subsequently test whether the inter-provincial convergence patterns deviate from those in Fraser. Certain assumptions, such as the relative stability of prices for imported items relative to the exported or home-produced goods, are likely to remain valid. Our provincial indices consist of seven sub-groups: Grocery, Dairy, Meat, Fuel and Light, Clothing, Housing, and Miscellaneous. Discussed herein are four of the most important – Grocery, Dairy, Meat, and Housing – the remaining subgroups showed similar price patterns.

The individual items in each subgroup are supposed to comprise items that exhibit similar price trends and are related to the assigned group. Most of the

Grocery group items are goods that were either imported or produced for domestic consumption (e.g. sugar, tea, coffee, potatoes); only wheat and flour were exported to some extent. Frequent fluctuations in the Grocery index series (see Figure 2A) reflect the seasonal volatility of bread, potato and flour prices, which are highly dependent upon the weather and the harvest in a particular year. Bread and flour together comprised around 10 per cent of the overall expenditure and about a third of the grocery basket. Fraser found that the retail prices of home produce items such as bread, flour, oatmeal, potatoes and onions were largely responsible for the annual fluctuations in the Grocery group. Notable from the new Grocery series are the common peaks and troughs of the provincial prices.

The plot of the coefficient of variation, Figure 2B, shows no major local variation in prices (the dispersion slightly increased during 1889–1900 and declined thereafter), which points towards the existence of one general market for New Zealand groceries. The general trend is indicative of a price decline in the late 1880s–1890s and subsequent recovery, which seems consistent with the world price deflation of the 1890s.

One distinction that can be drawn is the prevalence of low prices in the Canterbury region (on average the lowest among the four provinces). During the nineteenth and early twentieth century, South Island farmers produced most of the country's agricultural produce (cereals, wheat etc.) and Canterbury was predominantly the centre of wheat production in New Zealand due to the abundance of fertile land, easily accessible and readily cultivable. Flour prices, which remained the lowest in Canterbury until 1901, serve as an indication of Canterbury's agricultural dominance during that era.

The second subgroup in the Food group is Dairy produce, which is more homogeneous in its composition than the Grocery group. Figure 3A shows that the fluctuations between provinces pre-1900 do not co-vary. Dairy prices experience considerable local divergence prior to 1900 (Figure 3B). Post-1900, however, prices begin to fluctuate together. As with the Grocery series, relatively lower Canterbury prices prevail in the dairy market until 1900.

Until 1900, nominal prices of buter and cheese in Canterbury were markedly lower than the national average. During the period 1885–1913, the most butter came from Canterbury, due to its large farming population and the large area in Banks Peninsula devoted to dairy farming (New Zealand Ministry for Culture and Heritage, 2003). Unlike the Grocery series, there is a distinct increasing trend in dairy prices for all four provinces post-1900. Under the Dairy category, both cheese and butter were export commodities. The success of refrigeration prompted the establishment of the fast steam service between New Zealand and England, which also benefited both the butter and cheese industries. By 1890, dairy exports had reached 7 per cent of total exports, and they continued to increase in the twentieth century.

Figures 2A: Provincial Grocery Index Series, and 2B: Grocery Series Coefficient of Variation

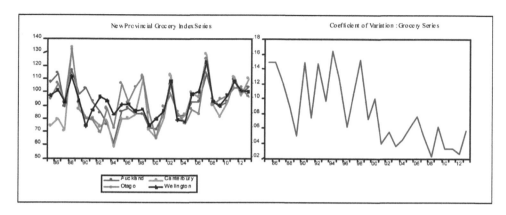

Figures 3A: Provincial Dairy Index Series, and 3B: Dairy Series Coefficient of Variation

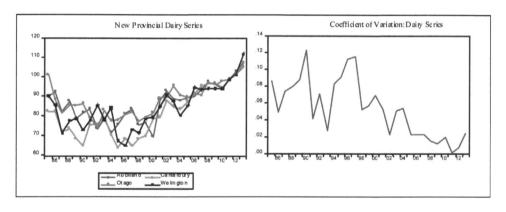

Meat was also an important export commodity in New Zealand. The first shipment of frozen meat in 1882 revolutionised the New Zealand economy and triggered the simultaneous development of freezing works in Dunedin, Christchurch, Wellington and Napier (New Zealand Ministry for Culture and Heritage, 2003). The number of freezing works in the colony gradually increased, and by 1891 it had risen to approximately 21, with 12 in the North Island and nine in the South Island. Most freezing works were located at ports, since it was more expensive to transport frozen meat than live animals (Hawke, 1985). These works were collectively capable of freezing up to four million sheep per annum (New Zealand Department of Statistics, 1893). However, it was not until the mid-1890s that the country began to experience any real economic benefit from the frozen meat trade. The yearly exports of frozen meat increased in volume from 19,339 pounds in 1883 to 1,033,377 pounds in 1892. As the frozen meat trade flourished, large areas in the south (Canterbury and Otago) that had been growing crops switched to pasture, with Canterbury dominating the frozen meat trade until the First World War. In 1900, 50 per cent of the frozen sheep carcasses exported were shipped from Canterbury. Over 83 per cent of lamb was shipped from the South Island and Canterbury's meat prices reached their lowest point in the 1890s (Figure 4A). Fraser's series, however, identified prices in Dunedin to be the lowest throughout the period 1891–1914. In both sources (Fraser and Department of Statistics retail price series), Auckland prices were consistently above those of the other regions or centres.

The world price of meat increased dramatically in 1895. Fraser noted that retail prices did not fluctuate according to the variation in export prices, and the local causes, peculiar to the meat trade, did not have any connection with the variations in the price of dairy produce, for instance. He also found that the local divergence in the 1890s was apparent across the four largest centres, which is consistent with the provincial results (Figure 4B).

Figures 4A: Provincial Meat Index Series, and 4B: Meat Series Coefficient of Variation

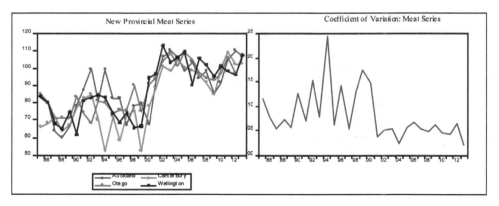

Consistent housing price data were derived from two sources: *Statistics New Zealand* pre-1902 (calculated from the number of boroughs and the rental value of rateable property), and the prices reported in Fraser (from 1902 to 1913, rental prices, based on the number of rooms in the house, were assigned different weights and averaged). Expenditure on rent contributed about 10 per cent of overall expenditure prior to 1900, and increased subsequently to approximately 20 per cent in 1910–11.

The Housing index identifies the greatest dispersion prior to 1900 (see Figure 5B). The relative absence of yearly fluctuations is due to fixed-term leasing, common for that period (Fraser, 1915). According to Fraser, the movement of rent over time tended to remain conservative even among those who rented on a weekly tenancy. Post 1898, Fraser recognised the greatest increases in rent for Auckland and Wellington, while Dunedin experienced the steadiest rent movement, and Christchurch had a boom in 1906, followed by a sharp fall in 1912. The new provincial Housing series exhibit marked differences from the Fraser series. Dunedin's housing prices are consistently higher than those in other provinces until 1898 (Figure 5A).

If we draw a North-South comparison, Wellington's housing prices appear to be higher than those in Auckland, but lower than in Otago or Canterbury. In fact, Auckland's housing prices were consistently lower than those in other provinces pre-1898, but post-1898 they rapidly increased; Auckland's likely due to rapidly growing population and positive rates of net inter-provincial migration.

Figures 5A: Provincial Housing Index Series, and 5B: Housing Series Coefficient of Variation

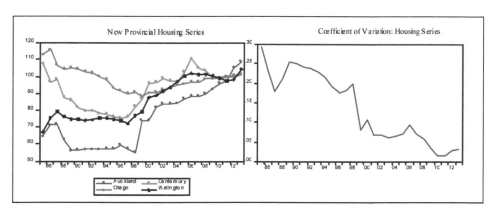

By the end of the 1890s Auckland's economy was booming, mostly due to the pastoral land expansion in the north, which triggered an increase in dairy and meat production. In contrast, Otago and Canterbury housing and rental prices fell throughout 1885–1898. In 1897, regional economies underwent a general increase in the cost of living, where the prices for most exported goods increased (flour and bread prices were at their peak then, probably due to an increase in export flour prices). The spike in the Canterbury housing prices in 1906 is consistent with Fraser's series. Overall, housing prices exhibited the greatest dispersion during the period 1885–1898, subsequently converging in the 1900s (see Figure 5B). This is perhaps not surprising, given the fixity of property once built.

To summarise the above, local price discrepancies were the highest during the 1890s, and world price deflation in the 1890s had the most impact on

New Zealand's traded sector. Food groups, in particular, underwent the most rapid decline of the seven subseries considered. Grocery prices in 1889 were 20–30 per cent higher than the average in 1909–1913, and by 1894 the cost of groceries in Auckland and Canterbury fell by 50 per cent and in Otago and Wellington by 25–30 per cent. Coefficient-of-variation analysis showed no major local variation in grocery prices, where the common peaks and troughs in the Grocery series might be best attributed to seasonal fluctuations in wheat and bread prices, which constituted approximately 30 per cent of the overall expenditure on grocery items.

Some dispersion in the cost of dairy produce was found across provincial markets, although they were not as widespread as for the Grocery series. The provincial Dairy series declined from around 1885, in contrast to the Grocery series trend, with dairy produce prices increasing in 1891, only to decline again in 1895. The lowest prices for dairy produce were found in Canterbury, which was consistent with the lower prices of butter and cheese in Canterbury compared to the other provinces. Dairy prices experienced considerable local divergence across regional markets prior to 1900, which was particularly apparent during the periods 1886–1891 and 1895–1898. The local costs of dairy produce appear to be converging by 1900, which is supported by an 80 per cent decline in the coefficient of variation from 1897 to 1901.

It is interesting to note that meat prices show a different trajectory to dairy prices. Prior to 1889, the fluctuations in meat prices were fairly homogeneous. Between 1889 and 1894 the level of dispersion among provinces greatly increased, reaching 25 per cent in 1894. As in the Grocery and Dairy series, a significant decline in the variation of prices among provincial markets achieved by 1900, is also observed in the Meat series.

The Housing price series declined in Canterbury and Otago and increased in Wellington and Auckland. Our findings deviate from those of Fraser (1915), who found that the highest prices existed in Wellington and the lowest in Auckland (until 1900). Our results, however, are consistent with population movements towards the North from the South. The cost of food relative to the cost of housing was declining in Auckland and Wellington, and slightly increasing in Canterbury and Otago (Figure 6). As housing prices in Auckland and Wellington were rising, a relatively larger proportion of the budget was spent on paying rent than on buying food. The opposite was true for Canterbury and Otago. The relative price effects induced an increase in the housing share, which corresponds to the reported increase in the expenditure on Housing and decline in the expenditure on Food (see Table 1). Figure 6, below, plots food to housing ratios for the different provinces.

From the analysis above, it seems clear that some prices varied significantly across provinces and time. Most price series converge or begin to converge by

1900, suggesting (via coefficient-of-variation analysis) that the markets became relatively more integrated by the beginning of the twentieth century. This contrasts with McLean's findings on Australia, which reported that annual fluctuations in price levels between the pairs Sydney-Adelaide, Melbourne-Adelaide and Melbourne-Sydney moved less closely from 1890 than before. This was true for all items combined and for food items separately. The only exceptions were the markets for bacon and potatoes, which became more integrated after 1890.[7] McLean suggested that these two food items were less perishable than butter or bread for instance, and so transport costs might have played a role here.

Figure 6. Relative prices, Food to Housing ratio (1885–1913)

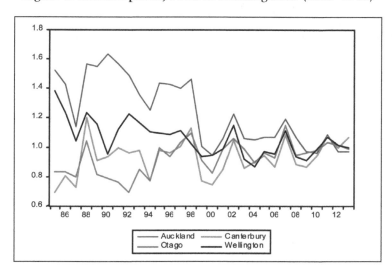

4.2 A new provincial CPI series

The final subseries were combined and weighted to produce a new composite provincial CPI series. From Figure 7A, we can see that for the period 1888–1891, there is a universal (i.e. common to all four provincial districts) decline in consumer prices. During the time when prices were falling, they were also diverging the most from the provincial average (Figure 7B). Food items constituted the largest percentage in the overall expenditure basket, such that peaks and falls in the composite series are typically mirroring the fluctuations in the Grocery, Meat and Dairy prices. Bread and flour were heavily dependent

---

7   McLean (1999) used correlation coefficients for the two periods, 1865–89 and 1890–1914, to compare the fluctuations in the price index series for the three metropolitan centres Sydney, Melbourne and Adelaide.

upon the weather and the harvest in a particular year, as well as external shocks for example, the 1902 Australia-wide Federation drought drove up flour prices in 1903, and very large increases in flour prices in 1907 in New Zealand were in response to Australia's protective duties of 9d per bushel of wheat.[8]

Figures 7A: Composite Provincial CPI Series, and 7B: Composite Provincial Series Coefficient of Variation

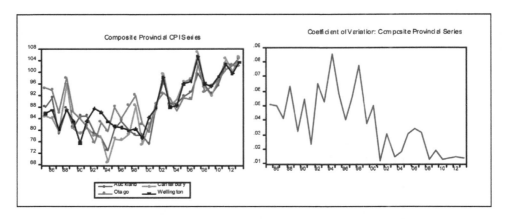

New Zealand's protective legislation also had an effect on the prices of imported and manufactured products and from 1895, there was a steady movement towards a reduction on the duties levied upon imported foodstuffs, and an extension of the tariff levied upon imported manufactured goods. The Preferential and Reciprocal Trade Act 1903 in New Zealand introduced preferential rates of duty in favour of the produce of the British Dominions, by imposing extra duties on certain imports that were produced or manufactured by other countries. The list of preferential items was materially extended by the New Zealand Tariff Act 1907, from 31 March 1908 (Knibbs, 1911).

Similarly to the Australian experience, New Zealand's economy emerged gradually from the integration of several regional economies, which initially were small and separated by significant transport costs. McLean suggested that a trend towards a more integrated market arises if disparities in the level of prices of a commodity across regions are reduced, or the fluctuations in prices become more highly (positively) correlated. McLean conducted pair-wise comparisons for Adelaide, Melbourne and Sydney for two periods: 1865–89 and 1890–1914, but his anticipated increase in the degree of market integration was not observed during 1890–1914. In New Zealand, price trends between 1900 and 1913 were very different from those between 1885 and 1899. The introduction of refrigeration from the 1880s led to substantial changes in the pattern of regional fluctuations:

8   *Appendix to the Journals of the House of Representatives*, 1912, H-18, p.354.

whereas prior to 1900 provincial differences were more apparent across all sub-index series, after 1900 these differences decreased markedly. And, unlike in Australia, these turning points in price trends coincided across all subseries.

Table 3 demonstrates a marked increase in the degree of market integration among provincial pairs of aggregate CPIs (combined subseries). It is apparent that Auckland became more integrated with all provinces between 1900 and 1913.

Table 3. Measures of market integration (correlation coefficients)

		1885–1900		
Correlation	Auckland	Canterbury	Otago	Wellington
Auckland	1.00			
Canterbury	0.63*	1.00		
Otago	0.63*	0.80**	1.00	
Wellington	0.29	0.34	0.20	1.00
		1900–1913		
Correlation	Auckland	Canterbury	Otago	Wellington
Auckland	1.00			
Canterbury	0.92**	1.00		
Otago	0.94**	0.88**		
Wellington	0.90**	0.98**	0.90**	

*, ** significant at 5 per cent and 1 per cent levels, respectively

Of particular interest is the change in significance of the correlation coefficient between Auckland and Wellington. Auckland was quite isolated until 1906, when the main trunk railway was built connecting Auckland to the other localities in the North Island where railways had risen in importance around the time of the growth of the freezing works. Negative rates of net inter-provincial migration in the South, and positive rates in the North, indicate that during the period 1886–1911, the population was following the shift of economic activity northwards.

4.3 The South–North convergence story: Benefits from refrigeration

The historical literature emphasises the key role refrigeration had on the economic development of New Zealand. The extensive exportation of pastoral products that began in the 1890s boosted the economy and helped it recover from 'the long depression'. While aggregate price and income trends are well known, regional analysis remains very limited and does not involve continuous time-series analysis. Previously, we presented regional price data on various grouped commodities where some common features mirrored national trends. Previous findings point towards idiosyncratic markets pre-1900 and sharp provincial inequalities, especially during the price deflation period (1879–1896). Particularly interesting is the central role of Canterbury prior to 1898, which was typified by low retail prices of traded commodities (meat, dairy, and some grocery items, such as bread and flour).

Prior to the refrigeration boom, most of New Zealand's agricultural and pastoral produce was concentrated in the South Island. Canterbury had an abundance of fertile land, easily accessible and readily cultivable, and it produced three quarters of the wheat, half the barley and one third of the oats grown in New Zealand. Cereals were almost entirely neglected in the North Island, where farming in general was not economically important pre-1900, owing partly to climatic and political conditions, but also to the difficulty of bringing the more heavily timbered lands of that island under cultivation. The kauri harvest dominated the economy of the upper North Island until 1910 and, with kauri gum, accounted for 58 per cent of Auckland's exports in 1885. Soils and climatic conditions in the North did not suit the pasturing of sheep, and there were only local markets for the production of butter and cheese.

For similar reasons (e.g. because the basic system of breeding and fattening suitable sheep breeds was already in place), the refrigeration boom initially benefited the South more than the North. Historically, sheep farming was the principal economic activity in the South Island during the nineteenth century, and as the frozen meat trade flourished, large areas in Canterbury and Otago that had been growing crops switched to pasture. Canterbury dominated the frozen meat trade until the First World War. In 1900, 50 per cent of frozen sheep carcasses exported from New Zealand were shipped from Canterbury, and over 83 per cent of lamb exports were shipped from the South Island, again mostly from Canterbury.

The response of dairying to refrigeration was less rapid than for the meat industry (Hawke, 1985). Some of the reasons related to the more advanced technology required for mass milk and cream separation, storage and cheese-making. As a result, the regional impact of dairying differed from that of meat production. Although initially the response to intensive dairy farming occurred in the far south (Otago/Southland), the better-suited lands in Wanganui, South Auckland and Taranaki began dairying after 1900 (Hawke, 1985). The role of transport in dairy farming played a very important role, as milk fat had to be moved to dairy factories daily until refrigerated storage became available on the farm. Again, initially, the South Island was better connected prior to 1900, and Auckland was particularly isolated from the rest of the North Island until the main trunk railway was completed in 1906, connecting Auckland with Wellington and other localities.

The domination of the South began to diminish post-1898 as the new trade reshaped agricultural production and more land became suitable for farming. Dairy, beef and sheep farming became the predominant industries in the North Island (dairying expanded into the better lowlands, while sheep and beef farms moved into the hill country). This transformation shifted the bulk of production and farming to the North Island, where the attraction was promoted by the progressive clearing of the bush for farmland,[9] the cessation of overt Māori resistance to European land settlement, the mining of gold near Thames, and above all, unprecedented scope for new developments and rationalisation of agriculture (Neville and O'Neill, 1979). The refrigeration boom stimulated diversification of agricultural production, which also led to an expansion of farming in the North Island and encouraged more intensive settlement.

The specificity of the New Zealand's regional climatic differences and economic development presupposes certain variability in consumer prices and living standards across provinces, especially before 1900, when production and transportation costs were higher. As one of the leading New Zealand economic historians, Gary Hawke (1985), pointed out: "despite the greater economic integration induced by Vogel's schemes (e.g. abolishing of the provinces in 1876), regional experiences were varied."

5 Time-series analysis: Common trends and leading provinces

5.1 Unit root tests

Previously, we considered whether regional prices were homogeneous and whether there was any evidence of price convergence in the form of a spatial integration of markets. The coefficient of variation was the measure of convergence and by implication, market integration. Here we use more sophisticated time-series methods for uncovering convergence, such as the original 'unit root'[10] tests of Dickey and Fuller (1979). Convergence is tested considering a panel data structure, where the provinces represent space (with a relatively small number of provinces, N), and time is measured with a relatively large number of years, T.

Examination of the time-series properties of the series typically begins with unit root testing to determine whether the series in question are stationary or non-stationary. Basically, a stationary series 'never wanders far away from its mean' or trend (if trend-stationary), while non-stationary series are characterised by long-term shocks that lead to idiosyncratic behaviour (such as the effects of tariff changes that lead to permanent increases in prices). In effect,

9   During 1892–1900 the Liberal Government acquired 1.3 million hectares of Māori land, which started a transformation of North Island hill country from bush to pasture.
10   A unit root is an attribute of a statistical model of a time series, the autoregressive parameter of which is equal to one.

stationarity allows for the regression estimates to be tested very closely along the well-known properties of a normal distribution.

Testing for non-stationarity in the variable is synonymous with unit-root testing, and the Augmented Dickey Fuller (ADF) tests are perhaps the most commonly used individual unit root tests. In the case of structural breaks in the series (a change in the direction of the trend or increase in the level of the series), discontinuities may lead to type I errors that will likely bias any further analysis. To account for any structural breaks, we include Perron-type unit root tests (Perron, 1989; Zivot and Andrews, 1992) in the pre-testing stage where appropriate.

Individual (for each panel separately) unit root tests indicate that Dairy, Meat and Housing are non-stationary for Auckland and Wellington; Dairy, Meat, Housing and Miscellaneous are non-stationary for Canterbury; and Housing, Fuel and Light, and Clothing are non-stationary for Otago (see Table 4 below). Other series appear to be stationary. An important result is that the export sectors (Meat and Dairy) seem to exhibit non-stationarity in the price series for more than one province, possibly due to changes in technology of production, or tariff changes that had permanent and persistent effects.

Table 4. ADF unit root tests in levels for the sub-series in each province

Index series by province	Auckland	Canterbury	Otago	Wellington
Grocery	v	v	v	v
Dairy	xx	xx	vv	xx
Meat	xx	xx	vv	xx
Housing	xx	xx	x	xx
Fuel and Light	v	v	x	x
Clothing	vv	vv	x	vv
Miscellaneous	vv	xx	vv	vv

Note: "v"– the series are stationary or I(0), "vv" – the series are trend-stationary, "x" – the series are non-stationary without a linear trend, "xx" – the series are non-stationary with a linear trend.

To check the robustness of the individual unit-root test results, we also use panel unit-root tests, where we consider four panels represented by the four provincial districts (Table 5). The Fisher-type panel test (Maddala and Wu, 1999) is likely to be the most appropriate for our data, as the effect of serial correlation is less severe for this test, and it has the highest power when performed in the presence of both stationary and non-stationary series in the group. In the panel environment, the test confirmed that the only non-stationary series are Dairy and Housing.

Table 5. Panel unit root test (Fisher-ADF)

Panel variable	Z-statistics
Grocery	−5.14*
Dairy	−1.53
Meat	−2.45*
Housing	0.645
Fuel and Light	3.672*
Clothing	−3.427*
Miscellaneous	−2.432*

Note: H_0 = existence of a unit root in the panel, H_1 = some cross-sections do not have a unit root.
* indicated rejection of the null at the 5 per cent level of significance.

Despite certain advantages of panel tests, they still do not account for the possible structural breaks or discontinuities in the series. In Section 4.1 we identified that most of the subseries experienced a change in the trend by the late 1890s. Where the 1880s were characterised as a period of 'depression' in New Zealand,[11] the following decade (1889–1899) was "a normal period in the Dominion history", where trade was steady, agriculture and manufacturing reached a high state of efficiency, the country was both politically and socially stable, and prices were expected to rise (McIlraith, 1911). Furthermore, protective tariffs and labour legislation changes[12] were likely to contribute to the increased cost of commodities by the start of the twentieth century. To identify whether such changes could be responsible for the possible discontinuities in certain subseries (only relevant for traded commodities), we utilise the Zivot and Andrews (1992) unit root tests. Table 6 shows that the Dairy, Meat and Housing sectors remain non-stationary for Auckland and Canterbury, while some changes are observed for the results in Otago and Wellington.

Structural changes in 1895 and 1900 were the most commonly identified breaks (i.e. Housing and Clothing in Otago; Dairy and Meat in Wellington). The provincial Dairy series all experienced a structural change in 1895, which had permanent effects in Canterbury and Auckland, when refrigerated rail facilities became available, making it possible to transport dairy products more easily. Before then, for example, Taranaki products were initially shipped to Wellington by coastal vessels for trans-shipment to ocean liners, due to inadequate roads in Taranaki (Hawke, 1985). As a consequence, the production of butter and

11   A period of almost $20 million debt (from the previous decade), falling prices for agricultural and pastoral products, a decline in the production of gold, and industry-wide stagnation.

12   In 1894 the first Industrial Conciliation and Arbitration Act was passed; it was amended in 1895, 1896 and 1898, and a new Act passed in 1900 (Collins, 1912).

cheese greatly increased from 1896 and for the period to World War I, butter production increased nearly five-fold, and cheese more than ten-fold.

Table 6. ADF unit root tests in levels (breaks considered) and first differences

Index series by province	Auckland	Canterbury	Otago	Wellington
Dairy	xx	xx		vv'
Meat	xx	xx		v
Housing	xx	xx	v'	xx
Fuel and Light			×	×
Clothing			v'	
Miscellaneous		xx		

Note: "xx" – I (1) series (first-difference stationary) with a linear trend in levels, "×" – I (1) series without a linear trend in levels (constant trend), "v'"– I (0) series, stationary with a crash and trend in the data (when the crash and trend in the series are taken into account).

Earlier, we argued that the Dairy and Meat indices had different growth trajectories due to differences in the technology involved in their production. Structural change in the Meat series across all provinces occurred around 1900, which is consistent with what can be observed in Figure 4A. By 1900, more land became available for pasture and greater quantities of mutton were being exported. The conclusion here is that the break tests suggest that the series are stationary around the break in a trend and/or intercept.

5.2 Testing for convergence in prices: Bernard and Durlauf (1995)-type tests

Among the sub-index series of the previous section, the most interesting were the non-stationary ones: Dairy, Meat, Housing, and Fuel and Light. Here, we consider the possibility of convergence or common trends, suggesting market integration, in those price series using time-series methods. Earlier, the coefficient of variation and simple correlation analysis revealed some interesting findings. These results suggest that New Zealand markets were relatively more integrated from 1900 to 1913 than from 1885 to 1900. This tendency was mirrored in most of the provincial subseries.

However, the coefficient-of-variation analysis is limited as a tool to examine the degree of regional market integration and serves only as a guide to changes in variation among regions over time. Economically, investigation of issues such as the Law of One Price (LOOP) can assist in our understanding of the disparities across specific regional markets and how integrated they were by the beginning of the twentieth century. The Law of One Price is more likely to occur for homogeneous, traded goods prices, and it is on these goods that we will concentrate. Tests for convergence typically differ depending on the time-series properties of the data, therefore we draw upon the results in the previous section to guide the choice of tests employed.

As raised in Section 5.1, non-stationarity gives rise to several econometric problems, but most importantly, non-stationarity in the levels of variables implies that a stable long-run relationship is not possible. However, if both variables are integrated of order one (stationary in their differences) there may exist a linear combination of them that is stationary, which implies that the two variables could be 'cointegrated'. Thus, if variables are cointegrated, they tend to move together and (statistical) convergence may occur faster than is the case for stationary series.

We test for cointegration by applying unit root tests on the bivariate differences of provincial prices, paired one at a time, following the Bernard and Durlauf (1995) approach. On the basis of the results (Table 7), the convergence hypothesis is not rejected for both the Dairy and Meat series for the Canterbury-Auckland pair, and the Housing series for the Canterbury-Wellington pair.

Table 7. Unit root test on the difference between each pair of provinces (without discontinuities) for the period 1885–1913

$\gamma_{i,t+k} - \gamma_{j,t+k}$	Dairy		Meat		Housing		Fuel and Light	
Provinces	ADF (2)	LM (SC)	ADF(0)	LM(SC)	ADF(0)	LM (SC)	ADF(0)	LM (SC)
Canterbury-Auckland	−4.66* (T)	1.92476	−4.779*	0.2646	−3.6287	1.194		
Canterbury-Wellington					−6.79*	0.0417		
Auckland-Wellington					2.4891	5.4307*		
Otago-Wellington							−3.486	0.225

* t-statistics denote significance at the 5 per cent level based on MacKinnon (1991).
ADF (2) and ADF (0) indicate the number of lagged differences of the variables (based on SIC criterion). (T) relates to trend significance at the 5 per cent level.
LM (SC) is a test for serial correlation: H_0 (null hypothesis) implies no serial correlation.

It is also possible to test for convergence in a multivariate setting utilising either panel-based unit-root testing techniques or cointegration methods, for example, Phillips and Ouliaris (1990) and Johansen (1988). Given that we do not have more than two provinces that exhibit non-stationarity for each price index, the bivariate testing is appropriate in this case; however, to check the robustness of the above results, we include estimates of the bivariate Johansen (1988) test for cointegration, which confirms that both the Dairy and Meat series for the Canterbury-Auckland pair each exhibit one significant cointegrating relationship (Table 8).

Table 8. Cointegration results: Auckland-Canterbury pair, Johansen estimates, 1885–1913 (unrestricted intercepts and trends in levels)

Number of cointegrated relations		Dairy (VAR=3) Lag intervals: 2		Meat (VAR=1) Lag intervals: 0	
H_0	H_1	Trace	Max Eigenvalue	Trace	Max Eigenvalue
r=0	r=1	21.25*	21*	23.07*	21.107*
r≤1	r=2	0.24	0.24	1.962	1.962

* indicates the rejection of the null hypothesis of no cointegrating relationship at the 5 per cent level. Lags selected were determined by prior estimation of an unrestricted VAR model in levels for each system of equations.

In addition, with the Johansen approach we can impose restrictions on the coefficients to identify if the series exhibit 'absolute' or 'relative' convergence (Bernard and Durlauf, 1995). The likelihood ratio (LR) test for binding restrictions for the Dairy series suggests that Auckland and Canterbury share a common trend, but do not converge to a common steady-state equilibrium. The results for the Meat price series indicate the opposite: the Auckland and Canterbury Meat series converge in a Bernard and Durlauf sense.

As discussed in Section 4.3, the response of dairying to refrigeration was less rapid than for the meat industry partly because of the more advanced technology required for the mass milk and cream separation, storage and cheese-making. Transport also posed more difficulties for the dairy industry than the meat industry. Sheep made only one journey to freezing works, but milk fat had to be conveyed to dairy factories daily until refrigerated storage was available on the farm. The regional impact of dairying thus differed from that of meat production.

As previously established by Greasley and Oxley (2010), both meat and dairy each had individual driving forces and formed separate development blocks: meat and cheese showed accelerating growth from the 1880s, whereas butter growth came in later, from the mid-1890s. Butter and cheese require different production technologies, and their growth paths could be dissimilar. Most dairy factories were producing only butter for commercial purposes (export) in the 1880s–1890s, and it was only in the late 1890s that many converted to produce both butter and cheese. Figure 8 shows that Canterbury had the lowest butter and cheese prices of the four provinces until around 1900.

Figure 8. Butter and cheese prices (per lb) for the four provinces (1885–1913)

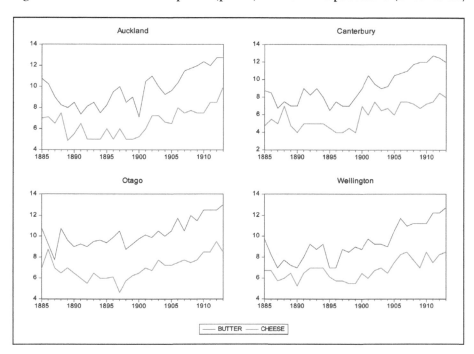

The common increase in butter prices in 1890 could be attributed to extra costs from the change in butter production technology: creameries were set up in the 1890s along with the skimming stations. By 1885, the manufacture of cheese was typically undertaken in factories, much more so than for butter. However, according to the Industrial Census, the returns from cheese factories were only 40 per cent of the total factory produce returns (New Zealand Parliament, 1887). Both butter and cheese series exhibit comparable trends, but the yearly fluctuations do not always coincide.

The same procedure of unit-root pre-testing that we used for the Dairy sector was applied to cheese and butter prices. The unit-root test results revealed that non-stationarity of the Dairy index (for Auckland and Canterbury) was driven by butter prices rather than cheese prices. The butter prices between Auckland and Canterbury appear to satisfy the properties of a long-run equilibrium relationship. However, such results are conditional on the chosen period, for example, cheese prices experienced accelerated growth earlier (at the beginning of the 1880s) than butter (in the mid-1890s), and it is possible that if we were to consider a longer period, cheese prices would be driving the dairy sector (Greasley and Oxley, 2010).

Moving to housing prices, Johansen's bivariate test validated the Bernard and Durlauf (1995) convergence result where the Canterbury-Wellington pair exhibit a 'cointegrating' relationship (Table 9). The implied restrictions for convergence suggest that Canterbury and Wellington experience long-run convergence, denoting that the long-run effect of shocks to housing prices impact Canterbury and Wellington similarly. It is interesting to note that by 1910–11, the net inter-provincial migration rate for Canterbury was negative 6, and in Wellington the opposite, positive 6. Christchurch rental prices boomed in 1906, followed by a sharp fall in 1912 (Figure 5A). Wellington is the only other province that had an increase in the cost of housing in 1906.

Table 9. Housing index series: Bivariate Cointegration results, Johansen estimates, 1885–1913 (unrestricted intercepts and linear trends in levels)

Hypotheses		Auckland-Canterbury		Canterbury-Wellington		Auckland-Wellington	
H_0	H_1	Trace	Max. Eigenvalue	Trace	Max. Eigenvalue	Trace	Max. Eigenvalue
r=0	r=1	21.251*	21.009	23.07*	21.107*	13.643	13.289
r≤1	r=2	0.2416	0.2416	1.962	1.962	0.354	0.354

5.3 Testing for causality: Leading provinces

The historical literature argues strongly that pastoral products, for example, beef, mutton, lamb, wool, butter and cheese, were the export commodities that had the most influence on New Zealand's economic performance for the period we are considering. New Zealand supplied almost half of the total quantity of frozen mutton and lamb imported into the United Kingdom between 1885 and 1993; by comparison, Australia contributed around one-tenth of that.

In Section 4.3 we discussed the leading position of the South Island, particularly Canterbury, during the nineteenth century, in both agricultural and pastoral produce. It was hypothesised that the refrigeration boom initially benefited the South more than the North, based upon its initial advantage of easily accessible and readily cultivable land. In addition, transport costs imposed restrictions on the exportation of meat from the more remote areas in the North Island. Railway and road construction was slow to progress in the North, with large areas of the North Island covered in bush. Most freezing works were located at ports due to the cost of transporting frozen meat compared to live animals (Hawke, 1985). The wholesale prices of frozen mutton for export were the lowest at the ports of Lyttelton (Canterbury) and Dunedin (Otago) in 1893 (New Zealand Department of Statistics, 1894). The quantity of frozen mutton exported was also the largest at the port of Lyttelton. Notably, Canterbury also benefited the most from the overseas trade, which had absolute surplus in the net exports.

Previously, we noted that meat and dairy prices followed different time paths. The initial response of dairying to refrigeration originated in the far South, which only later included North Island areas. Nominal prices for all dairy (butter and cheese) and meat (lamb, beef, etc.) products remained the lowest in Canterbury until 1900. Within the dairy sector, cheese and butter exhibited different growth paths. While meat and cheese showed accelerating growth from the 1880s, butter's faster growth came later, from the mid-1890s. In Section 5.2 the unit-root test results showed that non-stationarity of the Dairy index (for Auckland and Canterbury) was driven by butter prices rather than cheese prices.

To explore whether Canterbury was, in fact, a leading province in the Dairy price series, we can test for Granger causality. However, in the context of non-stationary data series, the standard Wald statistic does not follow its usual asymptotic Chi-square distribution. Therefore, we follow the Toda-Yamamoto (T-Y) procedure to test for Granger causality (Toda and Yamamoto, 1995). Table 10 represents the pairs of provincial Dairy series, where a rejection of the null hypothesis implies there is Granger causality. We should point out that if the variables are cointegrated then there must be a causal relationship in at least one direction, however, the converse is not true (Johansen, 1988).

In the case of the Meat series, Otago is revealed as the leading province (Table 11). The first shipment of frozen meat was from Dunedin in 1882, the number of carcasses of frozen mutton exported from Otago was the highest until at least the late 1890s, and some of the earlier freezing works were also built there. Thus, it is reasonable to assume that the changes in fluctuations in Otago meat prices preceded those in other provinces.

The South Island provinces were undeniably the more economically and resource advantaged during the nineteenth century. When profits from refrigerated shipping were realised, it was much easier to convert the readily available farmland from agriculture to pasture. Statistically, we find evidence of Canterbury leading the dairy sector prices, and Otago leading the meat sector prices, which is consistent with the historiography on economic development in New Zealand.

Table 10. VAR Granger/Block Causality Exogeneity Wald Tests: Dairy

Dairy Price Series Variable Pairs	Granger Causality Block Wald χ^2 tests (first variable: leader)	Granger Causality Block Wald χ^2 tests (second variable: leader)	Leading Province in the Granger Causality Sense
Auckland-Canterbury VAR=3	$\chi^2(3)=5.54$	$\chi^2(3)=7.68**$	Canterbury
Canterbury-Otago VAR=1	$\chi^2(1)=4.103**$	$\chi^2(1)=1.36$	Canterbury
Canterbury-Wellington VAR=1	$\chi^2(1)=18.82**$	$\chi^2(1)=0.242$	Canterbury
Auckland-Otago VAR=1	$\chi^2(1)=0.0016$	$\chi^2(1)=5.83**$	Otago
Otago-Wellington VAR=1	$\chi^2(1)=2.89*$	$\chi^2(1)=6.6**$	Bi-directional
Auckland-Wellington VAR=1	$\chi^2(1)=3.75**$	$\chi^2(1)=0.054$	Auckland

*, ** significant at 10 and 5 per cent levels, respectively

Table 11. VAR Granger/Block Causality Exogeneity Wald Tests: Meat

Meat Price Series Variable Pairs	Granger Causality Block Wald χ^2 tests (first variable: leader)	Granger Causality Block Wald χ^2 tests (second variable: leader)	Leading Province in a Granger Causality Sense
Auckland-Canterbury VAR=3	$\chi^2(3)=1.556$	$\chi^2(3)=13.29**$	Canterbury
Canterbury-Otago VAR=3	$\chi^2(3)=0.86$	$\chi^2(3)=10.6**$	Otago
Canterbury-Wellington VAR=1	$\chi^2(1)=0.231$	$\chi^2(1)=3.64*$	Wellington (Weakly)
Auckland-Otago VAR=2	$\chi^2(2)=0.27$	$\chi^2(2)=8.93**$	Otago
Otago-Wellington VAR=3	$\chi^2(3)=5.955$	$\chi^2(3)=7.44**$	Otago
Auckland-Wellington VAR=3	$\chi^2(3)=0.63$	$\chi^2(3)=18.37**$	Wellington

*, ** significant at 10 and 5 per cent levels, respectively

6 Consistency of the new aggregate index

Consistency of the new provincial series can be assessed by comparing the new aggregate with the existing national CPIs (from Arnold, 1982; McIlraith, 1911; Sauerbeck, 1895). Potential differences may arise for several reasons, including different estimation of certain expenditure items in the basket, minor weight changes within the subseries and an alternative index formula for our CPI calculation. In addition to the New Zealand CPI series, Figure 9 includes historical price indices for Britain (Sauerbeck, 1895) and Australia (McLean, 1999).

Figure 9. Aggregate price index comparison

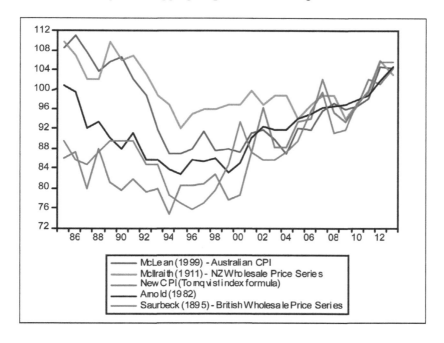

Notably, all CPI series move in the same direction and have similar trends. McIlraith's wholesale price index for New Zealand resembles McLean's Australian CPI, while Sauerbeck's British wholesale price index movements have more in common with Arnold's index and the new CPI series. Arnold's CPI is hypothesised to have the highest degree of correlation with the new index, as opposed to earlier alternatives, by way of construction and use of the same data source. Table 12 shows that fluctuations in the new CPI (Törnqvist index) are significantly related to the fluctuations in Arnold's CPI, but not to other indices.

Table 12. Correlation coefficient matrix (first differences)

Correlation Probability	Arnold	McLean	Törnqvist	Sauerbeck	McIlraith
Arnold	1.00				
McLean	0.35	1.00			
	0.07				
Törnqvist	0.63	0.23	1.00		
	0.00	0.23			
Sauerbeck	0.15	0.13	0.14	1.00	
	0.46	0.49	0.49		
McIlraith	0.33	0.35	-0.07	0.36	1.00
	0.09	0.07	0.73	0.06	

There are, however, marked differences between the new series and Arnold's series, for example, the new CPI exhibits sharper falls and increases (those could be outliers that are not apparent from Arnold's index, since her CPI is a weighted national average that included most provincial districts). Spikes around 1902, 1907 and 1911 may be due to certain well-documented New Zealand events, for example, manufacturing and tariff changes. Revision of the Tariff Act in 1907 imposed extra duties on manufactured items and equipment from countries other than Britain, which led to increased costs of production.

To make further comparisons and identify whether our derived aggregated consumer index[13] is 'similar' (in a statistical sense) to the Nesbitt-Savage/Arnold index ('the best' existing historical CPI), we follow the time-series analysis procedures introduced earlier. Unit-root pre-testing revealed that both series experience a common structural break around 1901. Exclusion of the other provinces in the new aggregate CPI calculation made the series more volatile to fluctuations of the grocery and other food items. To smooth the effects of the outliers, we used Holt-Winters (no seasonality with the lowest RMSE) exponential smoothing technique (Holt, 2004), with the results presented as in Figure 10.

We can test if the series co-move in the long run by using the Johansen method. The results revealed that the smoothed series do move together, but do not suggest a long-run equilibrium such that the series are effectively statistically identical.

---

13 Since the Törnqvist formula was used for deriving the aggregate index, we will refer to it as the 'Törnqvist index' for simplicity.

Figure 10. Holt-Winters exponential smoothing: the resulting series

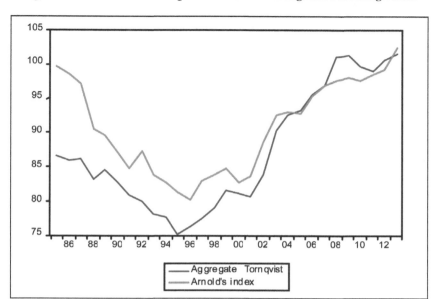

7 Some Concluding Remarks

Historical statistics in New Zealand, particularly prior to the 1950s, are largely unavailable in a readily usable form. Compiling and analyzing historical data can assist us in better understanding the living standards in in New Zealand, where the data on prices, wages, economic performance and health statistics were relatively consistently collected and published annually by the Department of Statistics for each province since at least the 1850s. Prior to the abolition of provinces in 1876, socio-economic and demographic data covered all New Zealand regions, but after 1876 the scope of data reporting for most indicators was restricted to the four largest provinces (in terms of population). Construction of regional deflator series and regional real wages[14] allow us to explore differences in regional dynamics and changes in the standard of living in different locations over time. This work, in particular, focused on establishing the degree of market integration within the New Zealand dairy and meat sectors, and whether the theoretical assumptions on the South-North convergence were supported statistically.

Statistically, we found that both meat and dairy price series (traded goods) either exhibited convergent behaviour in the long run (meat series) or 'catching up' (dairy series). This was only established for the Auckland-Canterbury pair, although the coefficient-of-variation analysis confirmed considerable declines

---

14   Not presented here, but constructed by the authors.

in dispersion post-1900 across all provinces. In addition, we established that Canterbury dairy prices were leading the dairy sector prices, and Otago meat prices led the meat sector prices. These findings are suggestive of South-North convergence, demonstrating that the refrigeration boom that initially benefited the South gradually involved the North. The dominating position of the South began to diminish post-1898 as the new trade reshaped agricultural production and more land became suitable for farming. Dairying, beef and sheep farming became the predominant industries in the North Island (dairying expanded on the better lowlands, while sheep and beef farming moved into the hill country of the North Island). This transformation has shifted a lot of the production and farming to the North Island.

Provincial analysis of the historical price series in this chapter highlights the disparities that existed among local markets due to a variety of reasons including transport, climate and geographical location. Not only were there differences between the North and South Islands, but also within the two islands. Lack of reliable transportation was one of the reasons why Auckland was relatively more isolated within the North Island. The importance of railways rose around the time of the advancement of freezing works, the introduction of refrigeration from the 1880s led to substantial changes in the pattern of regional fluctuations, and by 1900, New Zealand provincial markets became more integrated, especially between the North Island and South Island provinces. Negative rates of net inter-provincial migration in the South and positive rates in the North indicate that during 1886–1911 New Zealand's population was moving north with the shift of economic activity.

Provincial analysis undertaken here is important in its own right, but also for comparison to other countries, including Australia and Britain. McLean (1999) concluded that for the four capital cities in Australia there was no clear trend during the 1870–1914 period towards greater integration of commodity markets, with the exception of selected food items (bacon and potatoes). Thus, it is likely that the timing of the emergence of a national market for goods in New Zealand was quite different from that in Australia, suggesting that greater persistent disparities existed among Australian regional markets than among New Zealand markets well into the twentieth century.

References

Allen, R. (1994). Real Incomes in the English-Speaking World, 1879–1913. In George Grantham and Mary MacKinnon (eds) *Labour Market Evolution: The Economic History of Market Integration, Wage Flexibility and the Employment Relation*, London: Routledge, pp. 107–138.

Arnold, M. N. (1982). *Consumer prices, 1870 to 1919*. Discussion Paper, Department of Economics, Victoria University of Wellington.

Bambrick, S. (1973). Australian Price Levels, 1890–1970. *Australian Economic History Review, 13*(1), 57.

Bernard, A. B., and Durlauf, S. N. (1995). Convergence in International Output. *Journal of Applied Econometrics, 10*, 97–108.

Briggs, P. (2003). *Looking at the numbers: a view of New Zealand's economic history* (Vol. 69). Wellington: New Zealand Institute of Economic Research.

Brosnan, O. (1986). Net interprovincial migration, 1886–1996. *New Zealand Population Review, 12*(3), 185–204.

Collins, J. W. (1912). Inquiry into the Cost of Living in New Zealand 1910–11(Report and Evidence of the Royal Commission on). *Appendix to the Journals of the House of Representatives*, Session II, H-18. Wellington: Government Printer.

Dickey, D. A., and Fuller, W. A. (1979). Distribution of the Estimators for Autoregressive Time Series with a Unit Root. *Journal of the American Statistical Association, 74*(366), 427–431.

Fraser, M. (1915). *Report on the cost of living in New Zealand: Being an Inquiry into the Course of Retail Prices During the Period 1891–1914*. Wellington: Government Printer.

Fraser, M. (1916). *New Zealand Official Yearbook*. Available at www3.stats.govt.nz/New_Zealand_Official_Yearbooks/1915/NZOYB_1915.htm

Greasley, D., and Oxley, L. (2004). Globalization and real wages in New Zealand 1873–1913. *Explorations in Economic History, 41*(1), 26–47. doi: 10.1016/s0014-4983(03)00044-5

Greasley, D., and Oxley, L. (2010). Knowledge, Natural Resource Abundance and Economic Development: Lessons from New Zealand 1861–1939. *Explorations in Economic History, 47*(4), 443–459.

Hawke, G. R. (1985). *The making of New Zealand: An economic history*. Cambridge: Cambridge University Press.

Holt, C. C. (2004). Forecasting seasonals and trends by exponentially weighted moving averages. *International Journal of Forecasting, 20*(1), 5–10. doi: 10.1016/j.ijforecast.2003.09.015

International Labour Organization, International Monetary Fund, Organization for Economic Cooperation and Development, United Nations Children's Fund, Eurostat, and Bank, T. W. (2004). Consumer price index manual: Theory and practice. *International Labour Review, 143*(4), 403.

Johansen, S. (1988). Statistical Analysis of Cointegrating Vectors. *Journal of Economic Dynamics and Control, 12*(1), 231–254.

Karamea Store Book, 1875–1876, NP Series 23, Box 5, item 6, Archives New Zealand (ANZ).

Knibbs, G. H. (1911). *Inquiry into the Cost of Living in Australia, 1910–11*. Melbourne: Commonwealth Bureau of Census and Statistics.

MacKinnon, J. (1991). Critical values for cointegration tests. In R. F. Engle and C. W. J. Granger (eds), *Long Run Economic Relationships*. Oxford: Oxford University Press.

Maddala, G., and Wu, S. (1999). A Comparative Study of Unit Root Tests and a New Simple Test. *Oxford Bulletin of Economics and Statistics, 61*, 631–652.

McIlraith, J. W. (1911). *The Course of Prices in New Zealand: An Inquiry Into the Nature and Causes of the Variations in the Standard of Value in New Zealand*. Wellington: Government Printer.

McLean, I. W. (1999). Consumer prices and expenditure patterns 1850–1914. *Australian Economic History Review, 39*(1).

Mitchell, B. (1988). *British Historical Statistics, 1845–1966*. Cambridge: Cambridge University Press.

Nesbitt-Savage, R. (1993). *A long run consumer price index for New Zealand*. Working paper, Department of Economics, University of Waikato, Hamilton.

Neville, R. J. W., and O'Neill, C. J. (1979). *The Population of New Zealand: Interdisciplinary perspectives*. Auckland: Longman Paul.

New Zealand Department of Statistics (1873–1935). *New Zealand Census*. Wellington.

New Zealand Department of Statistics (1893). *The New Zealand official year-book*. Wellington: Government Printer.

New Zealand Department of Statistics (1894). *The New Zealand official year-book*. Wellington: Government Printer

New Zealand Department of Statistics (1911). *The New Zealand official year-book*. Wellington: Government Printer.

New Zealand Ministry for Culture and Heritage (2003). Te Ara – The Encyclopedia of New Zealand.

New Zealand Parliament (1884). *Appendix to the Journals of the House of Representatives*. Wellington: Government Printer.

New Zealand Parliament (1887). *Appendix to the Journals of the House of Representatives*, Vol. 2, H-01. Wellington: Government Printer.

New Zealand Parliament (1965). *Index to the Appendices to the Journals of the House of Representatives of New Zealand 1954 to 1963: being a continuation of indicies 1854 to 1913, 1914 to 1922, 1923 to 1938, and 1939 to 1953*. Wellington: Government Printer.

Perron, P. (1989). The Great Crash, the Oil Price Shock, and the Unit Root Hypothesis. *Econometrica, 57*(6), 1361–1401.

Phillips, P. C. B., and Ouliaris, S. (1990). Asymptotic Properties of Residual Based Tests for Cointegration. *Econometrica, 58*(1), 165–193.

Sauerbeck, A. (1895). 'Index numbers of prices. *The Economic Journal, 5*(18), 161–174.

Thorns, D., and Sedgwick, C. (1997). *Understanding Aotearoa/New Zealand: historical statistics*. Palmerston North, N.Z: Dunmore Press.

Toda, H. Y., and Yamamoto, T. (1995). Statistical inference in vector autoregressions with possibly integrated processes. *Journal of Econometrics, 66*(1), 225–250. doi: 10.1016/0304-4076(94)01616-8

Tremblay, M. S., Pérez, C. E., Ardern, C. I., Bryan, S. N., and Katzmarzyk, P. T. (2005). Obesity, overweight and ethnicity. *Health Reports, 16*(4), 23–34.

Zivot, E., and Andrews, D. (1992). Further evidence on the Great Crash, the oil price shock, and the unit root hypothesis. *Journal of Business and Economic Statistics, 10*, 251–270.

Acknowledgements

The author gratefully acknowledges the helpful comments received from Kris Inwood, Evan Roberts and David Greasley. In addition, the author thanks Marsden Fund grant UoC807, 'The long and the short and the tall: Measuring health and wellbeing in New Zealand', for funding this research.

Conceptualising the CPI: A Note

Gary Hawke & Antong Victorio

Abstract

The CPI is commonly regarded as a measure of how the prices of consumer commodities change over time. Behind this regard are many conceptualisations. These range from the CPI being an index for preserving purchasing power to it being a gauge for enhancing the well-being of its country's citizens.

Introduction

Interest in price movements – and in prices relative to those of the United Kingdom – began as soon as European settlement occurred in New Zealand, but it became more intense once the State took an interest in wage determination. One antecedent was the Industrial Conciliation and Arbitration (IC&A) Act, a piece of industrial relations legislation enacted by the New Zealand Parliament in 1894. The IC&A Act created a specialist employment court, the Court of Arbitration, which was originally intended to prevent recurrent strikes rather than to determine a basic wage. For New Zealand, however, the dream of a land without strikes proved to be transitory. Unions became ever more popular, perhaps as an unintended consequence of the court giving them 'recognition' (see e.g. Bain and Price, 1983). Union growth and the experience of inflation combined to help pave the way for determining a 'just wage' for a male New Zealander of modest means, married and supporting three children.

The IC&A Act formed conciliation councils to assess appropriate wage levels in each of New Zealand's main centres. The court would then ensure that 'good' employers in one centre would not be inappropriately undercut by those in other centres. While these councils eventually collapsed – for reasons having to do with greater national integration, and perhaps union/employer impatience – interest in a just wage never waned. In 1906, the influential socialist organisation, the Fabian Society, lobbied for a British 'minimum wage'. In neighbouring Australia, a landmark was set when, in 1907, an arbitration court ruled against the Harvester Manufacturing Company in favour of a minimum wage that was based upon the cost of food, shelter and clothing. Thus emerged the notion of a wage that had to be linked to some cost-of-living index.

Early conceptualisations

An early New Zealand price index was constructed by McIlraith (1911) for the years between 1861 and 1907, using export and import prices. This reliance upon external indicators was characteristic of early work. Domestic retail and wholesale prices were conceptualised as being largely governed by New Zealand trade and by the activities of large industrial economies like the United Kingdom (see e.g. Condliffe, 1927). For example, Condliffe's first economic history, *New Zealand in the Making* (1930), was mostly about international influences and local responses. This conceptualisation continued on even after World War II. In the 1960s, a great deal of discussion revolved around how domestic prices would rise with a devaluation, thereby potentially nullifying the intended competitive effect, and making it even more difficult for authorities to arbitrate a just wage. Until the floating of the New Zealand dollar in 1985, it was common for macroeconomists to think of growth as being constrained by export markets and available foreign exchange – a 'foreign exchange constraint' – lending even more credence to the idea that New Zealand's wages and CPI were largely determined by external prices (see e.g. Wells and Evans, 1983; also Buckle and Pope, 1985).

The CPI and inflation

The importance of the CPI in determining a just wage was eroded with the eventual development of a welfare state, which offered more direct means of ensuring adequate living standards, and with the eventual dissolution of the Court of Arbitration in 1973, although the notion of a centralised 'wage round' lasted for 10–15 years beyond that. With the economic reforms of the 1980s and the Reserve Bank Act of 1989, the CPI's conceptualisation changed from being a local variant of international prices to being a way of ensuring a low level of nationwide inflation. This heralded a new independence in its treatment. In 1988, Minister of Finance Roger Douglas boldly proposed that New Zealand inflation should be brought down from 9 per cent to no more than 1 per cent per annum over the next two years. In 1990, the Reserve Bank formalised this proposal with an inflation target of 0–2 per cent per annum, expanded later on to 3 per cent per annum. This target was achieved by an average inflation rate of 2 per cent per annum for the next ten years (Brash, 2002).

The CPI continues to be regarded as an instrument within a mechanism for achieving low inflation. However, its conceptualisation has been further broadened in scope to include 'informing monetary policy' (Statistics New Zealand Consumers Price Index Advisory Committee, 2013). This view is shared by many Western democracies but not by all of them. In the United States, the government no longer regards its CPI as primarily a means of containing inflation or of preserving purchasing power. A US Government commission in 1996 recommended that the main purpose of the United States CPI should be changed to that of maintaining the cost of a given standard of living (Boskin et al., 1997). This differs from either containing inflation or preserving purchasing power because the basket for a given standard of living continually changes, and also because the standard itself might change independently of inflation. Much research has since been conducted concerning how the United States CPI may have since diverged from a standard-of-living index (see e.g. Gordon, 2006; also Victorio, this volume).

Group-based conceptualisations

Because the CPI of any economy is calculated on the basis of an average market basket, it does not serve the interests of everyone. Many sectors, such as education and health, are apt to claim that the CPI does not apply to them because the market basket does not reflect the expenditures of their constituents. There is some merit to such claims and they raise many distributional considerations. They reinforce the view that the CPI consists of many underlying conceptualisations, the interests behind which are virtually impossible to satisfy with a single number.

Because of the many competing conceptualisations, there is always a danger that the CPI is misused. Thus, advance briefings to senior public servants may arise from an incentive to mould expectations and reactions in order to preserve a political agenda. Or the timing of releases could be changed in order to cater to the wider demands of economic management. This is ubiquitous in public indexation and it is to be distinguished from any corruption of underlying sources. But it demonstrates the importance of regarding the CPI as a window on key economic and social developments, rather than as an icon whose purity must be preserved.

A straightforward solution is for the CPI to be complemented by specific variants that are justified by some analysis of what constitutes a proper conceptualisation. For example, a special index for the elderly ought to capture their altered spending habits, especially in terms of their greater reliance upon medical care (see e.g. Hobijn and Lagakos, 2003). In every case, the price index is no more than an instrument which assists analysis; the notion of a ready-made answer to policy questions is a mirage.

Welfare-based conceptualisations

Debates concerning the CPI should consider that it is only one economic measure relating to a broader concept, which is that of economic welfare. Other measures include household income and value added in the context of a nation's trade. Household income has some advantage over the CPI and many of the other measures because it captures the welfare-improving liberties of being able to make spending choices. A discussion of household income and its many proposed alternatives (such as indices of life satisfaction) is especially useful because the discussion frees the CPI from bearing some of the brunt of measuring economic welfare.

While the CPI and its alternatives may not always achieve their underlying conceptualisations, they all imply practicable policy considerations that would otherwise not have been discussable. Should we prohibit sellers from raising their prices in the interest of containing overall inflation? Is spending against household income consistent with setting aside enough resources for the future? Should we expand trade so as to capture the welfare benefits to consumers of being able to use illegal drugs? These and other policy considerations can only be answered if any attempt to measure welfare is complemented by the social, moral and distributional dimensions of an economic society.

References

Bain, George S., and Robert Price. 1983. The Determinants of Union Growth. In William E. J. McCarthy (ed.) *Trade Unions*. Harmondsworth, England: Pelican, 245–71.

Boskin, Michael J., Ellen R. Dulberger, Robert Gordon, Zvi Griliches and Dale W. Jorgenson. 1997. The CPI Commission: Findings and Recommendations. *The American Economic Review*, May 1997, 87:2, 78–83.

Brash, Don. 2002. Inflation Targeting 14 Years On. Speech presented at the Annual Conference of the American Economic Association in Atlanta, Georgia, December 2002. Available from http://www.donbrash.com/inflation-targeting-14-years-on/

Buckle, Robert A. and Mervyn J. Pope. 1985. Inflation and the Terms of Trade in a Foreign Exchange Constrained Economy. *New Zealand Economic Papers*, 19:1, 1–20.

Condliffe, John B. 1927. An Index of Industrial Share-prices in New Zealand. *Transactions and Proceedings of the Royal Society of New Zealand*, 57, 883–891.

———. 1930. *New Zealand in the Making*. London: Allen & Unwin, and Chicago: University of Chicago Press.

Gordon, Robert J. 2006. The Boskin Commission Report: A Retrospective One Decade Later. *National Bureau of Economic Research Working Paper 12311*, June 2006. Available from http://www.nber.org/papers/w12311/

Hobijn, Bart, and David Lagakos. 2003. Social Security and the Consumer Price Index for the Elderly. *Current Issues in Economics and Finance*, May 2003, 9:5, 1–7.

McIlraith, James W. 1911. *The course of prices in New Zealand: an inquiry into the nature and causes of the variations in the standard of value in New Zealand*. Wellington: Government Printer.

Statistics New Zealand Consumers Price Index Advisory Committee. 2013. *Report of the Consumers Price Index Advisory Committee 2013*. Available from www.stats.govt.nz.

Victorio, Antong. 2014. The CPI versus a Cost-of-Living Index: Some Sources of Bias. In Antong Victorio and Sharleen Forbes (eds) *The New Zealand CPI at 100: History and Interpretation.* Wellington: Victoria University Press.

Wells, G., and Lew Evans. 1983. *Issues and Estimation of the Impact of Traded Goods Prices on the New Zealand Economy,* Occasional Paper No. 18. Wellington: New Zealand Institute of Economic Research.

Contributors

Editors

Sharleen Forbes

sharleen.forbes@vuw.ac.nz

Sharleen Forbes has four children and four grandchildren and has had a variety of research, policy and management positions in New Zealand state sector agencies including the Ministries of Agriculture, Māori Affairs and Māori Development and more recently a split position, working half-time as Adjunct Professor of Official Statistics in the School of Government, Victoria University and half-time as General Manager, Statistics Education at Statistics New Zealand. She has a long-standing interest in statistics education with a PhD on the measurement of gender and ethnic differences in school mathematics. She has been a member of the International Statistics Institute's Committee on Women in Statistics, President of the New Zealand Statistics Association, and Vice-Director of the International Statistical literacy Project and. Her recent research has focused on ways of increasing statistical literacy, particularly the teaching of conceptual understanding in statistics. Her current research interests in official statistics include the teaching and dissemination uses of data visualisation tools and the history of, and influences on, these statistics.

Antong Victorio

antong.victorio@vuw.ac.nz

Antong Victorio, who also writes as Andres G Victorio, is Senior Lecturer at Victoria University of Wellington, having previously obtained a Master of Public Policy and PhD in Economics from Harvard University and Boston College. He teaches applied economics, public economics and quantitative methods for public policy. His published contributions, in economics science, have been in understanding financial crises, fiscal policy, non-market insurance, school leaving, trade liberalisation, altruism in the presence of externalities, bargaining in housing demand, and union power in the face of globalisation. He is the author of *Applied Models in Public Policy* (2005), *The Benefits and Wider Costs of Leaving School* (2006) and served as editor of the *Journal of Business and Governance*. He lives in Wellington and travels regularly to Asia and the Americas.

Other Contributors

Alan Bentley
Senior Statistical Analyst, Statistics New Zealand, alan.bentley@stats.govt.nz

Brian Easton
Economist and author, www.eastonbh.ac.nz

John Gibson
Professor, Department of Economics, University of Waikato, jkgibson@waikato.ac.nz

Gary Hawke
Honorary Fellow, School of Government, Victoria University of Wellington, gary.hawke@vuw.ac.nz

Corin Higgs
Victoria University of Wellington, corinh@gmail.com

James Keating
Victoria University of Wellington, hemikeating@gmail.com

Frances Krsinich
Senior Researcher, Prices, Statistics New Zealand, frances.krsinich@stats.govt.nz

Les Oxley
Professor, Economics, Waikato Management School, University of Waikato, loxley@waikato.ac.nz

Chris Pike
Prices Manager, Statistics New Zealand, chris.pike@stats.govt.nz

Michael Reddell
Special Adviser, Reserve Bank of New Zealand, michael.reddell@rbnz.govt.nz

Evan Roberts
Associate Professor, Department of History and Minnesota Population Center, University of Minnesota, eroberts@umn.edu

Ekaterina Sadetskaya
University of Canterbury, ksadetskaya@gmail.com

Grant Scobie
Principal Adviser, The New Zealand Treasury, grant.scobie@treasury.govt.nz

Acknowledgements

Gratitude is extended to all the contributors in this book and to all others who helped so greatly in the various phases of its writing and editing: Richard Arnold, Alan Bentley, Fergus Barrowman, Peter Campion, Len Cook, Vince Galvin, Gary Hawke, Kyleigh Hodgson, Mohammed Khaled, Nick Martelli, Les Oxley, Chris Pike, Chelly Plaza, Chris Slane, Thomas Stapleford, and many others we may have forgotten to mention. Gratitude is also extended for the institutional support provided by Statistics New Zealand, StatScience Limited and the Victoria University of Wellington School of Government.